COCKTAIL

WIRED'S ALCHEMIST PAUL HARRINGTON
AND
LAURA MOORHEAD

COCKTAIL

The Drinks Bible for the 21st Century

DESIGNED AND ILLUSTRATED BY DOUGLAS BOWMAN

VIKING

WIRED

VIKING
Published by the Penguin Group
Penguin Putnam Inc., 375 Hudson Street,
New York, New York 10014, U.S.A.
Penguin Books Ltd, 27 Wrights Lane,
London W8 5TZ, England
Penguin Books Australia Ltd, Ringwood,
Victoria, Australia
Penguin Books Canada Ltd, 10 Alcorn Avenue,
Toronto, Ontario, Canada M4V 3B2
Penguin Books (N.Z.) Ltd, 182-190 Wairau Road,
Aukland 10, New Zealand

Penguin Books Ltd, Registered Offices:
Harmondsworth, Middlesex, England

First published in 1998 by Viking Penguin,
a member of Penguin Putnam Inc.

1 3 5 7 9 10 8 6 4 2

CIP data available upon request.

ISBN 0-670-88022-1

This book is printed on acid-free paper.

Printed in the United States of America
Set in Bembo
Designed by Doug Bowman

Acknowledgments

A toast and a special thanks to all those who have helped make this book possible. Tops on the list are Douglas Bowman, for his fine design and the illustrations in this book; and Mark Durham, for his first-rate editing, spirit, and literary spunk; and Martha Baer and Gary Wolf, for their edits and encouragement throughout the production of both the book and the Web site (*www.cocktailtime.com*).

The contributors to this book cannot be praised sufficiently for their work and their willingness to sample any drink: Jill Atkinson, for her passion and style from the git-go (she gave the Web frames as they should be); Brady Clark, for illustrations like the Aviation and the Floridita; Graham Clarke, for his patience and his ability to crank out one-liners worth a thousand words; Cate C. Corcoran, for her writing on the cool Mojito and the steamy Sazerac; the band Combustible Edison, for its music and drink; Michael Cudahy (better known as The Millionaire of Combustible Edison fame), for his willingness to work with us on more than one occasion; Jeff Eaton, for his tasting and his comments; Paschal Fowlkes, *Cocktail*'s New York correspondent, for the Manhattan and the Pimm's Cup; Alex Huneeus, our native Chilean and writer on the Pisco Sour; Jonathan Louie, for setting the design direction and online navigational system at *Cocktail*'s beginning; Steve Silberman, whose early edits and one-liners made a lasting impression; Pamela Statz, for her musings on the original Daiquiri; and Gary Wolf, for his writing on the Aviation, the Bronx, the Jasmine, and the Sidecar.

Of course, there are many others who also contributed to *Cocktail*. There are the fact-checkers — Amy Bourne, Kristen Philipkoski, Jennifer Sullivan, and Sean Williams — who had the Herculean task of verifying a history better left in the dark corners of the bar, and Emily Hobson, who kept the Web site humming while we created the book. There are those whose eagle eyes kept us from embarrassing ourselves on paper — Emily McManus, who remembers the *Cocktail* Web site before it was, and Michael E. Ross, who worked holidays and was unwavering in his dislike of nouns used as verbs. And there are those who let *Cocktail* be — Andrew Anker, Lisa Gerhauser, Barbara Kuhr, Beth Vanderslice, and David Weir.

We share not only our glasses but our hearts with those who supported us throughout the process: Marta and Natalie, our families and friends — as well as those who have been an inspiration in life: Evan, Evelyn, and Joseph, and those at Enrico's and the Townhouse. None of them can be thanked enough.

CONTENTS

PART TWO:
THE DRINK CLASSICS WORTH IMBIBING FIRST

PART THREE:
DRINK RECIPES

Introduction

Anyone who remembers the sight of the parents' cocktail shaker as a portent of good company knows the power and the mystique of the cocktail – a modern-day archetype that's come to symbolize far more than a quick, friendly drink. Resurrecting the taste of these classics – as recalled from the occasional maraschino cherry or gin-soaked olive tossed one's way at those long-ago cocktail parties – isn't easy. Indeed, for most of us, it has proved impossible. For all the talk of the cocktail revolution, we've seen neither a resurgence of good drinks nor a renewed sense of their enjoyment, though it has certainly fattened the ranks of the abominable and the mundane. Like the *nouveaux riches* created by the California gold rush or the latest spate of Silicon Valley IPOs, today's cocktail drinkers have occasionally been overzealous. Annoying the world's better bartenders and intimidating the beer-and-wine crowd, they've squandered their orders on sickly-sweet drinks without spirituous flavor and unsavory Martinis, oversized and parched. In the face of all this, lovers of the cocktail require a helping hand.

Cocktail: The Drinks Bible for the 21st Century is for those imbibers who would rather play host in their own homes than belly up to a public bar for yet another round of mediocre drinks – if only to avoid seeing the cocktail's good name defiled. For the more tenacious spirits among you, *Cocktail* is a tool to improve your chances of getting a first-rate drink when you're out on the town and willing to tip well. You won't find the Chocolate Martini, the Beer Buster, or any drink whose name contains the word *sex*. In fact, you'll find little here outside the realm of cocktails, and the occasional exceptions serve to punctuate our sense of these drinks as accents to a life well lived. The cocktails in this book – including a well-balanced Martini, the quintessential Sidecar, and the soothing Sazerac, along with more than a few modern classics – provide a benchmark against which all drinks can be judged.

Unlike most potables, the cocktail is not the drink for gung-ho tipplers whose evenings out cut a broad swath from bar to bar and from drink to drink. The cocktail caters to those who view the drink as a complement to food, the celebratory ritual, and the culinary tradition – not a perspective honored at every corner bar. Fads come and go, but the cocktail is timeless, anchored in the art and the customs of great cuisine. That said, it's inevitable that the cocktail should fall from favor among the flippant.

But those among us who recognize this drink as sleek, refined, and limitless in variation will take no notice as we continue to explore these tasty classics.

Years ago, journalist and cocktail connoisseur H. L. Mencken and a friend recruited a mathematician to calculate how many cocktails a reputable establishment could make. The hired hand came back with a total of 17,864,392,788 possible drinks. We've included only a few hundred of these on the principle that refinement and selectivity are crucial to the art of the bar. A well-received drink, after all, owes its success as much to its appropriateness and timing as to its recipe, however brilliantly inspired and deftly executed. But even the 275 formulas collected here make for a dizzying array when all you're really looking for is one good drink. To help a host decide which libation best suits the occasion and the tastes of the guests, each drink is rated by its mixing difficulty and taste complexity. In Part One, Paul Harrington walks you through the intricacies of drinkmaking and defines the cocktail's place in the world of mixed drinks, educating you for a life of subtle pleasures. Paul – known as the Alchemist to his fans at the modern-day speakeasy of the Web, *www.cocktailtime.com* – has poured much of his young life into exploring the lure and lore of the perfect cocktail. He approaches bartending as a lost art, one to be revered by civilized, cunning, and curious drinkers determined to become savants of the cocktail. To make his day, ask him what the *capos* liked to sip in Havana during the '20s, or what secret ingredient made absinthe the dissipation of choice for painters and poets. As the last word in imbibing etiquette, Paul demystifies distillation from the host's perspective, explains the finer points of glassware, and gives you the perfect crib sheet for figuring the mathematics of a party. You'll come to know that a perfectly portioned drink doesn't happen by chance, and that good ice is more than frozen water. You'll also learn to spot a greenhorn behind the bar in ten seconds flat and discover why an opened bottle of peppermint SCHNAPPS should be cause for concern.

The next section of *Cocktail*, compiled by the enthusiasts of Bacchus, gives the *vitae* of more than 60 cocktails – worthwhile reading for anyone who demands a drink with a story as good as its taste. From the showy Blue Blazer of the 1800s to the 1950s Vesper (a favorite drink – and beloved double agent – of the notoriously particular James Bond), each drink is described in an entry that highlights its history as well as its flavor and its charm. The stories of these cocktails are presented with the same subtlety required to mix such classics. For instance, the Manhattan's highlights include the geographical and seasonal protocol that's part of serving this tasteful delight – which hails from a time when the Dow was less than 200, the Dodgers were in Brooklyn, and a joint was still your local bar.

An uninhibited celebration of potent potables, *Cocktail* takes you through the ages of drink with appetizing historical tidbits, bracing anecdotes, and mixing instructions as lucid as a double shot of the good stuff. Since long before the 20th century began, the cocktail has been a sign of taste and sophistication. Crossing class lines, it is one of the world's most affordable luxuries, allowing for both cheer and reflection even on the bleakest of days. A volatile mixture that can sting, smart, and swing, *Cocktail* proves that the DARK AGE OF AMERICAN DRINKING has finally come to an end and the REVIVAL is upon us.

It's time to chill the glasses – the Cocktail Nation has come of age.

Mixing Advice
from the Alchemist

The Cocktail, by Definition

The cocktail – an elusive phenomenon not easily defined – certainly wasn't the first way humanity found to enjoy distilled spirits, but today it's counted among the most sophisticated, the embodiment of civilized refreshment. The cocktail's supple nature lets mixers adapt it to almost any setting and mood; as a consequence, this classic has come to the fore of the drink world, as its acolytes continue to mix, shake, and stir to accommodate the most subtle of tastes. Even so, the purpose of studying the cocktail's finer points is not to settle on a single obscure potion and stick to it, but to know what to drink when. No one should be branded with one token concoction – that monotonous and inevitable drink, ordered irrespective of hour, weather, frame of mind, or local custom. Such a person is endured, not respected, by true aficionados of the bar.

The cocktail hour has traditionally marked the transition between work and home – that time of day when the pressures of the office are left behind and life's pleasures just beginning. But as today's office environment changes, so does the cocktail hour: These drinks are now considered the appropriate embellishment to many times and many settings. Cocktails – sleek, refined, and limitless in variation – have become the perfect accessory to almost any gathering, adding a dose of cheer along with a measure of reflection.

Back in 1806, *The Balance*, a New York newspaper, defined the cocktail as "a stimulating liquor, composed of spirits of any kind, sugar, water, and bitters … vulgarly called bittered sling and supposed to be an excellent electioneering potion." Later definitions more closely resembled the recipe of the Martini, though the usage of the words *Martini* and *cocktail* remained distinct. Today, however, *Martini* is often incorrectly substituted for the word *cocktail*. As mixers and imbibers took note of the Martini's seductive appearance, they even began to refer to the cocktail glass as a Martini glass, and many bar owners and restaurateurs now use *Martini* in place of the more general name. Without doubt, nothing compares to the clean lines of a well-prepared Martini and its iconic olive, but its moniker should not replace that of the cocktail. While the Martini is indeed the best-known cocktail, that certainly doesn't make it the only member of the family.

Most of the drinks in this book are classed as APÉRITIF cocktails – drinks devised to stimulate the taste buds and the stomach. Apéritifs, in general, can be wine- or spirit-based and are often bitter in taste. Flavored with a broad variety of herbs and extracts, traditional apéritifs are served at the outset of a meal, usually with hors d'oeuvres.

Although the French may have given the world more memorable apéritifs (and cuisine) than any other culture, keen travelers will be wise to note the native apéritifs of every country and region. Many of these libations can be enjoyed straight from the bottle, poured over ice, or mixed in a drink. In the United States, the tradition of apéritifs stems from the period of PROHIBITION. Although cocktails certainly existed before the Noble Experiment, they were not common. But once the drought hit, the cocktail became entrenched in American society as clandestine mixers sought ways to make palatable drinks from the likes of bathtub gin. Most cocktails of this era, made overly sweet to disguise the poor quality of the liquor, didn't survive past Repeal. But we've found plenty of classic drinks from this time, along with others that deserve to be chronicled as notable contributions to the bar.

3

Most apéritif cocktails — whether they hail from Prohibition or from some other era — are easily identified by four key characteristics:

1. *The ideal cocktail is 3 to 5 ounces in volume and is served in a stemmed glass no larger than 6 ounces.* Just as wine is generally served in 6-ounce portions and beer in 12-ounce portions, the 4½-ounce cocktail helps ensure that you don't enjoy too much of a good thing. Keep in mind that a cocktail is not 5 ounces of an 80-proof spirit but of a finished product, containing a base, a modifier, an accent, and a generous portion of water. One of the cocktail's main advantages over other drink families, in fact, is its size: Generally served in smaller portions, cocktails don't overwhelm the appetite in advance of a meal. The misaligned trend of marketing 12-ounce Martinis only encourages drinkers to finish settled, lukewarm cocktails — they may have come for dinner, but by the final gulp, they're more likely to need a tall glass of ice water and a cab ride home.

Fig. 1 – cocktail glass

2. *The ideal cocktail must be well chilled.* Although a cocktail is never served with ice, it should always be served extremely cold, at a temperature between 20 and 32 degrees Fahrenheit. The icy edge of a good cocktail motivates the spirit as well as the palate. Even the most seemingly astringent cocktail will glide smoothly down the gullet when served correctly chilled. Harry Craddock, the mixologist of the Savoy Hotel in London

during this century's early years, once said that the best way to drink a cocktail is "quickly ... while it's laughing at you," and with that I must agree.

3. *The ideal cocktail is never sweet.* The sweetness of a cocktail must be subdued by the tartness of citrus juices, the briskness of BITTERS, and the potency of the spirit. If a cocktail is made too sweet, it only serves to coat the taste buds and dull the culinary instincts. A drink with too much bitters or juice can be resurrected with a touch of sweetness, but it is nearly impossible to retreat from the other extreme: If you err on the sweet side, the cocktail is better dumped down the drain and forgotten. In the case of complex distillates like whiskey and gin, few additives are needed to produce a balanced offering, and the maxim "less is more" decidedly applies – as exemplified by the refined nature of the Martini.

4. *The ideal cocktail is elegant.* Inspired by the shape and proportions of the stemware, cocktails are meant to be aesthetically pleasing, flirting with the eye while seducing the other senses. Every mixologist should pay close attention when building a cocktail, be it classic or modern, to ensure that the contents of the glass remain true to the character of the vessel. Simply combining ingredients in a shaker and straining them into the proper glass does not make a cocktail – but the balance struck in a well-mixed, well-presented cocktail raises its stature above any other type of mixed drink.

DRINK FAMILIES

If you have already perused this book, you may have noticed that not every drink presented fits the strict definition of a cocktail. We have included drink options outside the cocktail family in order to provide a more generous repertoire of recipes. You will have many occasions to celebrate in your life, and not all of them will call for an apéritif cocktail. The cocktail is just one family of mixed drinks; others that top the list of those worth drinking include tall drinks, punches, grogs and toddies, poussecafés, and pick-me-ups.

TALL DRINKS

The best tall drinks are usually well-prepared cocktails poured over ice and then topped with fresh soda – so if your thirst requires more than a cocktail, take any recipe from these pages and give it that treatment, using a tumbler larger than 8 ounces. As the tiny carbon bubbles are released, they will aid the drink's other ingredients – most notably the citrus juice – in dusting a dry mouth. The family of tall drinks is a large one whose members have their disposition and appearance in common – in fact, many of these summer SLINGS are distinguished more by nomenclature than by taste. Their common denominator: carbonated water or soda, a distilled spirit, and citrus juice. Among the best-known tall drinks are the Collins, the fizz, the sour, the rickey, the julep, the Buck, and the highball.

COLLINSES AND FIZZES

The Collins and the fizz require as much care to prepare as the most sensitive of cocktails – never let anyone tell you differently, just as you should never let anyone sell or serve you premixed concoctions from a bottle or a squirt gun. The true delight of any properly prepared iced beverage is that you get to enjoy it longer than you would a cocktail. If you're at a gathering or a bar where the host's skills are suspect, a drink on the rocks will be your safest bet – in any refreshment, melting ice is a great equalizer of mixing errors.

Having the expertise to differentiate a Collins from a fizz may be an indication of excessive leisure, but for most serious imbibers, it simply shows an awareness of what they're putting into their bodies. The basic difference between the Collins and the fizz is ice – with a Collins you get it, with a fizz you don't. A Collins should be presented in its namesake glass, between 10 and 14 ounces in size, while a fizz should be served in a glass smaller than 9 ounces. Unfortunately, the current disregard for the nuances of glassware confuses matters even more, since a fizz is all too often mistakenly served in a Collins glass.

SOURS

Not as tart as it sounds, a sour is a tall drink whose closest kin is the fizz; some, in fact, would argue that a fizz is merely a sour with soda water. Made with a distilled spirit, sugar, and lemon juice – and occasionally a DASH of orange juice – a sour is shaken with cracked ice and is typically served in the glass of the same name. A sour glass is short and squat, holding about 6 to 8 ounces. When made with 2 ounces less, the more respectable sours can be served as cocktails.

Fig. 2 – soda siphon

RICKEYS, JULEPS, AND BUCKS

The rickey resembles both the sour and the fizz, though its definition insists that the citrus juice used be lime. This drink is usually served with ice in a glass smaller than 9 ounces. The Buck, unlike these tall drinks, doesn't contain sugar, and is mixed with ginger ale and a citrus wedge. The julep, with its recipe of spirits, water, and syrup or soda, only adds to the confusion. To 15th-century English pharmacists, the julep was a sweet draft used to disguise the taste of unpleasant medicine. Today, most people immediately think of a mint-laced drink commonly found in Kentucky. When you combine a julep with a Collins, you have the Mojito, the crowning jewel of any drink card. To master this drink is to tease Zeus himself.

HIGHBALLS

The most popular tall drink is the highball, which has the ridiculous reputation of being far more complex and bewildering than it really is. Many people fondly recall elders speaking of this drink, or have come across it in a favorite novel, but haven't the slightest idea how it's prepared. Does scotch and soda sound familiar? A highball is any mixed drink composed of one spirit and one mixer (traditionally soda water or ginger ale) that is served in a highball glass – short and stubby by nature and typically holding 10 to 12 ounces. In most cases, a highball will be ordered by its base ingredient, but some of these drinks – such as the Cuba Libre and the Presbyterian – do have proper names. The addition of any citrus juice will turn a highball into one of the other tall drinks. In the early years of bartending, the only variation on the highball was to use soda water or ginger ale and a twist of lemon – but in today's world, where Snapple is king and restraint a fond memory, other sodas can be mixed with vodka or rum to create highballs of another stripe.

PUNCHES

When contemplating punch, most people envision a crystal bowl, ice molds, and a liquid sure to stain silk. It's true such party punches are popular, but there are many single-serving punches worth offering, especially at more formal gatherings. The word *punch* derives either from the Persian word *punj* or from the Hindu *panch* – both words meaning "five" – and as you might guess, punches typically include five or more ingredients, not all of them spirits. During the mid-1600s, the English – having traded punches of another sort with the Spanish over their claim to Jamaica – began concocting their own versions of this mix, based on the use of rum and water. By the 18th century, punches had become far more elaborate and contained a great variety of fruits and liquors, particularly brandy and wine; around the turn of the century they even began to take on miraculous medicinal qualities. Though no longer thought to cure disease, a punch will do wonders for hosts who doubt their mixing skills or lack the resources to acquire elaborate barware. A party punch also permits substantial economies of effort, whereas single-serving punches are quite time-consuming to make.

GROGS AND TODDIES

Grogs – spirituous liquors diluted with water – are the most basic of hot drinks. Brandy, dark rum, and whiskeys are all prime candidates for this drink. Because no sugar is added, grogs are ideal before a winter meal of fondue, and are attractive when garnished with a lemon or an orange twist. Toddies take grog one step further: With the addition of sweeteners, spices, and juices, toddies are the perfect treatment for that lingering winter cold. Usually enjoyed right before bed, a good, potent toddy will ensure that even the most congested sufferer sleeps like a baby. One of my favorite toddy variations is the Hot Bonnie, made with bourbon, honey, lemon juice, and hot water.

POUSSE-CAFÉS

This showy family, with its layers of differently colored cordials and syrups, has been despised by mixologists for years. Although the name means a drink to go with coffee, the pousse-café was diverted from its original coffee-pushing purpose long ago, as Charles H. Baker points out in his *Gentleman's Companion* of 1939: How could "anyone imagine following a good demitasse of strong black mocha with half a dozen sweet cordials roosting on the yolk of an egg"? The layering effect of a pousse-café results from the differing densities of the various LIQUEURS or syrups in the drink. These different liquids, if mixed in a DIGESTIF cocktail and left to stand, would take hours to separate into layers on their own, but a steady hand and the proper technique can create a drink colorful enough to rival any Fourth of July fireworks display. It would be difficult at best to specify the density of every liqueur, since different brands of the same liqueur can vary in density. But a mixer will fare well by noting two general guidelines for FLOATING cordials and syrups: The higher the sugar content, the higher the liquid's density; the greater the PROOF, the lower the density. Sweet syrups like GRENADINE will keep to the bottom of a pousse-café, while 151 rum will remain at the top of the glass.

PICK-ME-UPS

If you've sampled from several of these drink families in a single evening, perhaps the pick-me-up – that legendary but unconfirmed hangover remedy – should be your next selection. Most frequently drenched in bitters, pick-me-ups were invented to postpone the awful (though inevitable) side effects of too much drinking. If you're familiar with the aching head, sour stomach, and general distress that accompany a classic hangover, you may want to flip through these recipes, if only to find a sympathetic friend. Just keep in mind that a good pick-me-up can contain little more than water – in fact, even the spirit can be dispensed with. Traditional pick-me-ups are the potions that inspired the saying "a hair of the dog that bit you," which refers to the practice of welcoming a bit of the same spirit that previously did you in. As the *Esquire Drink Book* of 1956 points out: "The hair of the dog is a downright assassin; most have just enough truth in them to be plausible – and enough untruth to make them poisonous." As a general rule, I strongly advise against this practice; however, there are occasions – most just barely dependent on the previous evening's excesses – when a slight drink is an appropriate way to turn one's afternoon mood around.

The Techniques of Drinkmaking

Cocktails are the most honest of all mixed drinks. They hide nothing, and their delicate nature demands ingredients of the highest quality. Any deficiency in their preparation inevitably comes through in the final product. Even the best bartenders have a difficult time masking the flavor of unripe fruit or inferior spirits, and no one can expect to render a cocktail noble by relying on one ingredient to redeem the others. Inexperienced hosts are often overly concerned with the labels on the bottles they present to their guests, while completely ignoring the other components of the cocktails they serve. These mixers assume that using expensive spirits will save any drink they make. But as common sense suggests, such an approach will rarely be successful if the mixer's skills are weak or unpracticed. Choosing the right base is a valid concern, but it's just as important that the fruit be ripe, the juice fresh, and the cream uncurdled.

BASES

In mixing cocktails, extremely delicate or complex spirits are simply not needed, and brand recognition, as much as anything, will dictate what you buy – with personal taste, aesthetics, and your budget also coming into play. Fortunately, making cocktails demands a greater investment of effort than of money; the per serving cost is slight compared to that of a fine wine, and an

Fig. 3 – mixing tin

average bottle of spirits is sufficiently versatile to use on any occasion, in any season. When buying spirits for a gathering that calls for cocktails, plan to spend $12 to $35 per liter for your base ingredient. Many base spirits are typically 80 proof (the legal minimum) but may be much higher. The most common of these spirits are gin, rum, vodka, whiskey, brandy, and tequila. There's great variety among brands in this price range, but if you honor these limits you need never be embarrassed by the spirits you serve – even if you ultimately select a spirit for its wax seal or the shape of its bottle. Although some guests may challenge your choice if it doesn't happen to be their brand, most will gracefully defer to your opinion. Don't be intimidated by pretentious imbibers; the best spirits – cognac, armagnac, and single-malt scotches – should never find their way into a cocktail or other mixed drink, where their key qualities would be wasted. Reserve these spirits for reflective moments.

If serving cocktails for a crowd of one hundred, you probably won't opt for the $25 bottle when picking a whiskey for your Rob Roys, but if it's only your boss and a few associates, it might be wise to splurge. And just as the intimacy of your party can dictate which spirit you'll invest in, so can the evening's chosen drink. Spend more on brandy if you're serving a drink like the brandy Manhattan that highlights the distillation, or if you intend to serve the brandy as an after-dinner nightcap. If you're making a drink like the Sidecar, whose citrus fruits and sweet liqueur mask the delicate qualities of a premium spirit, by all means spend less.

MODIFIERS

These ingredients, also called mixers, are the complementary ingredients in cocktails that blend with the base to create a new flavor. Modifying agents may be distilled spirits (usually 40-proof liqueurs), fortified wines (as in the case of VERMOUTH, port, or sherry), juices, or carbonated water. Regardless of the boldness of the modifier or the slightness of the base, a mixer should never mask the character of the main ingredient.

CITRUS JUICES

When using juice as a mixer, it's always best to rely on fresh-squeezed citrus. These juices complement both the high-proof base and the sweet spirituous mixers of a cocktail because of their high acidity and tartness.

Fig. 4 – citrus

Fortunately, citrus is available to most of us year-round, though its quality can vary greatly. A fresh lime, lemon, or orange should have a vibrant color, and when squeezed, it should "give" easily but return quickly to its previous shape. If you can roll the fruit against a hard surface and soften it without difficulty, the fruit is just right for mixing in cocktails. A telltale sign of immature fruit – particularly fruit not ripened on the tree – is a rigid hull caused by an overly thick rind. The obvious solution for such fruit is to buy it several days before your party and let it ripen at home. If fresh juice is unavailable, don't even consider ordering or serving cocktails that call for it. Under such circumstances, a cocktail like the Martinez will be far better appreciated than a drink like the Daiquiri, which simply can't be made palatable without good limes.

CORDIALS AND SYRUPS

In many cases, a cocktail's mixer will include more than one ingredient – usually when the tart or bitter qualities of a citrus juice need buffering. There are three ways to sweeten a cocktail, the most effective being the addition of a liqueur. A cordial's proof, complex taste, and sweetness will enhance most drinks. Some liqueurs, such as PARFAIT AMOUR, are called for in classic recipes but are no longer produced or are difficult to find. If you lack the appropriate cordial or if your guests lean toward a lighter variation – even one without alcohol – reach for a flavored syrup instead of a sweet spirit. If this is impossible, simply add sugar to the drink. The best way to prepare this sweetener for use in cocktails is in the form of simple syrup. Made with two cups of sugar dissolved in one cup of boiling water, simple syrup should have the consistency of motor oil to be an effective sweetener – but at this concentration, take care not to oversweeten a drink. For the inevitable moment when you run out of simple syrup, keep a box of superfine sugar on hand; with smaller granules than regular sugar, this type dissolves more easily in drinks. For hot drinks like the toddy and the Irish Coffee, use sugar cubes – they're easy to portion and will dissolve in the warm liquid. The easiest brand to use for drinkmaking is Dots, which comes in convenient half-teaspoon-size cubes. Other brands offer larger cubes that make subtle sweetening difficult.

CREAM AND EGGS

For obvious reasons, always exercise care when using eggs and cream as modifiers. Soured milk will spoil a palate long after the drink is gone. Cocktail gatherings can last for several hours, so take care to protect the quality of these somewhat fragile ingredients. Still, don't use their fragility as an excuse to cut corners. A pet peeve of mine is to get an Irish Coffee from a bartender who neglects to use fresh cream for the topping. When the cream has soured or comes from a can or a plastic tub, it's enough to make me want to pass on the drink entirely. Always use heavy cream when mixing a cocktail. Usually labeled "whipping cream," it can be found in the

Fig. 5 – swizzle stick

dairy section of most grocery stores. To prepare cream for cocktails, lightly whip or FLASH BLEND it to the consistency of honey. If plain cream is too bland for your taste, add a dash of white CRÈME DE CACAO or vanilla before blending the drink.

To many novice drinkmakers, eggs are an unwelcome ingredient in a cocktail. But a teaspoon of egg white will give a drink a lovely froth, and its slight taste will go unnoticed by guests. However, it's still a good idea to tell imbibers about the addition of this ingredient, in case one of your guests is a vegan or allergic to eggs. Gin and egg may not sound appetizing, but when the two are mixed well it is a heavenly blend.

ACCENTS

As the cocktail's most subtle element, accents will tell you if your drink was prepared by a rookie bon vivant or a mixing master. The addition of the right accent can make a good drink recipe sublime. Bitters, herbal liqueurs, peels, and flora are all used, some to improve a cocktail's taste and others to enhance its appearance – whether they change the drink's color altogether or simply provide a contrast to the mixture's hue. While a sprig of mint floating on the surface may not affect a cocktail's flavor, its presence shows a sense of style, and its scent will elevate the experience from pleasing to remarkable.

Depending on the accent, you may want to add it as you mix the cocktail or wait until the drink has reached your guest's linen. Bitters are best shaken with a drink, while a dash of ANIS or a squeeze of fruit should be added later to create an additional layer of flavor. While you may easily grasp the recipes and techniques needed to prepare cocktails, the mastery of accents is an education without end. Should you set out to excel in this domain, you'll want to invest in atomizers, melon ballers, specialty cutlery, possibly even canning equipment – devices that will let you make any recipe your own. Atomizers, for instance, are perfect for misting your drink with exotic flavors such as vermouth, gin, or herbal liqueurs, while pickling and canning will let you replace the rosy pimento in an olive with such baby vegetables as carrots, peppers, or asparagus.

MEASUREMENT

A great bartender's motions are as subtle as a cocktail's edge, and only forceful when appropriate. Compare it to ballroom dancing: Every dancer follows similar steps, but it's their subtle execution that makes one dancer more graceful and elegant than another. When it comes to cocktails, the key to execution is measurement. Memorizing drink recipes is one thing, but adhering to them requires true discipline and is crucial to the artistry of the bar – just as a dancer is thrown off when a partner missteps, so too will your guests be when they taste a drink made with imprecision. Measurements are meant to be exacting and should be respected as such, while improvisations should be made with care. A little extra here and a little less there really will make a difference.

If you were to watch a true professional over the course of an evening, you would see several methods of measurement at work. Very practiced and disciplined bartenders "free pour." To the novice, they don't seem to

Fig. 6 – jigger be measuring at all, but many of them rely on imaginary markers on the side of a pint glass, while others "count" as they pour the spirit. By finding the proper cadence, they note a beat as each quarter-ounce flows from the bottle. Of course, the home host for whom drinkmaking is only an occasional practice will do better to eschew such shows of bartending bravado.

STANDARD BAR PORTIONS

The most important information to glean from a drink's measurements is the proportions of the ingredients to be used. Experienced mixers will often break a recipe down into "parts" – for instance, two parts strong to one part sweet and one part sour. Many cocktail books printed before the '50s use this formulation; nowadays the use of ounces is more common. Either way, it's easy to convert measurement in ounces (or other units of liquid measure) to parts and vice versa. A moment's calculation will tell you that a cocktail calling for 1½ ounces gin, ¾ ounce Cointreau, and ¾ ounce lime juice contains 2 parts gin to 1 part Cointreau and 1 part lime juice, or 4 centiliters (cl) gin, 2 centiliters Cointreau, and 2 centiliters lime juice. It's worth noting that we've broken most of the recipes down into ounces, splashes, and dashes that fit nicely into a 6-ounce cocktail glass; if your glasses are of a different size, you'll need to adjust the quantities accordingly.

STANDARD BAR PORTIONS		
Dash	⅛ ounce	0.5 cl
Splash	¼ ounce	1.0 cl
Tablespoon	½ ounce	2.0 cl
Pony	1 ounce	3.0 cl
Jigger	1½ ounces	4.0 cl

TERMS OF MEASUREMENT

The most useful of all cocktail accoutrements – and the one to purchase first – is the jigger, a liquid measure that holds up to 1½ ounces. This nifty device's name is often used in drink recipes as a unit of measure, such that one jigger equals 1½ ounces. The best of them are really two small cups end to end, one holding exactly half as much as the other. This makes it easy to follow recipes given in parts rather than in specific amounts. Although a simple stainless steel jigger is adequate (and commonly stocked at liquor stores), a sterling silver jigger is far more impressive, though you may need to scour the antique stores to find one. Whatever its composition, a well-made jigger will add clout and confidence to your mixing efforts.

Other common terms of measurement are *pony*, *splash*, *dash*, and *drop*. A pony equals 1 ounce, while a splash is equal to two teaspoons, ¼ of an ounce, or as little as you can pour out of a liquor bottle. A dash equals two drops, or ⅛ of an ounce. Practically speaking, a dash is one vigorous shake or two mild shakes of a bottle with a shaker top. A drop is just that: one drop. In practice, the measurements of a splash and a dash can vary greatly in quantity. Let your instinct and the course of an evening determine how you treat such measures. Until you understand the taste and pungency of each ingredient, start conservatively – you can always add more. The most common mistake in measurement is to make a cocktail overly strong, falsely assuming that your guests' main desire is intoxication. In fact, too much base spirit in a drink only makes for a half-sipped cocktail.

METHODS OF MEASUREMENT

To avoid costly errors in measurement, add less expensive ingredients first, followed by ingredients called for in smaller quantities. In most drink recipes, this means beginning with the last ingredient listed and continuing through the ones above it. This little ploy will prevent an early slip-up from forcing you to toss an entire drink down the drain – at most, you might lose an inexpensive mixer such as citrus juice.

By becoming an exacting technician of the bar, you'll be able to compare and catalog the qualities of various cocktails. You'll soon learn how a dash can change both the taste and the name of a cocktail – for instance, a dash of grenadine transforms a Daiquiri into the sweeter Bacardi Cocktail. But the most valuable tool in perfecting your recipes will be the facial expressions of those who try your cocktails. A face can't conceal the effects of an overly sour or bitter cocktail. Keep an eye on the jowls of your guests through their first two sips – if they appear to pucker or seem otherwise uncomfortable, some adjustment is probably required.

Fig. 7 – jiggers

EQUIPMENT

Although your "guinea pig" friends may prove to be your most useful resource in learning to make delectable drinks, there are plenty of accoutrements available to make mixing easier and more exact. The bar is like any other vocation: It's quality equipment that separates the craftspeople from the hobbyists. Fortunately for the minimalists among us, the jigger, the shaker (with a strainer), and the hand juicer are really the only necessary tools; most other bar paraphernalia are just specialty items, and while they do make mixing easier, you can typically find workable substitutes among your kitchenware.

A good stainless steel shaker with an integrated strainer top will give you years of cherished service. Should you come across a shaker with the bottom stamped "Mr. Bartender," buy it. Although this company is out of business now, many of its products still exist, and they are by far the easiest to use. Not all shakers are as valuable as they appear – some houseware chains have begun to sell poorly engineered imitations. The most important feature of any shaker is a tight-fitting top that won't leak – wet spots on the host's shoulder are as distasteful as drool on a pillow. However, the shaker's lid shouldn't fit so snugly that it becomes stuck when chilled. Elegant glass shakers are like uncomfortable but attractive clothes: best left in the closet. Though often more decorative, glass shakers do not chill as well as metal mixing tins. Glass pitchers, with a spout to hold back the ice, are fine for serving Martinis and Manhattans, but not for much else.

Chances are the most difficult of these tools to find will be a simple hand juicer. Although common in Mexico, good hand juicers are not readily available elsewhere. I've always expected to find a beautiful, well-machined or cast version produced in Germany or Switzerland, but, alas, I have not. My current squeezer, bought at a flea market years ago, was made in America, perhaps during the '50s, by a company called Ebaloy. I treasure its way of squeezing the slightest bit of oil from the peel into each drink. When using a mechanical juicer, take care to extract only the juices, leaving behind the pith and the pulp, which will make the juice bitter. A juicer that's too aggressive in the hands of an inattentive person will produce bad-tasting juice, unsuitable for mixing.

EQUIPMENT FOR THE HOME BAR

Jigger
20- to 24-ounce metal or glass shaker
Stainless steel strainer
Citrus juicer
Pint glass
BARSPOON
Sharp knife
Cutting board
Dull knife or ice pick
Ice scoop
Ice crusher (optional)
Wine opener
Bottle opener
Clean towels

15

Fig. 8 – barspoon

PORTIONING COCKTAILS

Just as visitors migrate to the kitchen when they smell a perfected soufflé, your friends will flock when they hear the cocktail shaker tinkling. But their raised expectations can be dashed just as quickly when it comes time for you to pour. Watching a host struggle through the portioning of drinks can be as deflating as watching a soufflé fall moments after it's been pulled from the oven. Beginning bartenders are often thrown for a loop when asked to mix a quantity of drinks that deviates from their norm. Preparing a round of six or seven drinks is quite different from making a batch of two. Often the mixer ends up over or under by a noticeable amount. Make too little and you'll look nervous and inexperienced; too much, and your guests will ask if you know what you're doing. Either way, the cocktail's quality and presentation are almost always at risk.

Fig. 9 – muddler

If a round of drinks comes out short, the host is usually faced with making another half a drink to top off the glasses that lost out. The extra bit, usually mixed in a hurry, rarely tastes right and never melds with the original batch. However, the way a host handles surplus can be more disastrous. Any extra drink should be served only as a reward to enthusiastic imbibers who take an initial gulp. A leftover cocktail in a shaker will quickly melt the ice, overdiluting the drink. Topping off a half-finished cocktail with such a mixture is a gesture akin to serving half-cooked seconds. To prevent such shortcomings, plan ahead by choosing a glass volume and a serving size that will be forgiving. The portion of the glass between the top of the liquid and the rim is the collar, and it should measure one quarter of an inch. By allowing a generous collar, you can vary the amount of liquid in each drink by about half an ounce.

Another technique important to portioning cocktails equally is decanting. When pouring a round of three or more cocktails, do it in more than one pass – usually two. On your first pass, fill each glass halfway, gently shaking the mixture as you go. Before making a second pass, assess how much cocktail is left in the shaker so you'll know how much to pour into each drink. Make your way back down the line, last glass first, filling each glass to within that quarter-inch collar. If you've done this correctly, the last drop will just top off the glass you started with, and your guests will gape in amazement. Not only will you portion them equally, but by following this sequence, you'll also ensure that each drink will taste exactly like the others.

As you get bolder and more sure of your skill, you may want to heighten the challenge. When serving cocktails like the Martini or the Manhattan, with easily melded ingredients that are stirred rather than shaken, attempt to fill the glasses equally and within the collar on the first pass. Since the ingredients of such drinks don't separate rapidly, each serving will taste the same without a second pass.

CHILLING

When a cocktail doesn't bite your throat, it's either too warm or too sweet – and more often than not, it's too warm. Though there are no secrets to making the perfectly chilled cocktail, there are a few tricks; ignore them, and you'll sacrifice the edge that cocktails rely on so heavily. Drinks served at a temperature between 20 and 25 degrees Fahrenheit will survive the scrutiny of the most demanding imbiber, and those served at temperatures up to 32 degrees will still be enjoyed. Of course, temperature is a relative thing: the ambient temperature, the temperature of any food you're serving, and the season will all affect how well guests receive your cocktails. Generally speaking, the colder the drink, the more diluted it's likely to be. But even at the same dilution, a colder beverage tastes less pungent than one served at room temperature. For most drinkers, slight dilution is a fair trade for an icy-cold cocktail, though Martini drinkers might argue otherwise.

17

ICE

Of course, ice is the key element in chilling a cocktail. Most people are aware that water freezes at 32 degrees Fahrenheit (0 degrees Celsius), but few realize that ice can achieve even lower temperatures. Some bartenders claim the dilution of cocktails is controlled by whether you shake or stir them during the chilling process. I've never subscribed to that; an overly diluted cocktail is the result of using old, relatively warm ice, easily identified by its coating of water. Wet ice is just reaching 32 degrees at its surface, and is thus about 20 degrees too warm to make a well-chilled, potent cocktail. Storing the mixing ice in the freezer until moments before it's needed will keep it properly chilled. Ice buckets are handy when serving tall drinks but ineffective in keeping ice truly cold for cocktails.

Fig. 10 – strainer

How rapidly you're able to chill your cocktails will also depend on how much of the ice's surface area comes into direct contact with the beverage. Cracked or chipped ice, having a greater overall surface area, will do a much quicker and more thorough job of chilling than those clumsy cubes formed in typical residential ice trays. If you do use homemade ice, break up the cubes with a small mallet or meat tenderizer. Another advantage of using small, delicate pieces of ice when shaking or stirring cocktails is that a few chips will always slip past the strainer and into the drink, adding to the perception of frostiness.

SHAKING VS. STIRRING

The age-old debate over whether to shake or stir a cocktail really hinges on one question: Is it more important that the drink be stinging cold or free from cloudiness? Typically, cocktails that only call for a blend of spirits with no juice added should be stirred – although, setting aside questions of temperature and appearance, there's no difference in taste between a cocktail stirred and one shaken. With either method of blending, the ice must be moved around in the liquid forcefully for the drink to be sufficiently chilled. When shaking, the ice should be thrown against the metal sides of the mixing tin. When stirring drinks, make certain that each ice cube makes at least one trip from the top to the bottom of the glass. By moving them up, down, and around in such a fashion, you'll be sure they've done their job. Note that if the liquid and the ice move at the same rate relative to one another, very little chilling or mixing will take

place. When chilling in a glass container, continue to stir until you feel the glass become cold; when using metal mixing tins, shake until it's painful to hold the chilled container. These are the basics no matter what mixed drink you choose to prepare – the methods are given below. Just keep in mind that each method requires ice at 10 degrees Fahrenheit.

Fig. 11 – mixing glass

Method 1: Stirred. This is the method of those Martini aficionados worldwide who still believe it's possible to bruise gin. But it's more related to the handling of clear cocktails like the Martini, since shaking makes them cloudy. Even though stirring is not as vigorous as shaking, you should achieve results similar to Method 2 if you do it properly. A cocktail adequately stirred will typically be about 30 degrees Fahrenheit.

Method 2: Shaken with a pint glass. This classic method of professional bartenders is done with a pint glass fitted snugly into an upside-down metal shaking tin – just like you've seen in the movies and at your local bar. This method typically results in 25-degree cocktails.

Method 3: Shaken with a stainless tin. Common sense will tell you that metal is a better conductor than glass, and indeed, this method makes for the coldest cocktails. Using a completely metal shaker, instead of one that's half glass and half metal, produces cocktails at a truly chilly 20 degrees.

Method 4: Parade-waving wrist jiggle. This method is preferred by every lazy host or bartender. It's also used by a few priggish ones who like to make the job of mixing look easier than it ought to be. Barely jiggling the ice back and forth in a pint glass, this tactic introduces the ingredients to one another but never makes them comfortable with the ice. Not only does this fail to chill a cocktail, it also fails to blend the ingredients. This method is the equivalent of pouring the ingredients over ice and then straining them into a glass. The temperature of a drink made using this method is typically between 39 and 42 degrees.

FLASH BLENDING

For chilling large drink batches from recipes that call for egg, cream, or fruit juice, consider flash blending to ensure properly cooled and blended drinks. The key difference between flash blending and shaking is the tin. A shaking tin is made of thinner stainless steel and is designed to fit around a pint glass, while the type of tin used for flash blending is larger and has a rolled lip around it, much like the milkshake tins you see at the soda fountain. Add enough ice so that the cocktail's ingredients fill the tin three-quarters full. Keep in mind that if you put too much liquid or too much ice into the tin, centrifugal force will push the contents right out again. Once you have the ingredients and the ice in order, put it all under the blade and give it two or three short whirls in the blender. Your goal is merely to crack some of the ice and to whip up a little froth on top of the cocktail; flash blend too long and the ice will disappear, leaving you with a liquid cesspool.

GLASSWARE

Another common mistake that leads to cocktails being sipped without their icy edge is failure to chill the glassware. A cocktail portioned into a warm glass will waste much of its chill on the vessel. When playing host, remember to stock your freezer with glassware before a gathering. (If you want glasses with a picture-perfect frost, polish them well before placing them in the freezer.) Merely storing glasses for a few minutes in the freezer will do the trick. If the party's a success and its pace won't allow for such luxuries, have extra ice on hand to chill the glasses as you prepare the drinks. To frost a glass in this way, simply fill it with ice a few minutes before mixing the cocktail that will go into it. When you're ready to use it, toss out the ice and any residual water.

MIXERS AND THE LAST RESORT

Although it rarely affects a cocktail's final temperature, using mixers at room temperature instead of refrigerating them can make for diluted beverages. Soda water and other mixers should be well chilled, or they'll melt most of the ice used in the drink. However, if you plan on squeezing fresh juice, do not store the fruit in the refrigerator – chilling citrus fruit diminishes the quantity of juice. If you must prep the juice the night before a gathering, store it in the refrigerator, but only in a well-sealed container that's filled to the top; as with fine wine, an abundance of oxygen in the bottle will oxidize the liquid.

When you find yourself unable to get a cocktail cold enough, there's nothing wrong with enjoying it on the rocks – a properly made drink on ice can be particularly refreshing, especially on a relaxing or extremely hot day. But never take the easy way out when serving drinks in this fashion. Do not simply pour the ingredients over ice in a tumbler without bothering to mix the drink, leaving your guests to fend for themselves with a undersized stirrer. Even worse is to shake a drink, only to empty it into a glass without using a strainer. To serve a drink on the rocks, follow the same steps as you would to serve it up, but strain the mixture into a tumbler or goblet filled with ice. If the cocktail is cold and well mixed when it comes in contact with an ice-filled glass, its flavor and integrity will be preserved. By the time an imbiber finishes the drink, there should still be plenty of ice left in the glass. Even a Martini, mixed by a master and then strained over fine lumps of ice, will retain many of the classic qualities for which this drink is idolized. After several minutes, the drink's character will change, but if the drink is mixed properly, the imbiber will have gotten the needed kick in the first few sips, while still having his or her thirst quenched. The exceptions to this rule are such drinks as whiskey on the rocks, which benefits from slow dilution. Part of the experience of ordering a single spirit served over ice is that the drink starts out as a very strong beverage that soothes quickly but ends up as a thirst-quenching delight – just about the time a second round arrives.

SERVING VARIATIONS

People who learned bar diction from James Bond and other Hollywood heroes use the word *neat* interchangeably with *up*. But for the record, *neat* means a liquid is served unmixed and undiluted – in other words, the beverage is poured straight from its bottle or decanter into a glass with no ice. Port wines and cognacs are good examples of digestifs that are typically served neat. You would never order a Martini neat, unless you just wanted Martini & Rossi vermouth in a glass. Vodka, however, is ideal neat, and demonstrates why *neat* doesn't necessarily mean *warm*. A bottle of vodka, Genever, or aquavit, for instance, can spend its life in the freezer, making appearances only at the outset of meals featuring borscht. *Up*, on the other hand, implies that the ingredients of the drink will be mixed, typically with ice, before being strained into a glass without ice. The bartender will usually stir or shake the beverage with ice and strain it into a stemmed glass. True cocktails, like Martinis and Manhattans, are served this way unless a guest requests otherwise. If a bartender asks whether you'd like your order up or on the rocks, assume your cocktail savvy's been slighted.

Over describes one of the most relaxing concoctions ever – a drink composed of one or two spirits *poured* directly into a glass filled with ice, like a whiskey on the rocks. When served promptly, the first sip of a drink made as an over tastes strong, as if straight. After a few seconds, though, the ice melts a bit, and the spirit becomes refreshing. A bit of advice: Never take a glass of ice from a whiskey drinker – the ice is the reward for finishing the drink. Very similar to a drink ordered over is a *mist* – the only difference, in fact, is the type of ice used. A mist calls for shaved or finely crushed ice, while a drink served over calls for cracked ice. Drinks ordered as mists are much colder than beverages served on the rocks or over, because more of the ice's surface area touches the spirit. Mists are perfect for hot summer afternoons, as every sip brings with it a flotilla of small, refreshing chips of ice.

GARNISHES

Like a flattering hat, a cocktail's garnish is the crowning touch, a bit of flair to complete a properly prepared potable. Though it's not uncommon to see a host follow a drink's recipe to the letter only to leave off that final detail that defines the cocktail, the wise mixer will never neglect it. It's a sublime addition that only a few palates will detect, but one that every eye will miss if it's been forgotten. The garnish shows your guests that you've thought of every detail – and is, in certain cases, much more than an accessory. For instance, the Old Fashioned's flavor relies heavily on its garnishes and their proper treatment, and the same is true of the Mojito.

Garnishes are accents – never make them showy or overpowering. They should have a subtle presence – not in your face, but floating calmly atop a drink or lurking at the bottom, soaking up the last bits of spirit before offering themselves to the taste buds. Fortunately, garnishing a drink isn't

Fig. 12 – garnishes

difficult. In fact, you need only be familiar with the fundamentals: twists, squeezes, wheels, olives, onions, maraschino cherries, mint, and fresh-picked innocuous flowers. Once you've mastered these garnishes, your drink recipe box will expand further as you discover that a simple garnish substitution can result in an entirely different drink. For example, a Martini, when garnished with an onion instead of a green olive, becomes a Gibson; if a black olive is used, the drink is a Buckeye.

TWISTS

Cut from the peel of a lemon, the twist contains all sorts of aromatic oils. In a lucid cocktail like the Rob Roy or the Martini, it adds just a hint of bitter lemon. (Lime twists, though used quite often, are less elegant.) When preparing twists, remember to remove as much of the pith (the white part of the fruit) as possible – it's very bitter, and too much will spoil a drink.

The wonderful thing about the twist is that, unlike extravagant garnishes like cherries and large wedges of fruit, it's so sublime that you can't overdo it. As long as your fruit is fresh, your knife sharp, and your creativity willing, any shape or style will be welcome. To make a twist, take a sharp knife and cut the ends off the lemon, just to the point where the fruit begins to show. Next, insert a stainless-steel ice pick about ⅛ inch into the lemon between the yellow peel and the fruit, positioning the tip of the pick as close to the peel as possible. Gently circle the lemon with the ice pick to separate the lemon peel from the pith and the fruit. As you make your way around the lemon, gradually insert the pick farther into the fruit. (You'll probably have to repeat this process, this time starting from the other end of the lemon.) Once you've separated the hull completely from the fruit, the core may pop out easily; if not, make a single cut along the peel from one end to the other, then remove the fruit. Roll the peel into its natural configuration, but much tighter; then use your sharpest knife to cut ¼-inch sections of the peel. The ideal twist is long, curly, about ¼ inch wide, and ⅛ inch thick. The twists will be only slightly curled at this point; when it's time to serve the drink, retwist or roll the zest to curl it better. Twist or snap the zest above the glass so more of the aromatic oils are mixed into the drink, then rest the fruit gently on the side of the drink – the perfect, practical accessory.

Fig. 13 – juicer

SQUEEZES

This garnish, also typically derived from a lemon, is reserved for tall drinks like the Pimm's Cup that require a touch of fresh juice as an accent. Usually the lemon squeeze is a sixth of a whole lemon with both ends cut off; anything larger detracts from the drink. When serving a drink with a squeeze, cut a small slit into the side of the fruit and rest the garnish on the lip of the glass. Let your guests do the squeezing unless the drink's recipe directs otherwise.

A lime squeeze is smaller than its lemon counterpart, using only an eighth of the fruit. It's the perfect garnish for any cocktail calling for fresh lime juice and rum or tequila. The squeeze in a Daiquiri, for instance, adds a little unadulterated juice and a slight bitterness that helps balance the drink's overall sweetness; and it's the standard garnish for tall drinks like the Cuba Libre and the gin and tonic. To prepare this garnish, first cut the lime lengthwise in quarters, then cut each quarter in half crosswise.

23

WHEELS

Called for when a drink needs nothing more, a wheel or a half-wheel gives the imbiber something to eat or suck on after a sip of the cocktail. Wheels are difficult to squeeze juice from but make refreshing asides to many tropical beverages and are the perfect accompaniment to slightly sweet drinks in need of a little bravura. Use your sharpest knife to prepare them – like tomato slices, they're beautiful when precisely cut but look horribly sloppy otherwise. Slices ⅛ to ¼ inch in width will do nicely – merely rest them on the rim of a drink's glass.

MISCELLANY OF THE GARNISH TRAY

Olives and onions are almost always interchangeable, depending on the drinker's preference, and both follow the simple rule: One is elegant, two is proper, and three is a meal. The brine in which they're cured adds a little saltiness that complements gin drinks. One technique cherished by those who prefer very DRY Martinis is to pour the brine from the olive or onion bottle and replace it with dry vermouth. If olives are not to your liking, other pickled vegetables may be substituted in cocktails – though such garnishes are not traditional.

Maraschino cherries – commonly swiped from the host's garnish tray by ill-behaved guests – have a lamentable tendency to take a drink over with their syrupy-sweet essence, so use them sparingly and one at a time. The "juice" from the bottle can act as a sweetener or a coloring, but resort to it only if specifically requested.

When it comes to flora, mint is an all-time favorite for finishing the presentation of a drink. The uppermost sprig is one of nature's greatest gifts to the bar. Atop almost any tall drink or floating in a cocktail like the Stinger, mint adds a delicate aroma. If you're a connoisseur of edible flowers, use blossoms to top a cocktail or mixed drink.

Distillation

Mother Nature deserves the credit for inspiring distillation, but it was adventurous alchemists who perfected it. Yearning to understand the nature of matter – and somehow certain it would turn to gold when heated – they boiled a host of different liquids. No precious metals resulted, but they got something almost as good: distillation, a process of refinement that has enriched cocktail culture beyond measure.

Although it has come a long way since its crude early days, distillation is still used to produce alcohol. Some of the resulting distillates are burned as fuel or used as antifreeze, while the potable product is reserved for the cocktail hour. Of course, there have been instances – most notably during Prohibition – when imbibers turned a blind eye to this distinction. But nowadays, strict laws and a mild surge of common sense have set clear boundaries for the classification of distillates, and the closest most of us will ever get to sipping subpar spirits is ordering WELL drinks at the local dive.

Now that the landscape is studded with boutique wineries and microbrew pubs, plenty of people are willing to give you an earful about how these fermentations are produced. Both beer and wine are made through a chemical reaction that produces carbon dioxide and alcohol when the right amounts of sugar, water, and yeast are present. Distillation picks up where fermentation leaves off: Once alcohol is present in a liquid, applying heat will cause the alcohol to boil, eventually turning it into a gas that rises from the remaining liquid. Because water's boiling point is higher than that of alcohol, it's possible to separate the two substances by keeping the liquid's temperature between these two points. The volatile vapors are then recaptured and concentrated. Once distilled, the alcohol is still relatively unpalatable – it's through aging and blending that distillers arrive at the final, saleable spirit. Distillates vary widely according to the raw materials used – fruit, grain, malt, and yeast – and the different methods of production and aging employed.

LABELING OF SPIRITS

When shopping for distilled spirits, you may notice that most are labeled 80 proof, though they can range from about 30 to 190 (anything lower than 80 proof, in fact, must be labeled as a diluted spirit). In the United States, *proof* expresses the concentration of ethyl alcohol in a given liquid; the number is exactly twice the percentage of alcohol present (80 proof, for instance, equals 40 percent alcohol). As the minimum required by law, 80 is the most profitable proof at which to bottle spirits. But rarely does a spirit's bottled proof reflect anything about how the spirit was distilled or aged. When rating the quality of distillates, remember that the lower the distillation proof, the more *fusel oils* and *congeners* are carried with the alcohol. Although fusel oils and congeners sound like unfriendly terms, they're actually natural elements that help drinkers identify the origin of a spirit. They give distillates their character, as in the notable cases of whiskey and brandy. When buying spirits, you'll get more for your money if you choose those with a low distillation proof and a high bottled proof – in other words, spirits that haven't been overly diluted with water. Keep in mind, though, that spirits with proofs higher than 160 rarely display distinct characteristics.

Even though a country may choose to regulate production of spirits within its borders, U.S. trade and distillation laws dictate much of the information on the labels of distilled spirits imported and sold in the United States. This is largely a response to the early days of the whiskey trade, when distillers would ship their products in casks, along with one empty bottle that was used for display. As consumers purchased the product, they would simply fill their own jugs from the cask – a practice that kept the cost of packaging down but was also an invitation to fraud on the part of the retailer. It soon became impossible to guarantee that the product dispensed from the barrel was what had arrived in it originally: a shopkeeper could easily dilute the original spirit or replace it with a product of a lesser grade. During the early 1800s, brand recognition was not an attribute of distillers but of reputable resellers. In 1870, however, George Garvin Brown began bottling his bourbon – known as Old Forester – in clear, sealed bottles that weren't easily tampered with. Although Mr. Brown's whiskey cost more, it started a trend among distillers, and cask distribution soon fell by the wayside as spirit makers began bottling, sealing, and labeling their wares to ensure that consumers would get what they expected.

Nowadays state inspectors from the Department of Alcoholic Beverage Control visit establishments at random to verify that the spirits behind the bar are true to the proofs marked on their labels; any variation, and the bottles are confiscated and the proprietor fined. The much beloved Bureau of Alcohol, Tobacco, and Firearms is responsible for the classification of all liquor sold in the United States. Of the main groupings on the books, the ones pertaining to cocktails and other mixed drinks are whiskey, brandy, gin, rum, neutral spirits, tequila, and cordials. This system is designed to help consumers interpret the different variations in these spirits. *Cask strength*, for instance, is a rare measure of quality; the term means that water wasn't added to the spirit during bottling to lower its proof and increase its volume. Cask strength doesn't guarantee that the spirit was never diluted, but it's a good sign of a more flavorful whiskey. *Bottled in bond* is another term you'll see on the labels of spirits, but this phrase provides no indication of a distillate's quality; it merely lets you know that the distiller has paid its taxes, and that the product has been stored in a bonded warehouse for four years at no less than 100 proof. Simply put, bonding a spirit is how distillers avoid owing tax on a whiskey before it's ready to be bottled and sold.

The age marked on a bottle or a label is the length of time the distillate was allowed to mature before bottling, most typically in oak barrels. There the distilled spirit reacts with the natural qualities of the wood and the oxygen, which mellow its taste. Once the spirit has been bottled, the aging process comes to a halt; except for slight oxidation or evaporation, the spirit will change little after this point. If the label reads "not less than ten years," the spirit is a blend of distillates of various ages, the youngest having been aged ten years. When it comes to age, older is not necessarily better. Some spirits derive no benefit from aging after the third year, and though some robust spirits like cognac can stand for 25 years in various barrels, most will turn woody and bitter long before that. Buying and sampling distillates is a lifelong effort. As your expertise grows, you'll learn to strike a balance between age, quality, and price in the spirits you buy.

WHISKEY

Unless you've already acquired a taste for whiskey – or whisky, if you prefer the spelling used by the Scots, the English, and the Canadians – you'll find it the most difficult spirit to buy. So many brands and types exist that you'll inevitably feel you're missing some key bottle, and you probably are. In simple terms, whiskey – made throughout the United Kingdom and North America – is a spirit distilled from a mash of cereals that has undergone various stages of fermentation and distillation.

This rich brown spirit is most often requested by its region of origin – as in the cases of Irish or Canadian whiskey, scotch, and bourbon – or by its major components, such as rye, sour mash, or single malt. If all that fails or seems somehow insufficient, a whiskey may be ordered by its brand name. Many other factors contribute to the unique tastes of each type, and when you add the lore that surrounds each label and variation, you can see how so many whiskeys survive in today's fickle market.

SCOTCH

One of the most familiar whiskeys in the world, scotch is made only in the small nation of Scotland. While the prominence of this spirit is due more to marketing than to the whiskey's great history, Scotland's excellent natural resources and the superior craft of its distillers have kept single-malt scotches at the pinnacle of the whiskey world. Revered for their unique flavors, single malts are the choice of most connoisseurs and others willing to spend more for their tipple, though historically these scotches have been unpopular with the average drinker, who prefers the smoother taste of blended scotch.

Until the 19th century, the exportation of whiskey from Scotland was not common, and malt whiskey was mainly a drink for the Scots themselves. In 1820, barely 5 percent of all distilleries in Scotland were selling their product in the nearby English market. Single-malt scotch, the product of malted barley distilled in a simple POT STILL, was both expensive and time-consuming to make. But all that changed with the invention of the patent still by Robert Stein in 1826 and the Aeneas Coffey still in 1830. These innovations raised the rate of production and let distillers produce more spirits faster and at less expense using corn, rye, and oats. This new distillate, called grain whiskey, was much lighter than the more robust malt whiskey, though it was still known as scotch. This shared title disturbed the malt distillers, who lobbied the English Parliament to define whiskey by law. But in the end it was the industrious renegades selling blended whiskey who benefited from the government's definition of scotch as "a spirit obtained by distillation from a mash of cereal grain, sacchrafied by the diastase of malt" – a definition that did little to distinguish single malts from immature blended scotches. Single malts continued to be produced and enjoyed in the homeland, while the less expensive blended whiskeys were exported, spreading the name "scotch" around the world.

BLENDED SCOTCH

Understanding the value of blended scotch whiskeys in today's market is not nearly as simple as evaluating single malts, whose price is usually a good indicator of quality. With the rise in popularity of aged single malts among the cigar crowd, blended whiskey producers have joined in, hoping to profit from that fad. By blending grain whiskey with very old single malts, they've created an image that chases the top dollar. Johnnie Walker's varied labels – Red, Black, Gold, and Blue – are a case in point. Red Label is a blend of relatively young malt whiskey and grain whiskey. It's an excellent scotch for cocktails, and can be enjoyed on the rocks or with water. Black Label, a blend of whiskeys aged 12 years or more, offers a more refined taste when sampled straight, but when mixed in a cocktail, its higher cost (about $15 a bottle) is simply wasted. The two premium labels, Gold and Blue, are blends of older whiskeys commanding even higher prices, but are too smooth and nondescript for my taste. I side with the single-malt distillers when choosing a premium whiskey: If you plan to sip your scotch, spend more than $30 a bottle and sip single malts – blended premium whiskeys just aren't as interesting.

IRISH

The Irish have been credited as the first whiskey distillers, but today their spirits are among the least popular for sipping and drinkmaking outside the island nation itself. Light in body, most Irish whiskeys are made not from a single malted grain but from a blend of lighter grains, whose distillations typically produce an undistinctive taste. The malt used during fermentation is not smoked over a peat fire, as is the case with scotch. Although similarly distilled in a pot still and aged only slightly less than scotch, an Irish whiskey rarely stands up in character to a single malt. Not commonly used in cocktails, Irish whiskey is most often enjoyed straight or in a cup of coffee at meal's end.

NORTH AMERICAN

Soon after the arrival of the first European colonists in North America, the craft of whiskey distillation began on this continent. The migration to the grain-rich west conveniently coincided with the advent of the patent still, and so early western settlers found it relatively easy to produce grain whiskey in the New World. Less concerned with tradition than with practicalities, this resourceful group of settlers looked to the plentiful harvests of grain and corn for its raw materials. For this reason, North American whiskey is classified more by the ingredients of a particular mash than by distillation method. The whiskey produced on this continent is similar to the grain whiskey produced in Scotland and Ireland – but instead of being blended with a heavier-bodied whiskey for bottling, it is simply aged and bottled by itself, making for a very light and palatable spirit.

BOURBON

The father of North American whiskey, bourbon gets its name from the county in Kentucky where it was disputably (at least from the Virginians' perspective) first distilled. Bourbon still hails from the Bluegrass State, but the original county from which it came has since been divided into more than 30 counties – each of which can legally label its whiskey as bourbon. Federal liquor regulations require that bourbon be distilled from a sour mash containing 51 percent corn and be aged in charred oak barrels for a minimum of two years – a practice that gives bourbon a distinct smokiness. Although the law doesn't govern the type of still to be used, bourbon cannot be distilled legally at proofs higher than 160.

Jack Daniel's is probably the most distinguished sour mash whiskey that doesn't bear the bourbon moniker. Tennessee whiskeys such as Jack Daniel's and George Dickel are too proud of their own heritage to buddy up to the bourbons. To set themselves apart from their neighbors, these two Tennessee whiskeys use charcoal produced from maple trees, which adds a sweet finish to their distillates. Though not as cloying as whiskey liqueurs like Southern Comfort, George and Jack do not mix well in cocktails, but they continue to be favorites of the shot-and-beer crowd.

MASH

Bourbon distillers employ the sour mash method of fermentation, which requires that some of the "spill back" – the previous day's mash or spent beer – be added to the fermentation. As a general rule, one quarter of all yeast needed for the mash comes from the spill back. By deriving some of the yeast required for fermentation from an earlier batch, distillers achieve greater consistency in their product while conveniently saving money. Sweet mash, on the other hand, refers to whiskey produced from a fermented mash created entirely with fresh yeast. Today, this method – slightly more expensive and less consistent in quality than the sour mash method – is rarely used for mass-produced whiskey. Although the aromas of sweet and sour mash batches may differ, any differences in the final distillations will be indiscernible to the average drinker.

RYE

As one might guess, rye whiskey is defined as a distillate made from a mash containing 51 percent rye. Some consider rye a lesser grain, but a straight rye whiskey will display more character than a bourbon of equal rank. First produced in Pennsylvania and Maryland, rye whiskey is still most closely associated with those states. Those not fond of bourbon's smokiness will appreciate the full-bodied American straight ryes made by Jim Beam, Wild Turkey, and Old Overholt.

CANADIAN

Thanks to Prohibition in the United States, Canadian whiskeys gained great popularity during the 1920s, and their light nature continues to please – particularly those drinkers just beginning to appreciate whiskey. A blend of grains, this distillate is marketed in varying qualities. Light-bodied whiskeys such as Seagram's V.O., Canadian Club, or the premium Crown Royal are all perfect for cocktails.

BRANDY

Grapes are blessed with a natural balance of water, yeast, and sugar, so it's scarcely surprising that wine was one of the first fermented beverages known to humanity. Since those first grapes were crushed, volumes have been written about wine production. Today, wine is still treated with a reverence unique in the world of food and drink – with its distillate, brandy, holding its own and garnering more than mild respect.

A robust spirit, brandy is best when distilled in an old-fashioned pot still hammered out from sheets of copper. This type of still, also known as an alembic still, simply consists of a pot to heat the wine, a gooseneck tube to transport the vapor to the condenser, and a container to collect the liquid. Similar in style to the stills used to produce single-malt whiskey, the alembic still is a sensitive apparatus that produces relatively low proofs, between 120 and 140. At such proofs, enough congeners are present in the distillation that aged brandies will display distinct qualities depending on where they were produced; accordingly, each brandy is classified by the country or district from which it hails. The finest brandies are still made in Cognac, a region in the south of France near Bordeaux. High-quality cognac is too expensive (and too full-bodied) to mix in a cocktail; reserve it for sipping straight. In California, a few small distilleries produce superior brandies for the same price as an average Hennessey or Courvoisier. Carneros Alambic Distillery and Germain Robin make wonderful brandies using the same processes as their French counterparts.

Brandy is the distillation of fermented wine, but not the kind of wine you sip with dinner. Wines high in acidity and in alcohol content are heated in a still to produce this distillate. Most brandies go through at least two distillations. The first yields a liquid that's about 30 percent alcohol, while the second pass results in an *eau de vie* of 70 percent alcohol. A colorless, fiery liquid, *eau de vie* must be aged in oak for at least three years before it is drinkable. Most brandies, however, benefit from 10 to 12 years of aging in oak. Distillers may choose to age superior brandies for as long as 55 years, but if they misjudge a spirit's quality, they run the risk of bittering it.

As the brandy matures, it will be transferred to various barrels in the course of the aging process. If a new oak barrel is used, the brandy will remain there for only a year, since the wood will react quickly with the spirit. As brandies are moved from barrel to barrel, most are blended with other vintages to enhance the spirit's taste. The oak containers, like those used to age other spirits, are highly porous and allow evaporation to occur throughout the aging process, resulting in a decrease in volume and proof. As a consequence, the brandy becomes a more mellow and refined spirit, evolving from a colorless, coppery-tasting liquid to a smooth, amber liquor with only a hint of grape. If a sweeter taste is desired, the brandy can spend its last two months of aging in a barrel used previously to age sweet wines like port or sherry.

EAU DE VIE

Although most commonly associated with grapes, brandy can be distilled from the fermented mash of any fruit. *Eaux de vie blanches* – or young brandies – are distilled from many fruits and are especially popular in Europe. POIRE WILLIAM, kirsch, and framboise are all examples of traditional *eaux de vie* – colorless brandies with aromas and flavors reminiscent of fruit blossoms. Unfortunately, most people are put off by the fiery finish of these spirits. An acquired taste, *eaux de vie* are aged minimally and are cherished by aficionados for their refined yet rough edge. Rarely called for in cocktail recipes, an *eau de vie* is typically reserved for evening's end, when a brisk nightcap is in order.

CALVADOS, or apple brandy, is classified as an *eau de vie*, but in taste, appearance, and experience it's much closer in character to an aged grape brandy. Made in Normandy from small bitter apples, Calvados can be aged to rival the best cognacs. When gently warmed in the palm, a snifter of fine Calvados will take the winter chill out of anyone's cheeks. If fine brandies haven't been to your liking in the past, hunt for a bottle of *Pays d'Auge* Calvados, the top-of-the-line apple brandy. To appreciate a lesser Calvados, mix it with coffee or in a cocktail that calls for APPLEJACK.

POMACE BRANDIES

The country cousins of brandy, these distillates are produced from the remnants of a wine crush. Once the wine has been expressed for aging, fermented seeds, stems, and other parts of the fruit remain and can be distilled later. The pomace is distilled into an unrefined, highly aromatic spirit. In Italy, this brandy is known as grappa, while it goes by marc in France and pisco in South America. These regional spirits were first enjoyed by farmers and workers who wisely gathered the grape refuse for their own winemaking. Marc and grappa have since developed into a digestif fad in culinary circles, and pisco remains a popular beverage among South American locals and tourists alike. Very similar in quality to its European counterparts, pisco is the defining ingredient in such popular cocktails as the Pisco Sour.

RUM

No other spirit is as closely tied to human suffering as rum. Even its name makes reference to mayhem: from an archaic English dialect, *rumbullion* means "kill devil; a hot, hellish liquor." Rum's troubles began in the 15th century, when sugarcane from East Asia made its way to the West Indies (at about the time our favorite imperialist, Cristóforo Colombo, hit the scene). What followed over the next 400 years – the sugar trade and the discovery of rum – contributed to the enslavement of millions of people. But rum has made great strides in the cocktail world, despite its dark past. These days, most suffering associated with this liquor is self-inflicted.

Distilled from molasses, rum is made in every tropical region that produces sugar, but where quality is concerned, Cuba is to rum as Cognac is to brandy. As with any distillation, climatic and geographical differences will be evident in rums produced on different islands or in different countries after they've been aged and bottled. Much like whiskey and brandy, rum is classed first by the country of its origin and secondly by its style or color.

Sugarcane consists of 90 percent pulp, only about 20 percent of which becomes refined sugar. The byproduct of refinement is molasses, which has an abundance of usable sugars. Combined with yeast, these sugars create a fermentation ripe for distillation. Since no yeast is present in cane sap, distillers add their own, and many rum makers consider the yeast their secret ingredient – though other flavorings, such as raisins or vanilla, may be added later to give additional aroma and flavor to the rum.

Fermentation greatly affects a rum's taste – the longer the fermentation, the more intense the distillate's flavor. Lighter-bodied rums (such as those produced in Puerto Rico or Cuba) ferment quickly, in about 20 to 30 hours, while heavy-bodied rums (like Myers's from Jamaica and aromatic French-styled rums from Martinique) are often seethed up to 12 days. Distillers can control the length of fermentation by carefully selecting an efficient yeast. If a slower fermentation is desired, the distiller may choose to let Mother Nature work her magic on her own.

Naturally occurring yeast travels through the air, finding its place among the mash. Different strains of yeast will produce different styles of fermented mash. If they react quickly, the mash will demonstrate lighter qualities than if the yeasts were allowed to develop over a long period of time. The still used after fermentation will also greatly affect a rum's body and taste. A pot still, for instance, produces a full-bodied – though rustic – low-proof distillate that displays a maximum of flavor. The column still, on the other hand, makes for a lighter-bodied rum in a larger quantity that can be flavored later in the production process. After two passes through either still, a clear, fiery spirit will result. This raw spirit, called AGUARDIENTE, is unpalatable to most; however, with a style reminiscent of pomace brandies, *aguardiente* can be a great component of cocktails. In Brazil, *aguardiente* goes by the name cachaça, and is the main ingredient in the Caipirinha and the Batida.

Most *aguardientes* go on to become refined rums, typically aged for three years in oak casks or large stainless steel vats. Although you might suppose that brown rum is aged in oak while white (or clear) rum is aged in stainless steel, you can never be certain. Some rums are aged in oak but later filtered so that any color is stripped from the spirit. It's also common to flavor rum aged in stainless steel with molasses, caramel, raisins, and other additives that naturally impart color to the spirit. After aging the rum, the *maestro de ron*, or master blender, dictates the final qualities of the spirit by mixing it with various batches of rum aged from three to six years. When judging rums, don't be fooled by their color. White rums, which originated in the former French colonies, are often quite aromatic. But aromatic rums rarely make a good addition to a cocktail because they tend to overwhelm the other ingredients.

NEUTRAL SPIRITS

Unlike brandy, whiskey, and rum, there's little mystery or lore about the production of gin and vodka. No country or region bases its claim of cultural superiority on having created superlative versions of these spirits. By law and tradition, neutral grain spirits are distilled at higher than 190 proof. At such a high concentration, these spirits retain no natural qualities that would identify their source. Potatoes, rice, and grains all produce similar, tasteless distillations, labeled as neutral grain spirits. Keen palates might detect slight variations in finish, but most will note no difference at all. Aside from the high distillation proof, U.S. law requires that neutral spirits go through a charcoal-filtering process to remove any impurities left after distillation. This filtering characterizes the final product as much as the distillation does. Vodka producers, depending on the quality desired, will redistill and filter the spirits up to three times before blending them with water and bottling them. In the case of gin and other flavored spirits, the distillate is further rectified to achieve its final flavor. By adding JUNIPER berries, herbs, roots, and other bitters, each distiller can create a mildly distinct character for its gin. Though more complex than most flavored vodkas, gin is rectified in an almost identical fashion. If you find guests reluctant to try gin, merely have them think of it as a flavored vodka; after all, vodka is in many respects an incomplete gin – sort of like food without the flavor. By classic cocktail standards, today's flavored vodkas – particularly the popular citrus and pepper varieties – are more similar in style to fruit-flavored gins, which makes me wonder how popular a juniper-flavored Absolut might be.

FLAVORING SPIRITS

Spirits, including liqueurs, can be flavored in a variety of ways. The simplest and least expensive way to flavor distilled spirits is to add oils extracted from a natural source – but only the lowest grade of spirits are flavored in this way, as it creates a taste that fails to blend with the distillate. The second, more common method of flavoring is as simple as making tea: steeping or macerating a flavoring agent in neutral grain alcohol to produce a spirit infused with natural flavors and color. Peppers, citrus rinds, whole fruit, and herbs can be added to a grain spirit for up to a month or until the desired flavor is reached. If the spirits are to become a liqueur, sugar and water are added before bottling. As a general rule, higher-proof spirits absorb essential oils and flavors better than lower-proof spirits do. If you intend to experiment with flavoring spirits at home, model your production after the steeping of tea, and think of proof as heat. A good cup of tea is the result of fresh leaves steeped in very hot water over a short time; if you use only warm water, the process will take too long to produce a brisk cup of tea, and the bitter character of the leaves will likely become evident. Likewise, if you want fresh-tasting flavored spirits, start with high-proof alcohol, greater than 100 proof. Once you achieve a good crisp flavor, you can dilute it to 80 proof with distilled water.

The most complex and expensive way to rectify spirits occurs during the distillation process itself. Picture a column still – a tall cylinder with numerous perforated shelves. Distillers place herbs, roots, and spices on these shelves, which are then heated by the rising of the gaseous spirits during distillation. As the heated gas rises, it also heats these flavoring agents, which release oils and essences that in turn bind themselves to the alcohol molecules before being collected and condensed into the final distilled spirit. Once the spirits have been flavored, they are aged, blended, and diluted until the bottled quality is achieved. Although this may sound elementary, it is very difficult for a distiller to achieve the same flavor with consistency, batch after batch – to obtain a reputable quality, the person in charge of flavoring must be constantly sensitive to the potency of the flavoring agents.

VODKA AS WHITE PAINT

Regrettably, gin has become less popular as a base ingredient than vodka. Somehow, gin has never quite succeeded in shaking off the shady reputation it acquired during Prohibition, and vodka – through the deep pockets of crafty marketers – has become entrenched in the American bar. Of the two spirits, gin is by far the more difficult to manage when mixing cocktails, and a well-made gin drink is a greater artistic feat than any cocktail made with vodka. The latter spirit certainly has a place in the world, and it sells incredibly well, but when it comes to producing classics, you won't find too many that contain it. After all, mix white paint with any other paint and it melds with that color. Similarly, mix vodka with anything and it becomes that ingredient. Any less than deft craftsperson can hide behind it, whereas the work of someone truly gifted will remain well hidden by it.

Perhaps it's vodka's tender years as a stateside distillation that are to blame. Although this spirit has been around other, colder parts of the world for hundreds of years, it only hit the States in the late '40s, nearly 30 years after the OLD SCHOOL OF AMERICAN BARTENDING ended, when the great classic cocktails had already been invented. Some old-time alchemists argue that even if vodka had been more widely available back then, no serious bartender would have added it to a cocktail, because it wouldn't have contributed anything to the mix – vodka merely spreads a drink out.

Back in 1949, the Bureau of Alcohol, Tobacco, and Firearms mandated that vodka be "neutral spirits … without distinctive character, aroma, taste, or color." One of the first vodkas to hit the States followed that decree: "Smirnoff WHITE WHISKEY. No Smell. No Taste." The distiller went on to sell its spirit as "breathless," and – as William Grimes, author of *Straight Up or On the Rocks*, points out – "more or less announced: 'Look, we all want a drink at midday, but it's starting to look bad.'" From the bartender's perspective, it did look bad. I occasionally enjoy buffalo grass vodka pulled straight from the freezer, or a modern-day cocktail like the Drink Without a Name or the Petit Zinc, but the concept of vodka masked by orange juice – let alone vodka on the rocks – is a bit absurd.

Some vodka proponents insist that if you can taste the difference between two brands in a blind tasting, one brand must have more "flavor." Nice try. You can do the same trick with two glasses of water, but few tasters would claim that their water tastes like anything other than pure H_2O. That's why most people don't quite buy the government's definition of vodka as odorless and tasteless. It's all relative, and when you stick your schnozz over a tumbler of vodka and then do the same to a glass of water, you do notice a difference.

TEQUILA

This fiery spirit has always been slighted by the traditional cocktail crowd. Though appreciated at the occasional cocktail event, this distillate's mixing reputation has been soiled by distillers pushing low-grade tequilas and by the buffoons who drink them. You'd think people would know better, but I've seen plenty of imbibers take a little salt to momentarily deaden the taste buds before shooting an ounce or two of tequila. Fortunately, as tequila continues to grow in popularity, distillers are improving their production methods. The more refined tequilas they're starting to produce could lead to new, popular cocktails that would expand the roster beyond such typical tequila drinks as the Margarita and the Tequila Sunrise.

Much as cognac is protected and regulated by the French government, the production of tequila is managed by the rulers of Mexico. Traditionally, spirits advertised as tequila could only originate in the state of Jalisco, but this spirit's popularity has led the Mexican government to expand the tequila region to include the states of Michoacán, Tamaulipas, Nayarít, and Guanajuato.

Many drinkers believe that mescal is tequila, but this is incorrect. Tequila is the best of mescals, just as cognac is the best of brandies. Mescal can be produced anywhere, from any variety of the agave plant, whether grown in Mexico or in the southwestern United States. Tequila, on the other hand, must contain at least 51 percent spirits distilled from the pulp of the blue agave plant, grown in one of the five states of the tequila region. Only 1 percent of all tequilas are 100 percent blue agave, and those brands proudly proclaim this fact on their labels.

The blue agave plant can take up to 12 years to mature. Once fully grown, its broad, swordlike branches are cut away. The remaining core, known as *la piña*, looks like an overgrown pineapple. The *piña* can range from 50 to several hundred pounds each. The larger the *piña*, the higher the sugar content and the more tequila it will produce. *Piñas* are harvested and transported to distilleries, where they are steamed like giant artichokes and crushed. In some of the smaller boutique tequila distilleries, the steaming is done in brick ovens called *hornos*. Among the better tequilas are some, such as Sauza Hornitos, that feature this brick oven in their name.

Once the *piñas* are crushed, the pulp is separated from any fermentable juices. As in the production of rum, some distillers ferment the mash slowly for a robust flavor, while large producers typically use a much quicker fermentation process that produces lighter-bodied tequilas. Because of the expense of harvesting blue agave, most tequilas are diluted before distillation with up to 49 percent sugarcane pulp, the raw material of rum. Silver or white tequilas are ready for bottling immediately after the second distillation and are the least refined of the tequila family. Unaged, most are blended with water to lower the proof for a more palatable taste. Gold tequila is just white tequila with caramel added for coloring and flavoring. Gold and white tequilas are essentially of the same quality, though some might argue that gold tequilas have a smoother taste. In fact, this smoother taste results from the addition of flavoring, not from a superior distillation.

Unlike whiskey and brandy, tequila does not benefit greatly from aging, though *Reposados* are aged in oak barrels for up to a year to impart a milder bite. They are then blended with water and bottled, having taken on a slight golden hue from the oak casks. Even the most expensive tequilas, or *añejos*, are usually aged in oak for only two to four years. These tequilas are the most mellow agave distillates and must meet strict regulations set by the Mexican government. *Añejos* are now being marketed as sipping spirits, like single malts. If you aren't on a low-sodium diet and insist on doing shots, restrict your consumption to brands with the words "100 percent blue agave" on the label. Of course, you'll be looking at about $40 a bottle, and you may still make an ass of yourself, a regrettable tendency of those who enjoy too much tequila.

LIQUEURS

Flavored spirits didn't become fashionable until King Louis XIV of France developed a liking for them. Soon after, France became the forerunner in the production of these liqueurs, and they caught on as aphrodisiacs, stimulants for the heart, and general cure-alls.

Nowadays, liqueurs are produced all over the world, and there are so many brands that a creative bartender on an unlimited budget would never have to mix the same drink twice.

Added in moderation, these high-quality spirits, flavored with the essence of fruits and sweetened with sugar, can smooth a bitter drink. Often called CORDIALS in the United States, they must have a minimum proof of 30 and contain at least 2.5 percent sugar to be labeled as such. This is actually a small amount, and many brands contain up to one-third sweeteners.

Before any sweetening agents are added, the base spirit of a liqueur – which may be any distilled spirit – is flavored, often in the same manner as gin. Generally manufactured with an eye first on profit and second on quality, many American-made cordials are prepared in the least expensive and crudest fashion, typically by the addition of oils and syrups. If you're looking for quality liqueurs, look to France, whose long tradition of perfume production has benefited its efforts in the production of spirits.

37

HERBALS

Whiskey and Martini aficionados rarely order drinks made with fruity cordials. When I sense that such guests won't budge from their staid ordering habits due to a perception – almost moralistic – of drink superiority, I take a chance and challenge their taste buds with a cocktail accented by an herbal liqueur. If you can get these fanatics to taste something they can't readily describe, they'll usually be intrigued enough to step down from their pulpit (without muttering of heresy) and try to classify whatever you've prepared. After a glass or two, they'll typically retreat to their old favorite, but only after they've thanked you for the experience.

Although herbal liqueurs and bitter spirits are more difficult to incorporate into cocktails than their confectionary counterparts, they do offer otherwise unattainable flavors. The labels of such sweet cordials as CRÈME DE MENTHE, crème de cacao, and CRÈME DE CASSIS tell you what basic flavors are in store, whereas the packaging of herbal varieties reveals little beyond the inevitable long lists of obscure ingredients. Some of these labels list more than a hundred ingredients that contribute to the bouquet.

French monks were the first to achieve such worthy herbal distillations as BÉNÉDICTINE, CHARTREUSE, and TRAPPISTINE. The persistent appeal of these liqueurs after hundreds of years testifies to their quality. Many distillers have tried to copy the complex flavors of the originals, but most have failed. (The Bénédictine Museum and Distillery in Fecamp, France, proudly displays bottles of the liqueur's impostors.) Today, most herbal liqueurs are made in France, Holland, Italy, and throughout eastern Europe. Some of the most common flavors include Chartreuse, Strega, KÜMMEL, ANIS, and Izarra. A 375-milliliter bottle of one of these cordials will cost approximately $8 to $20, but unless you develop a penchant for sipping them as digestifs, you'll never need a larger bottle.

BITTER SPIRITS

Closely related to the herbal liqueurs are bitter spirits like CAMPARI, FERNET BRANCA, and PUNT E MES. Bitters, like most liqueurs, have their roots in early medicine. The predominantly acrid flavor of these European spirits derives from QUININE, a bark extract of the South American cinchona tree. Roots and herbs are typically added for flavor and coloring. Bitter spirits can be used as primary liquors or secondary liquors, but are called upon most often in cocktails as accents. As in the case of Campari, some people prefer bitter spirits mixed only with soda; others request them with gin and sweet vermouth, as with the Negroni; and some want only a drop for a dry finish, as in the Jasmine. Don't be put off by the taste of straight bitters – when included in a cocktail, they work wonders. Their high acidity can mask flavors better pushed to the background – for instance, a cheap vermouth in a Manhattan.

Bitters also work well to settle an upset stomach. A glass of soda water drenched in bitters can lessen the strain of a stomach vexed by an evening of too much tipple. And if overstuffing yourself before dessert is one of your weaknesses, look to bitters for a little comfort. One quick shot of Fernet Branca after a large meal may be exactly the pick-me-up you need.

VERMOUTHS

Wine-based apéritifs, with their rich herbs, taste nothing like most people's idea of wine. In fact, they're considered wine only because they're fermented from grapes, though in a process far different from the making of table wine. The herbs are what qualify these apéritifs as digestive tonics with the power to clear the palate. Vermouths are the most common variety of apéritif wines internationally, though in the United States they're served as a mere aside to gin and bourbon. In Europe, vermouth occupies the niche held in the United States by chardonnay.

Long before Americans began mixing, muddling, and shaking cocktails, their European forebears were concocting true apéritifs. Vermouth dates back thousands of years to the time just after wine was first fermented – but even though the ancient Greeks and Romans were already sipping it, it wasn't until Antonio Benedetto Carpano of Turin came along in the 16th century that this peerless appetite-enhancer was produced commercially. Much later, in the hands of stateside mixologists, vermouth became a favorite ingredient for classic cocktails.

Like so many of the bottles behind the bar, vermouth was first billed as a medicinal cure-all. In fact, the *Esquire Drink Book*, in its 1956 plea for a resurgence of respect for vermouth by Martini drinkers, recalled a bit of history that underscored this aspect of the drink's appeal. Its authors told the tale of "a small band of crooks who went about plundering the homes of the dead and dying" during the deadly plague of 1720 in Toulouse. "According to the records," recounts *Esquire*, "they immunized themselves against the disease by drinking a blend of '…the tops of sea and Roman WORMWOOD, a touch of rosemary, sage, mint, and rue, two ounces of lavender flowers … cinnamon, clove, camphor … a gallon of wine….' It was called the 'Wine of the Four Thieves,' but by any other name it's homemade vermouth."

Still rumored to be infused with some 50 herbs and miscellaneous flavorings, vermouth – whether sweet or dry – is made from a white wine base of mild quality. After fermentation, aging takes place in the presence of these flavorings and can last anywhere from six months to four years. The vermouth is then aromatized and fortified before being bottled at about 18 to 20 percent alcohol. Fortification – simply the addition of alcohol to fermentation – occurs in almost every apéritif wine. The spirit usually used is a neutral grape distillation with no hint of brandy characteristics. Aromatizing is the blending of fortified wine with extracts of herbs, roots, and spices such as wormwood, vanilla, and gentian.

But sweet and dry vermouths are the Wonder Bread of apéritif wines. They're quite enjoyable, though their flavors are somewhat bland and characterless in comparison to other apéritifs. Throughout Europe, there are hundreds of other interesting apéritif wines to be enjoyed. They are generally more bitter than vermouth, though made in much the same way. Brands to try are AMER PICON, BYRRH, DUBONNET, Punt e Mes, and SUZE. These venerable apéritifs are often overlooked; those who favor them have usually been privy to an elder gifted in mixing and serving them. Although they can be sipped neat, you may wish to start by merely mixing the apéritif with soda water in a tall, chilled glass filled with ice.

OTHER WINES

If you have a penchant for sipping such fortified wines as SHERRY, MADEIRA, or port, you'll be glad to know that each has a place in the world of cocktails. All three are produced in Spain and Portugal, but historically they're closely tied to the English shipping trade. Typically sweeter than vermouths, these wines are often associated with after-dinner affairs, though they do make nice accents in cocktails. For anglophiles, I often recommend sampling a Martini with a dash of *oloroso* sherry in place of dry vermouth. The nutty quality in this very dry sherry buffers the juniper and blends successfully when a twist is dropped into a drink. For sweeter cocktails that call for brandy, champagne, and whiskey, both port and madeira make good accents.

Stocking the Home Bar

With a little knowledge and just a few bottles, you can make most of the great cocktails. Never let the vast mosaic of containers you see behind your local bar intimidate you when you're deciding what liquid wares you need. Years ago, H. i. Williams – artist, "dilettante drinker," and "elite bartender" – wrote the *Three Bottle Bar*, and as the book's title suggests, Mr. Williams had an especially stripped-down approach to mixing. Though I have yet to come across his artwork (or the story behind that lowercase *i*), his method for stocking spirits still holds water. In a foreword, the book's editor says Mr. Williams is "neither a collector of media nor a dabbler in media. He respects all media, but they are only an incidental interest. Primarily, H. i. Williams is an arranger of ingredients." As your evolving skills demand a more varied palette, you'll almost certainly end up with more than three bottles in your bar. But you shouldn't need much more than that to start out.

BASES

The primary or base spirit sets the tone for a cocktail and for an event. The other ingredients in a drink should harmonize with it: mixers and accents can battle for attention, but they should be in agreement with and sublimated by the base spirit. Primary spirits fall into two categories: light and dark. If you want to please the greatest number of people with the smallest investment, start your collection with white spirits. Gin, vodka, and (to a lesser extent) rum are all typically considered neutral spirits that blend with almost anything and can be substituted in most classic recipes.

GIN

Although it's the most classic of spirits, gin's distinct flavor is not as well appreciated today as in days gone by. The predominant flavor in gin is juniper, a pungent evergreen berry whose star has dimmed in recent years. As a consequence, you'll need only one bottle of gin in your cabinet – unless you plan to upset the status quo. Boodles, Beefeater, Bombay, and Tanqueray are all London dry gins of quality. Boodles is the simplest-tasting of the four, while Tanqueray highlights the spirit's juniper most. Unless you're familiar with these four already, try them all.

RUM

No spirit is easier to mix with than rum, and since it's almost always well received at a cocktail party, you should consider stocking a rum of every color: white (colorless to light yellow), brown (golden or amber), and dark (rich molasses). If you're only going to buy one bottle of this spirit, make it a white rum. The lightest-bodied rum in your cabinet should hail from Cuba or Puerto Rico; it needn't be absolutely clear, though any color it has should be negligible. A young light rum like Havana Club or Bacardi Silver won't offend even the most callow palate. Similar in color to whiskey, the medium-bodied rums offer the greatest variety. Here again, Cuba and Puerto Rico produce especially fine aged rums, though other islands, such as Barbados and the Virgin Islands, also produce nice medium-bodied rums. Mount Gay Eclipse from Barbados or Bacardi Añejo from Puerto Rico will be the easiest brands to find. If you intend to make many tropical concoctions, or if you like the layered look of rum drinks, round out your stock with a dark Jamaican rum like Myers's or Appleton. Dark rum adds a slight molasses flavor to drinks, but it's used most often for the sake of its appearance. This heavy-bodied rum works as an accent in some drinks and as a base in others. When choosing rum, don't fall for gimmicky spirits like coconut-flavored or spiced rums. Tropical distillates like rum have rich natural characters that need no tampering; the accents that do enhance them are used more creatively in the classic cocktail recipes.

VODKA

Of the spirits enjoyed straight, vodka is among the most popular, but its presence in your home bar won't do much for your reputation as a creator of cocktails. As for choosing a vodka, any brand will do as long as it's at least equal in price to Smirnoff. Absolut and Stolichnaya lead the market, but others, such as Ketel One, boast a smoother finish. Though vodka is meant to be tasteless, each brand has its own aftertaste or burn that sets it apart. Flavored vodkas are popular enough that you may want a peppered version for those occasions when a late-morning Bloody Mary seems like your best move. Many other flavors produced commercially are meant to be enjoyed on the rocks – notably those enhanced with citrus, cranberry, or the like. But resourceful hosts can flavor their own by steeping the desired fruit or herb in unflavored vodka.

WHISKEY AND BRANDY

When choosing brown spirits, personal preferences are especially important. Unlike neutral grain spirits, there are so many variables in their production that it's impossible to predict which brand or type will be most to your liking. As with any spirit that's dark and rich in color, there's a broad, complex range of flavors. Among scotches alone you'll find more than a hundred distinct flavors, though some are never sold outside the tiny glens where they're produced.

Stocking a variety of whiskeys and brandies shows an appreciation of these dark spirits — and a willingness to drop a pretty penny — but such a tactic may not serve your cocktail interests well. If you have an allegiance to a specific label, stand by it. You can always adjust the recipes to satisfy your friends' tastes.

Ideally, you should stock a bottle each of sour mash, rye, scotch, and Canadian blended whiskey. The sour mash you choose will most likely hail from Kentucky. Straight ryes to try first are generally those produced in the States, most notably Wild Turkey, Jim Beam, and Old Overholt. If rye is too strong for your taste, opt for a bottle of Canadian blended whiskey from Seagram or Crown Royal.

Less expensive than single malts, blended scotches are most commonly used in cocktails like the Rob Roy or the Highlander. These scotches can vary in flavor from very light yet smoky to quite robust and smoky. Johnnie Walker is a nice, well-rounded blend, while Dewar's White Label has a sharp, distinct flavor that is recognized worldwide as consistently superior. Others, like J&B or Cutty Sark, appeal to the crowd that wants its whiskey watered down in a highball.

When buying brandy, stay away from the inexpensive brands produced in California, such as Korbel, E&J, and countless others — historically, they've been nowhere near the top of the heap. However, California boutique distilleries produce fine alembic brandies costing anywhere from $20 to more than $100. If you

42

STOCKING THE HOME BAR

THREE-BOTTLE BAR
Rum
Gin
Cointreau

SIX-BOTTLE BAR
Rum
Gin
Whiskey
Sweet vermouth
Dry vermouth
Cointreau

NINE-BOTTLE BAR
Rum
Gin
Vodka
Whiskey
Sweet vermouth
Dry vermouth
Bitters
Cointreau
Maraschino liqueur

TWELVE-BOTTLE BAR
Rum
Gin
Vodka
Sour mash
Scotch
Rye
Brandy
Sweet vermouth
Dry vermouth
Bitters
Cointreau
Maraschino liqueur

have a penchant for cigars and cognac, go ahead and splurge – just don't leave the bottle near anyone who might be tempted to mix a Sidecar with it. Being jostled with lemon is fine for some liquors, but anything aged over ten years – be it a brandy or a single-malt whiskey – deserves a bit more respect.

OTHER DISTILLATES

Tequila, mescal, cachaça, and pisco, though not usually considered classic, are other legitimate bases. Although recipes calling for these South and Central American distillates are few, their popularity in certain circles is high. Margaritas and Caipirinhas are possibly the most effective cocktails for putting a little spice into a summertime soiree. A reputation for making either of these well will earn you a circle of fans in short order. If you're in a warm climate and plan to host outdoor events, make an effort to stock accordingly.

43

MODIFIERS

Once you've rounded out your selection of base spirits, there are a few more bottles you'll want to consider investing in before you host a cocktail party. Without these popular mixers, many of the world's cocktails will be just out of your reach. Two of these bottles – dry and sweet vermouth (also known as French and Italian vermouth, respectively) – are absolutely necessary. Boisierre, Noilly Prat, Cinzano, and Martini & Rossi all produce quality vermouths. If you ever become bored with the basic sweet and dry vermouths, experiment with the fruitier Bianco or Lillet. The latter is especially valuable when it's time to make James Bond's Vesper.

To give your cocktails a sophisticated edge that still satisfies those drinkers who seek something fruitier and more refreshing, stock bottles of both MARASCHINO and COINTREAU liqueurs. These two liqueurs will very likely be the most costly bottles on your bar, but they'll also be the party favorites every time. Fortunately, most cocktails containing these liqueurs call for less than an ounce. Although other fruit-flavored cordials exist, there are none as classic and well-balanced as these two. If you're forced to seek substitutes, keep in mind that the replacements must possess a good fruit quality, with no resemblance to sweet syrups. Anyone can grab a bottle of peach schnapps and make a drink that tastes like peaches, but to use a subtle TRIPLE SEC or a maraschino well truly puts your skills to the test.

Modifiers needn't always be distilled spirits – in fact, they're often fruit juices or syrups. Because freshness is important, you'll want to gather most of these mixers on the day they'll be used. When buying sodas, opt for those packaged in small bottles – a liter of soda inevitably goes flat before a party ends. If you'll need a variety of mixers, such as ginger ale, soda water, and tonic water, consider purchasing the 10-ounce bottles sold in packages of six. What you don't use won't be wasted.

ACCENTS

Add a bottle of bitters to your bar and you'll be ready to create 90 percent of all apéritif cocktails. Angostura is the industry standard, but there are other brands of bitters that will work just as well. If you're looking for variety, instead of buying new brands of whiskey or gin, experiment with more exotic and complex flavors. PERNOD, Campari, PIMM'S, and Amer Picon are all good examples of international apéritifs that can be enjoyed alone or as an addition to a cocktail. Keep in mind that the flavors of these spirits may not be universally accepted – but once you find those friends who appreciate the complexity they add to libations, you'll have your A-list of invitees.

Slightly more expensive, but just as effective for accenting a drink, are such herbal liqueurs as Bénédictine, Chartreuse, and DRAMBUIE. All are blended from dozens of herbs distilled into potions whose recipes only a handful of people know. It just takes a bit to give a fabulous finish to cocktails like the Rusty Nail, the Drink Without a Name, and the Frisco.

The Mathematics of Drinking

Since cocktails are only recently making a comeback, many of your compatriots won't grasp the potency of what you're serving them – and merely by playing host, you shoulder much of the responsibility to wise them up before their heads start to spin. When cocktail imbibers are sideswiped by libations too tasty to describe, they tend to blame the drink – or the host – and rarely themselves. I won't get into the human species' innate ability to concoct such creative alibis, but I will explain the common misconception that swilling merlot is somehow safer than sipping Martinis.

The bottom line, of course, is this: If you're drinking alcohol carelessly – whether it's wine, beer, or distilled spirits – you will become drunk. Basic math shows that a typical 4½-ounce cocktail like the Aviation has the same amount of alcohol in it as a 6-ounce glass of wine (with 12 to 14 percent alcohol) or a 12-ounce beer (with 6 percent alcohol), both typical serving sizes for those drinks.

In the Aviation, 1½ ounces of the liquid is gin, which is 40 percent alcohol, and ½ ounce is maraschino liqueur, which is 30 percent alcohol. Lemon juice and water from the melting ice make up the remaining 2½ ounces, or 56 percent of this drink. The entire concentration of alcohol in your average cocktail is typically about 17 percent. With any drink, if you multiply the concentration of alcohol by the number of ounces in a typical serving, you'll come up with a potency that shows cocktails to be dead even with wine and beer in their standard serving sizes.

DRINK POTENCY				
Cocktail:	4.5 oz	x .17	=	.765
Glass of wine:	6 oz	x .14	=	.84
Bottle of beer:	12 oz	x .06	=	.72

I suspect the reason people naively assume cocktails have more alcohol is that they enjoy drinking them more, and that the smooth taste of a cocktail encourages the imbiber to sip more briskly. In general, only one or two cocktails should be enjoyed at one sitting – or, at least, before food has reached the table. Another fallacy is that drinking a variety of cocktails, each containing a different base spirit, will make the drinker more sotnosed. The fact is that if you drink five Manhattans instead of two Aviations, one Sidecar, and two Rob Roys, you'll be just as bombed – and just as foolish. And when mixing drinks, never disguise the taste of alcohol from your guests (especially the rookies) unless you want them at your house for an unplanned slumber party.

One way to enliven a party – one that lets guests enjoy themselves without regretting it later – is to offer a glass of soda or still water after each cocktail while your guests await the next. Garnished with a slice of citrus, the water is a pleasant, elegant aside to any cocktail. Offering this SPACER has three advantages: it keeps your guests from enjoying too many spirits too quickly; it keeps them well-hydrated, which in turn helps fend off any nasty side effects the next morning; and it eases the burden that successful parties are prone to put on your pocketbook. And on that score, if the budget is a concern and close friends are being asked to bring a little something, it's better to request a specific ingredient than to leave the decision to them – an approach that often nets you a bottle you already have.

HOW MUCH FOR HOW LONG

When planning a cocktail party, from an impromptu after-work gathering to a formal reception, there's a certain amount of math to be done. Like balancing a checkbook, this tallying, while not complex, can have humbling consequences when calculations go awry. First, decide which cocktails or mixed drinks you'd like to serve. There's no need to mix more than two or three types, especially while you're still polishing your mixing skills. If you decide to serve only a few drink recipes, it's quite acceptable for all of them to have the same primary spirit. If you opt for a limited drink menu or one that's likely to offer cocktails new to your guests, it may be best to just put a drink into the hands of those who are willing. Once they taste it, they'll usually be delighted – even if it wasn't their familiar first choice. By the second round, they'll want to know what other specialties you have up your sleeve.

TEMPO AND DURATION

A successful cocktail party is well-focused – whether on a seasonal or a social occasion – and rarely lasts longer than three hours: an hour for everyone to be late, an hour for everyone to sound smart, and an hour for everyone to leave. Evening gatherings should start earlier rather than later; that way, if new friends are made, they can continue the evening over dinner or a movie. If you're planning to serve dinner after cocktails, drink time need only last an hour or so. If you're not planning a meal, at least serve hors d'oeuvres. The best strategy is to serve food that's enjoyed cold and prepared ahead of time. It will be easier to refill trays than to slave over the oven with a houseful of guests. Cocktail food should be slightly salty and moderately oiled. Heavy foods help coat the stomach, which buffers acidic drinks and slows the progress of alcohol into the bloodstream. If you'll be attending a cocktail party and the host is not known for his or her cuisine, enjoy some bread and olive oil at the very least.

SPIRITS

Bottled spirits will be your greatest expense at any cocktail party. A 750-milliliter bottle of a primary spirit will make about 16 drinks containing a jigger each of the liquor. If you plan on mixing cocktails featuring more than one spirit, be sure your calculations reflect the proper proportions of the chosen cocktail. A word to the penny-wise: Buy the best you can afford, but don't imagine you can afford more by selecting those very large, unwieldy 1.75-liter jugs. I'm not sure why manufacturers came up with this package for distilled spirits – unless you're making punch in a garbage can, these bottles do not work well for pouring. A liter-sized bottle is about all you'll want to handle when making drinks in front of others. Although they're slightly more expensive, a 750-milliliter bottle or a fifth will be much more manageable, cutting down on spills and the embarrassment of pouring from something you can hardly hold. Decanting a bottle of distilled spirits with two hands is amateurish. When pouring, remember this old school saying: "Hold your partner by the waist and a bottle by its neck."

How much should you afford? Most human bodies can process one serving of alcohol per hour. For guests particularly anxious to unwind, plan on serving two drinks in the first hour and one every 45 minutes after that. Of course, you'll also need to budget for those guests who will be driving. A typical party of 30 will consist of about 15 drivers and 15 talkers. Over three hours, plan to serve four drinks to each talker, and two drinks to each driver. Although that's 90 drinks, plan on 100 servings – a slight buffer for unannounced guests.

GLASSWARE

The most difficult part of throwing a large cocktail party is glassware. Paper and plastic don't complement a cocktail well and should be avoided at all costs. Depending on the occasion and the number of guests, you'll need between 20 and 100 6-ounce glasses. Close friends at casual gatherings probably won't mind washing their own glasses as they go – a small price for an evening's entertainment – but a formal gathering may require that you buy or rent additional glasses.

To rent glassware costs about 45 cents per item. For a group of friends or family, you'll need only one glass per person, plus a few extra to cover breakage. If these guests are slow drinkers and you want to impress them, two glasses per person will suffice; you can employ a friend or significant other to help you clean as you go. For formal gatherings, budget one glass for every drink you intend to serve. Paying a trusted neighbor or helper to wash glass-ware may be a cheaper alternative, assuming your kitchen or bar space will comfortably allow such work without intruding on the party. If you plan to serve beer and wine in addition to cocktails, 8-ounce goblets will be the perfect stemware for all three.

ICE, CITRUS, AND SODAS

When calculating the amount of ice needed, always round up. Running out of ice will end a party faster than running out of distilled spirits: Guests will volunteer to buy more spirits, but they'll leave before being drafted to get an awkward bag of sweaty ice. As a general rule, have one pound of ice per person for every three hours, and don't kid your-self into thinking you can make all the ice.

For citrus, remember that the typical lemon or lime contains about an ounce of juice, while an orange contains a little more. Most recipes call for less than half an ounce of citrus juice, so you can plan on making two drinks from one piece of fruit. Hand-squeezing citrus will require more fruit than the mechanical method.

Have alternative beverages on hand, such as soda water (flavored and plain), bottled juices, and beer. Plan on no more than two of these per guest, or the cocktails may seem like an afterthought.

The easiest way to handle all this math is to take the time to figure it out properly on paper, once each, for the two most common numbers of guests: 10 and 30. From there, roughly add or subtract guests as needed, always rounding up – just like you do with your checkbook.

COMPLEXITY AND DIFFICULTY

There's a reason you can't always get what you order at a bar – a reason you'll appreciate more with every cocktail party you host. After all, everyone has different tastes, though most are initially (if not ultimately) moderate. As host, you cater to this crowd – because it is a crowd – usually the majority. This group's tastes may not be exciting or challenging to your mixing skills, but if you keep them pleased – even if they're not sipping cocktails at a cock-tail party – then your gathering will have succeeded.

By their nature, cocktails inherently buck the status quo of the drink world: They're not mainstream and won't be appreciated by everyone. Accept this, and you'll enjoy hosting cocktail parties a whole lot more. But rest assured you'll always find at least a few com-patriots who will be drawn to your side by the mere tinkle of ice or the sheen of the mixing tin. Remember them, and invite them back for those intimate gatherings that allow for numerous, complex drinks. As for larger get-togethers, always consider the practical side of mixing. For instance, if you'll be the only one mixing at a gathering, make sure the drinks are simple and the guest list short – no more than 12. Even if you budget to hire bartenders, make sure their skills are up to snuff before confronting them with difficult recipes or a large crowd. When planning a drink menu, consult the drinks in this book. All are rated by complexity of taste and difficulty of mixing. Below you'll find further explanations of the rankings used for each drink.

TASTE COMPLEXITY

1   *Prosaic:* About as exciting as sipping ice water. These drinks are well received, though rarely remembered. Any guest who finds one of these drinks exotic has rarely (if ever) tasted a true cocktail.

2   *Tasty but artless:* Suitable for those who enjoy wine or beer occasionally but rarely order a mixed drink.

3   *Inspiring:* A true classic cocktail. Far from average (as its numerical ranking might imply), these drinks are sophisticated and will prove enticing to most. Serve them proudly, confident that they are always appropriate.

4   *Challenging and complex:* Serve only to friends who understand and trust your mixing talents. Before handing guests one of these cocktails, prepare them for what will strike their taste buds. Once you've become a master in mixing, you'll recognize the right moment to present a drink from this category, and you will almost always amaze your friends.

5   *Obscure – an acquired taste:* This category represents the upper echelon of cocktails. These drinks are perfect only on rare occasions, and even then, they will probably be enjoyed only by those who actually smoked cigars before the fad hit. These cocktails will never be trendy or popular, but they will definitely hit the spot when called upon. Typically, these drinks have heavy herbal undertones appreciated by those with developed palates.

MIXING DIFFICULTY

1   *Elementary:* As difficult as preparing a glass of ice water.

2   *Basic:* Simple enough to be made well by anyone with an interest in the bar or a little experience behind one.

3   *Moderate:* Easily made at home, but not without a test of skill. A fine restaurant would be able to prepare these drinks, but a dive bar would not.

4   *Difficult:* Requires some extra step in preparation. These are not your typical, run-of-the-mill drinks, and are best reserved for parties with no more than eight guests.

5   *Advanced:* As difficult to concoct as Number 4, but compounded by a hard-to-find ingredient or a more challenging step in their preparation. Never expect to receive one of these classics from a bartender you're meeting for the first time.

The Drink Classics
Worth Imbibing First

Americano

Derided as a "neutered Negroni" by one bar compatriot, the Americano never gets a fair shake from those who've adopted Italy's most notorious BITTER as the key to a good cocktail. (Even the Italians admit you have to try CAMPARI three times before acquiring a taste for it.) But as far as we're concerned, the Americano is a perfectly legitimate version of an especially drinkable Campari cocktail. Of course, imbibers of the Americano, lacking the superior air typical of the Campari fanatic, only rarely flaunt their mastery of this piquant APÉRITIF's somewhat difficult flavor. Instead, they're like the few remaining tipplers of the original Martini – determined to drink what they like, not what popularity dictates.

The Americano – 1 ounce Campari, ½ ounce sweet VERMOUTH, and soda water, garnished with an orange wheel – is said to have been served first around 1861 at Gaspare Campari's bar, a fashionable meeting place frequented by Verdi, Edward VII, and, later, Ernest Hemingway. But it wasn't until the time of the Noble Experiment that the Italians, subjected to an influx of Americans, noticed New World bons vivants favoring this drink and – in a dubious compliment – dubbed it the Americano. The Americans, in turn, took the recipe home, where they sipped this spirit (then classified as a medicinal product) legally throughout Prohibition. We sadly suspect the Americano hasn't enjoyed such popularity since.

The drink does have a reputation for impotence (although only by comparison with a Negroni or a Campari ON THE ROCKS). But even James Bond managed to sip this drink without scandal – though Ian Fleming didn't pass up the opportunity to criticize the French: "James Bond had his first drink of the evening at Fouquet's. It was not a solid drink. One cannot drink seriously in French cafés," wrote Fleming in *A View to a Kill*. "Out of doors on a pavement in the sun is no place for VODKA or WHISKY or GIN. No, in cafés you have to drink the least offensive of the musical comedy drinks that go with them, and Bond always had the same thing, an Americano."

If we knew what the rest of the musical comedy drinks were, we'd comment more directly on the matter. Instead, we'll just assure you that in our view, the Americano is a fine-tasting Campari drink, one we certainly wouldn't be ashamed to drink in public – though we'd probably still find some reason to criticize the French.

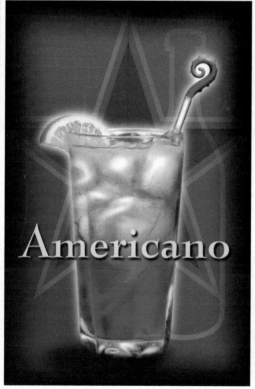

Americano

The Americano is an afternoon HIGHBALL that can be sipped safely at lunch by anyone with a scrap of common sense.

Serve this drink in a tall, thin glass to slow the escape of gas from the soda water. Like other tall drinks, always serve the Americano with a cocktail napkin, since this type of glass will perspire.

A swizzle stick may be placed in the drink, though a straw certainly should not. Sipping a mixed drink like this through a plastic tube tends to undermine the imbiber's measured pace, while the straw itself keeps the drinker's nose too far away to smell the pleasant fruitiness of the drink. One more word of caution: Over-stirring this concoction will encourage the soda water to go flat more quickly.

Similar drinks include the Picon Punch and the Negroni over ice.

RECIPE

1 ounce Campari
½ ounce sweet vermouth
Soda water

Add Campari and sweet vermouth
over ice in chilled Collins glass.
Top with chilled soda water and stir.
Garnish with an orange wheel.

O nce famed but now forgotten, the Astoria cocktail started out as a pampered pet, first poured by the barkeeps of the Old Waldorf-Astoria to commemorate the opening of the establishment's new main annex back in 1897. We've revived its simple recipe of GIN, ORANGE BITTERS, and dry VERMOUTH, a mixture that provides the perfect transition between office and Martini.

Chronicler Albert S. Crockett had higher hopes for the Astoria when he included its recipe in *The Old Waldorf-Astoria Bar Book* of 1934. In this tome, which he dryly describes as "something that might interest the researcher into American mores," Mr. Crockett says drinks like the Astoria have earned their place both at the bar and in books of record: "Their nomenclature belongs to [history], not only as part of our national chronicles, but as an index to certain social, industrial, and artistic achievements of an age. Brushing aside such mythological, ornithological, theological, zoological, or otherwise 'logical' designations as Adonis, ... Goat's Delight, Gloom Lifter, and Hoptoad – to name just a few samples of cocktails of other times – consider others that betray less of fancy and originality, but perhaps more of cause of origin."

But when we do consider others, particularly the Astoria, we remain perplexed by this smooth but inspiring drink's fall from favor. When a drink that's difficult to make or ridiculously named falls by the wayside, that's one thing – but the Astoria is neither. We can only suppose its pedestrian ingredients are to blame. "During the first two decades of the century, the commonly accepted American definition of a COCKTAIL was a mixture of gin and vermouth with bitters," writes Mr. Crockett. "Their composition is important to the historian ... who will no doubt find material for study and zealous contemplation, if not amazement, in the fact that men once were able, year after year, to get outside so many kinds of more or less ardent spirit, and in such quantity, and still survive." Well, they didn't all survive, and neither did all of their drinks.

We eventually called the Waldorf-Astoria in New York, certain that establishment would know this cocktail if anyone did. We started with the assistant beverage manager: "I'm not aware of the drink, and I know we don't make it now, but I do have a few bartenders left from the Middle Ages – maybe they can help." And they did try. Elijah, a Waldorf-Astoria bartender for more than a quarter-century, recalled that "a couple of years ago, we talked about the drink while behind the bar. It's not on the menu, so people don't know about it." Not quite satisfied, we tried Oscar, a bartender who's been there two decades. No luck. Finally we turned to Dennis Delaney, a maitre d' at the Waldorf-Astoria for upwards of 50 years, who testified that neither the drink nor its name had ever passed his lips. If nothing else, we hope we've inspired him to give it a try.

GLASS	TASTE COMPLEXITY	MIXING DIFFICULTY
Y	LOW ⊢──○──⊣ HIGH	LOW ⊢──○──⊣ HIGH
	DRINK ERA	
	GOLDEN AGE OF AMERICAN DRINKING	

RECIPE

2 ounces gin
½ ounce dry vermouth
1 dash orange bitters

Shake with cracked ice;
strain into chilled cocktail glass.
Garnish with a twist of orange or lemon.

The Astoria should be served during the early minutes of the cocktail hour, when guests can anticipate being offered a second, heavier-hitting drink, followed by a meal.

Showmen will want to rinse the Astoria's chilled cocktail glass with bitters rather than simply adding it along with the other ingredients; those more concerned with making a smooth-tasting cocktail should toss the bitters into the shaker.

Unlike most clear cocktails, the Astoria should be shaken, not stirred, to ensure that the ingredients mix well. If orange bitters are unavailable, substitute GRAND MARNIER, but be prepared for a sweeter drink.

Similar drinks include another New York classic, the Bronx, and its West Coast competitor, the Martinez.

Aviation

Aviation

T he Aviation is the prince of classic cocktails. Still served at the Rainbow Room in Rockefeller Center (where the staff will lend you a clownish jacket if you fail to dress up), the Aviation has no modern equivalent, and can only be obtained at establishments where the vanishing art of mixology is still pursued with zeal, if not fanaticism.

The Aviation has no known creator, though most drink historians agree that it was first concocted during the later days of the OLD SCHOOL OF AMERICAN BARTENDING, when civilized imbibers began to insist on more complex drinks. Nowadays, the difficulty of finding a good Aviation has been linked to the disappearance of MARASCHINO LIQUEUR, which is fundamental to the drink. Once a fairly common CORDIAL, maraschino is a clear cherry liqueur that's sweet, but not too sweet. It has nothing at all in common with the red chemical syrup found in jars of cherry garnishes – though if you order an Aviation in a common bar and mention the word *maraschino* as you recite the recipe, be prepared for some sickly consequences. Most mixers, left to their own devices, will grab for the bottle of CHERRY HEERING. Painfully sweet and syrupy thick, this cordial has little in common with the much preferred, significantly drier maraschino.

At older, fancier hotel bars, you may spy a bottle of maraschino that has survived unscathed from an earlier era. If so, and if you have a knack for making friends with bartenders (hint: tips help), you might give this approach a try:

"Got fresh lemons?"

"Uh, sure."

"If you squeeze one of those lemons and shake it over ice with a shot of GIN and a splash of that liqueur in the green bottle there, it will make one hell of a cocktail. You game?"

It's worked a few times, and it's failed a few times. The strict recipe is an ounce and a half of gin, a half ounce of maraschino liqueur, and three-fourths of an ounce of lemon juice, shaken hard and served up. The result should be softly opaque and inviting, with several chips of ice still spinning on the surface. The most wonderful thing about this drink? It makes you smarter. Trust us.

GLASS	TASTE COMPLEXITY	MIXING DIFFICULTY
Y	LOW ⊢─O──┤ HIGH	LOW ⊢───O─┤ HIGH
	DRINK ERA	
	OLD SCHOOL OF AMERICAN BARTENDING	

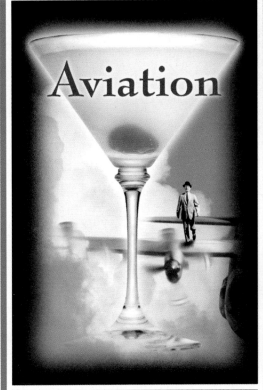

RECIPE

1½ ounces gin
½ ounce maraschino liqueur
¾ ounce lemon juice

Shake with cracked ice;
strain into chilled cocktail glass.
Garnish with a maraschino cherry or a lemon twist.

Occasionally accused of tasting like a Pixi Stix with a JUNIPER aftertaste, the Aviation is one of the most likable cocktails around. The drink's neutral base means its recipe lends itself to easy alteration, often endearing itself even to those who typically shun the taste of gin.

If you suspect that an Aviation might be too acidic for a particular guest's tastes, add a dash of a cordial, such as blackberry, peach, or apricot. Doubling the amount of maraschino liqueur will work as well, though some may find this overwhelming.

Garnish with either a lemon twist or a cherry. As a general rule, don't drink this cocktail after dark, unless a long night of dancing is in store.

Similar drinks include the Beachcomber.

Bacardi Cocktail

I t's not every day a cocktail appears before a high court, though Hunter S. Thompson did manage to get the contents of the Cosmopolitan cited in an affidavit. But the case of the Bacardi Cocktail was no minor mention in a random ruling: The drink's very recipe was the topic of heated debate, and in 1936, New York's Supreme Court defined this cocktail's formula, making it illegal to mix it without Bacardi rum.

In retrospect, the court's ruling suggests a defect of common sense, or at least a dearth of serious work in the lower courts. But let's not let our excellent hindsight blind us to the realities of the time: PROHIBITION affected imbibers' sensibilities long after its repeal. Always considered subtle and sophisticated, the Bacardi Cocktail came into high demand during the Noble Experiment as the chosen drink of those who could afford to spend the drought elsewhere. "After 1919, Havana became the unofficial U.S. saloon – a hive of hotels, casinos, and brothels," Magdalena Casero, curator of the Bacardi Museum in Miami, Florida, told us. "Bars like Sloppy Joe's and El Floridita became famous, and Bacardi became among the best known of their forbidden fruits." Even drinkers trapped on dry land got comfortable shaking up 1¾ ounces of bootlegged rum with 1 ounce of lime juice, a BARSPOON of SIMPLE SYRUP, and a dash of GRENADINE – all the while calling the concoction a Bacardi Cocktail.

The Bacardi family soon tired of missing out on well-deserved profits while watching its name become the generic term for a pink Daiquiri – particularly in Manhattan, where bartenders commonly advertised the drink by name but mixed it however they pleased. So to set the record straight – or at least obtain a restraining order preventing barroom charlatans from serving the Bacardi Cocktail without its original rum – the Bacardi family took the case to court in 1936, and the resulting ruling became the envy of the liquor industry.

We're not certain how the officers of New York State enforced the proper mixing of the Bacardi Cocktail. But given the stern ruling that "the Court finds as a clear, preponderating, and even that which would be exacted in a criminal situation, beyond a reasonable doubt, that Bacardi rum left out of a Bacardi Cocktail is not a Bacardi Cocktail, and that otherwise it is a subterfuge and fraud," we don't doubt the men in blue did their damnedest. Now, 60 years or so later, Bacardi rum is no longer considered a candidate for substitution. We order the Bacardi Cocktail when the taste of another drink seems too severe, or when faced with an untested mixer who needs grenadine's sweetness to temper a lack of skill. But unlike Bacardi Cocktail drinkers of yesteryear, we've never had a bartender replace the called-for rum with anything else, though we'd welcome the chance to put our expertise on the legalities of this drink to good use.

COCKTAIL

GLASS	TASTE COMPLEXITY	MIXING DIFFICULTY
Y	LOW ⊙ HIGH	LOW ⊙ HIGH
	DRINK ERA	
	OLD SCHOOL OF AMERICAN BARTENDING	

Bacardi
Cocktail

RECIPE

1¾ ounces Bacardi light rum
1 ounce lime juice
½ teaspoon simple syrup
1 dash grenadine

Shake with cracked ice;
strain into chilled cocktail glass.
Garnish with a lime squeeze.

Not quite as refreshing as a FIZZ or a COLLINS, the Bacardi Cocktail is still smooth and cool – perfect for impromptu gatherings inspired by good weather. Unlike those water-laden concoctions, the Bacardi Cocktail still manages to stir the appetite.

Traditionally shaken to the point of having visible ice flecks, the Bacardi Cocktail can also be FLASH BLENDED for a thicker, colder drink. If you're planning to make large batches of the drink, this blending technique saves time.

For a sweeter cocktail, substitute lemon for lime juice and garnish with a lemon wheel. If you leave out the grenadine, you have another cooling Cuban classic known as the Daiquiri.

Similar drinks include the Presidente, the Miami, and the Santiago.

Bellini

A t some point, alchemists were bound to match up the spirits of the bar with the mixers of the bar. Most drink creations, in fact, are inevitable and without imagination. Fortunately, the divining of a drink has only a speculative influence on its taste. We've seen plenty of enterprising mixers set out to invent a drink only to create a concoction showing a painful lack of restraint and topped with a ridiculous garnish. But the Bellini − a cocktail with no garnish, a deliberate author, and an ingredient more typically found far from the bar − is one lonely archetype from the Years of Reform that still elevates any occasion with its sophisticated simplicity.

Made with the nectar of white peaches and Italian sparkling wine, the Bellini is light on the tongue and soothing to the psyche. But like the bar from which it hails, it must be sought. With only "Harry's Bar" etched into the windowpanes, this Venetian establishment expects no casual passers-by, only those already familiar with its fine fare and reputation. A former haunt of Ernest Hemingway, Sinclair Lewis, and Orson Welles that dates to 1931, Harry's Bar has become a fixture in the cocktail culture. Yet, despite the stature of its birthplace, few establishments have promoted the Bellini, a drink inspired by the 15th-century Venetian painter Giovanni Bellini. Too time-consuming for most bartenders to bother with, the Bellini's recipe still survives unscathed long after its 1948 birthdate.

"I had no idea at the time that the pink glow my father had so admired in one of Bellini's paintings would be the inspiration for his famous cocktail," wrote Arrigo Cipriani in *Harry's Bar: The Life and Times of the Legendary Venice Landmark.* "… my father had a predilection for the white [peaches]. So much so, in fact, that he kept wondering whether there was a way to transform this magic fragrance into a drink he could offer at Harry's Bar. He experimented by puréeing small white peaches and adding some *prosecco* (Italian champagne)."

The drink was a sudden and strong success at Harry's, and soon Arrigo Cipriani's father, Giuseppe Cipriani, hired a crew solely to purée the peaches during the fruit's four-month season. Not surprisingly, today Bellinis can be had at Harry's Bar year-round. "[A]n entrepreneurial fellow Frenchman has made his fortune by setting up a business that freshfreezes the white peach purée," explains Arrigo Cipriani in his 1996 book.

Unless visiting Venice, we make our Bellinis at home, and only during the peach season. In 1990, a Mr. Canella was authorized to sell the Bellini as a ready-made mix with the same ingredients and the addition of raspberry juice for coloring. But Arrigo Cipriani soon realized that no good could come from a mix that followed on the heels of the wine cooler craze, and he took his case to arbitration in 1995. "So the bellini," he explains, "reverted to its original, pristine state, saved from possible extinction by an arbiter's common sense and good judgment."

GLASS	TASTE COMPLEXITY	MIXING DIFFICULTY
♟	LOW ⊶━━ HIGH	LOW ━━⊶━ HIGH
	DRINK ERA	
	YEARS OF REFORM	

Bellini

RECIPE

4 ounces *prosecco* (Italian sparkling wine)
1 ounce white peach purée

Peel and purée 3 to 4 very ripe white peaches;
mix nectar with 1 ounce simple syrup.
Strain through coarse cheesecloth;
refrigerate until chilled.
Pour 1 ounce of nectar into
frosted champagne flute;
top with *prosecco*.

Tradition dictates that any variation in the Bellini's recipe is a bastardization best shunned. But for those who ignore custom or have difficulty finding succulent white peaches, there are other options. The obvious though not necessarily recommended change in recipe is the use of regular peaches.

Almost any fresh fruit may be substituted if it's not overly sweet. The amount of SIMPLE SYRUP used may need to be altered, depending on the type of fruit used.

A Bombay Bellini is champagne with a splash of fresh mango purée. The nectar of pears, nectarines, and berries mixed with sparkling wine may also appeal to imbibers. A splash of lemon juice will make these drinks more refreshing.

Similar drinks include the French 75 and the Champagne Cocktail.

Black Velvet

We've been accused of lacking creativity when it comes to Saint Paddy's Day, and it's true: Every March 17, without fail, you'll find us at a decidedly non-Irish pub with a Black Velvet in hand, quietly honoring the Emerald Isle's patron saint, who banished small reptiles from the island about 1,500 years ago. We might be more likely to change our routine if there were some other cocktail with Irish ties, or if selecting an Irish WHISKEY didn't stir up so much trouble.

We always skip the annoying green beer, instead ordering one part Guinness stout to four parts champagne for a drink combining sparkling wine's *verismo* with the unaffectedness of Guinness. While we can't swear the Black Velvet is truly Irish, we've yet to come across an Irish person who's taken overt offense. On the other hand, the drink's best-known tale does link it to London's Brooks Club, not an establishment we think of as catering to the Irish. By most accounts, a barman first mixed this drink for the club's patrons in honor (or at least acknowledgment) of Prince Albert's death in 1861.

By the late '30s, the Black Velvet had made it as far as Manila, where drink historian Charles H. Baker was sipping it by the Mariveles, "an extinct volcanic peak cooling its heel across Manila Bay." In his *Gentleman's Companion* of 1946, Mr. Baker quotes Monk Antrim as once saying the Black Velvet "is an expensive sort of drink, but when you think it over, it's worth it." To which Mr. Baker added, "It will save life, nourish, encourage, and induce sleep in insomniacs."

We certainly can't top that, and won't try. But as we sip our Guinness cocktails, we're often inspired to broach (carefully) the topic of the Troubles associated with other Irish spirits, all the while noting one of life's great ironies: Bushmills and Jameson, two Irish whiskeys primarily distinguished by the politics of religion, have been owned by the same French company, Pernod, for about 10 years. To that, we're not sure if a toast or tears would be in order.

GLASS	TASTE COMPLEXITY	MIXING DIFFICULTY
🍸	LOW ⊢──○──⊣ HIGH	LOW ○───────⊣ HIGH

DRINK ERA
GOTHIC AGE OF AMERICAN DRINKING

Black Velvet

RECIPE

4 ounces chilled champagne or sparkling wine
1 ounce chilled Guinness stout

Pour chilled Guinness into frosted flute.
Add chilled champagne and
garnish with a lemon twist.

Serve the Black Velvet when champagne might be in order, but seems a bit too formal. When preparing this drink, pour the Guinness first, then follow with the wine. There's no need to stir – the wine's carbonation will "mix" the ingredients. Serve in a flute and garnish with a lemon twist, which will cut through the aftertaste of the Guinness and add a slight tang to the drink.

Any good sparkling wine can be used in this cocktail. Older recipe books, such as David A. Embury's *The Fine Art of Mixing Drinks*, insist on extra-dry champagne, preferably a *brut* or a *nature*; but this viewpoint, although certainly accurate for its time, is outdated. If porter is substituted for the stout, the drink is simply called the Velvet.

Similar drinks include Death in the Afternoon.

Blue Blazer

W hen everything else at the bar seems banal and uninspired, we request what a worn and weary miner first ordered back in the 1800s – then hope for the best, knowing the bartender will very likely kick us out, ridicule us, or accept our challenge but expect one heck of a tip. Named for its blazing blue flame, the Blue Blazer is despised by mixers scornful of gimmicks or partial to their fingers. But even they can't diminish this drink's masterstroke, performed with equal parts boiling water and scotch, plus a teaspoon of honey or a cube of sugar.

We first came across the Blue Blazer in Harry Craddock's *Savoy Cocktail Book* of 1933. An impressive woodcut shows the drink's creator with arms spread wide, tossing a thunderbolt of whiskey back and forth above the caption: "Professor Jerry Thomas, the greatest Bartender of the Past, mixing his famous 'Blue Blazer' at the Metropolitan Hotel in New York, in the Roaring Fifties." Later in the same volume, Mr. Craddock elaborates: "A beholder gazing for the first time upon an experienced artist compounding this beverage, would naturally come to the conclusion that it was a nectar for Pluto rather than Bacchus." But it was only after we learned that the good professor had first concocted the Blue Blazer at San Francisco's Occidental Hotel (or, as some would insist, the El Dorado) that we decided to mix a batch ourselves, despite reports that the aforesaid miner disappeared for three days, presumably to recover from the tipple's kick.

We've always prided ourselves on our mixing skill, but our initial attempts to make a Blue Blazer were disastrous, ending in a promise to the landlord that we'd not flame drinks on the property again. Good sense having won out, we called William Grimes, a food writer at *The New York Times* and author of *Straight Up or On the Rocks,* a book which states quite simply that "although diluted whiskey barely catches fire, the reciprocal pouring acts as a kind of bellows, and the result is a roaring fire." Mr. Grimes was somewhat shocked to hear of our ineptitude and assured us that mixing the drink did not require sleight of hand. Recalling his own first efforts mixing a Blue Blazer, he said, "I simply lit the liquid in one container and poured it back and forth. There was even a roar."

We were pleased with this information, but it was Mr. Grimes' passing mention of large mixing tins and asbestos gloves that gave us renewed hope, and on our next try, we succeeded. Of course, we now understand why Jerry Thomas considered this drink a tonic for cold weather, reportedly mixing it only when the thermometer stood at or below 10 degrees Fahrenheit. Knowing that such a rule would kill one's chances of obtaining the drink even in the town where it was created, we suspect Mr. Thomas' greatest skill was making patrons want a drink he'd never have to serve.

GLASS	TASTE COMPLEXITY	MIXING DIFFICULTY
	LOW ⊢━━O━━⊣ HIGH	LOW ⊢━━━━O⊣ HIGH
	DRINK ERA	
	GOTHIC AGE OF AMERICAN DRINKING	

Blue Blazer

RECIPE

4 ounces scotch whiskey • 4 ounces boiling water
2 teaspoons honey or 2 sugar cubes

For a flaming Blazer, use 16-ounce mixing tins or Pyrex pitchers. Mix honey with 4 ounces water; boil the mixture. (If sugar cubes are used, drop into the drink right before serving.) Simmer 4 ounces scotch in a chafing dish; ignite. Pour each into a mixing container. Dim the lights, and pour from one container into the other until the flame burns out. Portion drinks into 2 tumblers that won't crack from the heat. Let the Blazer cool slightly before drinking.

If you decide to serve the Blue Blazer in its full glory, remember that the key is to have the right equipment, foremost among which should be asbestos gloves. These may seem unsuitable cocktail attire, but they certainly look better than singed fingers wrapped in bandages.

Traditional metal containers work well enough, but they're also good conductors of heat, and may leave hands uncomfortably warm even through the gloves. Large Pyrex pitchers with handles work better and allow guests a better view of the flame. Some bartenders suggest using a silver platter to catch spills – a fine idea provided the plate covers a large area. Practice first with cold water. For a short cut when making this drink, don't ignite the concoction or dim the lights.

Similar drinks include the Combustible Edison.

Bronx

P | eople used to love to disrespect the Bronx, until the drink, like the borough, reached a state of general disapprobation rendering further criticism superfluous. We resist these trends, and whenever we come across a bartender possessed of a rare knowledge of history, we happily order a Bronx cocktail. It may be that the drink fell into disfavor during the '30s because it contains orange juice, a seeming affectation. But we insist the Bronx cocktail is an earlier, subtler version of the fruit-juice drink: just an ounce of fresh orange juice, equal parts sweet and dry VERMOUTH, and an ounce of good GIN.

Little did the purists realize how low mixologists would descend in later decades, when potent concoctions from '60s FERN BARS became popular. Of course, there was a time when the demand for the Bronx cocktail was so great that establishments like the Old Waldorf-Astoria went through several cases of oranges a day. Not surprisingly, it's said the Bronx was invented at that fine establishment, with credit going to Johnnie Solon, who joined the bar in 1899. This is Solon's own story of the creation, as recalled by historian Albert S. Crockett in the 1934 *Old Waldorf-Astoria Bar Book*: "We had a cocktail in those days called the Duplex, which had a pretty fair demand. One day, I was making one for a customer when in came Traverson, head waiter of the Empire Room – the main dining room in the original Waldorf.... Traverson said, 'Why don't you get up a new cocktail? I have a customer who says you can't do it.'... I finished the Duplex I was making, and a thought came to me. I poured into a mixing glass the equivalent of two JIGGERS of Gordon's Gin. Then I filled the jigger with orange juice, so that it made one-third of orange juice and two-thirds of Gin. Then into the mixture I put a dash each of Italian and French Vermouth, shaking the thing up. I didn't taste it myself, but I poured it into a cocktail glass and handed it to Traverson and said: 'You are a pretty good judge. (He was.) See what you think of that.' Traverson tasted it. Then he swallowed it whole."

Oddly enough, Mr. Solon didn't name the Bronx after the borough. He had visited recently the Bronx Zoo, where he noted many a strange beast. When Traverson asked him to christen the drink, Mr. Solon reflected on the strange animals his customers had seen – usually after too many mixed drinks. Following that thought, Mr. Solon named the drink after the zoo. Fortunately, we can testify that as long as no more than three Bronxes are sipped during a four-hour sitting, no strange animals will be sighted.

GLASS	TASTE COMPLEXITY	MIXING DIFFICULTY
Y	LOW ⊨⊨O⊨ HIGH	LOW ⊨⊨O⊨ HIGH
	DRINK ERA	
	GOLDEN AGE OF AMERICAN DRINKING	

A classic standby that's an acceptable precursor to lunch, the Bronx – as often as it has been sniped at – is always a crowd-pleaser.

Since this drink does not demand exacting measurements, let the imbiber's tastes suggest the drink's proportions. An extra dash of any ingredient will bring that flavor to the fore.

Fresh-squeezed juice is a *sine qua non*. Use Seville oranges whenever possible. Should the fruit seem overly sweet, add a dash of lemon juice.

The Silver Bronx – composed of double the sweet vermouth, no dry vermouth, and half an egg white – makes for a smoother drink if shaken well. For a sweeter drink, add a dash of pineapple juice.

Similar drinks include the Abbey, the Duplex, and the Leap Year.

RECIPE

1 ounce gin
½ ounce sweet vermouth
½ ounce dry vermouth
1 ounce orange juice

Shake with cracked ice; strain into chilled cocktail glass. Garnish with a maraschino cherry or an orange wheel.

Caesar

W e can't help feeling for this hearty Canadian pick-me-up, so often mistaken for a Bloody Mary in a FROSTED glass. As far as we're concerned, that's about as blatant a provocation as calling a Canadian an American. There may not be much difference to the naked eye, but taste is another matter – and frankly, we're siding with the Canucks on this one.

Never inclined to split hairs, mince words, or join in debates on the precise scope of the term *American*, we just call it as we see it, and eight times out of ten we'll order a Caesar over a Bloody Mary. Since both drinks are made with VODKA, it must be the clam juice that gives the Caesar its distinctive, zesty bite. Composed of 1½ ounces of vodka, 4 ounces of tomato-clam juice, and a dash of Worcestershire sauce with several pinches of horseradish, the Caesar is a substantial drink that – unlike the Bloody Mary – needn't be reserved for brunch.

Measured against the normal timeline for classic cocktails, the Caesar achieved an unusually sudden and enduring fame. In 1969, the higher-ups at the Calgary Westin Hotel asked their bar manager, Walter Chell, to mix a cocktail for a contest to mark the opening of their Italian restaurant, Marco's, in the Calgary Inn.

We'd be suspicious about a Westin employee winning this Westin-sponsored contest if the Caesar weren't so tasty. According to well-documented legend, Mr. Chell spent three months developing the recipe. From what we gather, mashing fresh clams into what Mr. Chell optimistically called "nectar" is no easy task. But his thinking demanded that his new beverage complement a menu of Italian foods made with vongole and tomato sauce. His rationale: If it's good to eat, it's good to drink.

Early on in his experimentation, Mr. Chell simply called this drink the Caesar. But one afternoon, an Englishman sampled his work. After purportedly hearing the man exclaim, "Walter, that's a damn good bloody Caesar," Mr. Chell expanded the name to Bloody Caesar. Now, this may be a direct quote, but we still don't like the story. Besides, adding the word *bloody* only confuses the Caesar with its competition, and we already have enough trouble getting this drink at any bar more than two states south of the Canadian border.

Most bartenders (or hosts, for that matter) are loath to grind tomatoes and clams, and since we're not about to either, we never take offense at a Caesar made with Clamato juice. As we struggle to imagine the first two years of the Caesar's life – before Clamato came on the scene – we're amazed the recipe survived at all. Although invented in California by Duffy-Mott, Clamato juice has yet to take off in the States with the same zeal as in Canada. In 1970, a Canadian broker brought the juice home from California, but the company he worked for sold only 500 cases in Canada that year. It wasn't until the importers followed a trail of Clamato to the Calgary Inn that they found their true market.

GLASS	TASTE COMPLEXITY	MIXING DIFFICULTY
	LOW ⊩O⊟⊟⊟ HIGH	LOW ⊟⊟O⊟ HIGH
	DRINK ERA	
	THE DARK AGE OF AMERICAN DRINKING	

This Caesar, too, has its Brutus – and it goes by the name of Mary. Never mind finding the perfect gathering for mixing this drink. All we ask is that you resist serving a Bloody Mary in its place.

For loyal GIN drinkers, substitute this spicier spirit for the Caesar's traditional vodka. TEQUILA or (surprisingly) RUM may also be substituted for vodka, but there is no substitute for Clamato juice.

Unlike other mixed drinks, the Caesar can be mixed in bulk and stored overnight. Frost the rim of the glass with celery salt, and don't make a meal out of the garnish – simplicity, as always, is the key.

Similar mixed drinks – besides the obvious Bloody Mary – include the Red Snapper and the Bullshot.

RECIPE

1½ ounces vodka
4 ounces Clamato juice
1 dash Worcestershire sauce
2 to 3 dashes horseradish
1 pinch of salt and pepper
Celery salt • Celery stalk

Shake first five ingredients with cracked ice; strain into chilled pint glass. Coat the rim of the glass with celery salt. Garnish with a celery stalk and a lemon wheel.

Caipirinha

H enry Ford outlawed the spirit in this classic drink – and all others, for that matter – in Fordlandia, his "Amazonian suburbia" in Brazil during the '20s and '30s. But for the natives of this cradle-to-grave company town, the thought of giving up their endemic tipple must have been the last straw. After all, when the auto tycoon's worker bees wandered in, the Brazilians had been more than accommodating. In *Americas* magazine, Mary A. Dempsey reports many of them learned to square dance, stayed awake through what would have left most Americans comatose – poetry by the likes of Henry Wadsworth Longfellow – and worked hard harvesting rubber for Model T tires. They accepted the QUININE, but most likely couldn't bring themselves to drink it the way Ford's Americans suggested – straight or with lime juice. Instead, they did what Brazilian common sense dictated – they mixed it with their fiery national spirit, CACHAÇA, in hopes, we presume, of creating something like a Caipirinha.

In tribute to them, we reserve this drink for occasions requiring both pride and determination, though we have been known to sip it on more than one lazy summer afternoon. Pronounced "kuy-per-REEN-yah," this cocktail is made with 2 ounces cachaça and a lime quartered and muddled with ¼ ounce of SIMPLE SYRUP. Served in a cool tumbler peaked with ice, the Caipirinha is a serious SLING, with a bite reminiscent of TEQUILA tamed by RUM.

If the bartender grabs a long wooden pestle quite a bit bigger than our standard MUDDLER to make this mixed drink, then we know we're in the presence of someone who upholds Brazilian custom. If he or she calls for a Caipirinha glass, we know the bartender is also familiar enough with this drink to recognize its namesake vessel.

Occasionally, in the absence of cachaça, we'll allow VODKA or rum to replace this clear sugarcane distillate, creating a Caipiroshka or a Caipirissima respectively. Although certainly not a true Caipirinha, it gives us hope that, contrary to Ford's motto ("You can have any color, so long as it's black"), we can have any flavor or mood, so long as it's sapid.

GLASS	TASTE COMPLEXITY	MIXING DIFFICULTY
	LOW ○━━━ HIGH	LOW ━━━○ HIGH
	DRINK ERA	
	YEARS OF REFORM	

Caipirinha

RECIPE

2 ounces cachaça
¼ ounce simple syrup
1 lime

Cut lime into quarters and place
pieces in the bottom of chilled tumbler, pulp side up.
Pour simple syrup over the lime, and muddle.
Add the cachaça, and stir. Fill glass with ice.

A good Caipirinha relies on the use of whole limes. Use medium-sized fruit with even coloring and thin skins – a sure sign of adequately ripe citrus. Although limes (and lemons) should always be rolled before slicing to extract the aromatic oils, this step is absolutely crucial when making the Caipirinha.

Those unaccustomed to sipping a fiery distillate may prefer less cachaça and more lime. A sweeter fruit than lime might also be to their liking. If mixing with passion fruit, replace the lime with the pulp of 1½ passion fruits. With pineapple, replace the citrus with a slice of fresh pineapple, diced, with the center removed. Add half a lemon if the pineapple is overly sweet. Oranges, grapes, and guava are other fruit alternatives.

Similar drinks include the Pisco Sour, the Batida, and the Mojito.

Clover Club

T his drink's luck ran out about 50 years ago. Like a has-been whose name is only vaguely remembered, the Clover Club – still included in all the revered records of classic cocktails – now garners respect only for its venerable age. But we like the Clover Club when it's made with 2 ounces of GIN, ¼ ounce of GRENADINE or raspberry syrup, 1 ounce of lemon juice, and 2 teaspoons of egg white. This APÉRITIF is as rousing as most made with gin, but its ambrosia of fruit syrups keeps the drink's edge from digging too deep.

Almost certainly invented during the OLD SCHOOL OF AMERICAN BARTENDING, the Clover Club began to brave mild baiting during the early '30s, starting with the Old School itself: "A Philadelphia importation," wrote Albert S. Crockett in *The Old Waldorf-Astoria Bar Book*, the drink "originated in the bar of the old Bellevue-Stratford, where the Clover Club, composed of literary, legal, financial, and business lights of the Quaker City, often dined and wined, and wined again."

In the hope of learning more about how this drink's fortune ran awry and its stature was diminished, we tried to go to the supposed source – the Clover Club. Although we came across plenty of references to the club in obituaries of seemingly fine fellows from Boston and Philly, we never found a live specimen from the organization. We soon began to question whether the club had anything to do with the drink at all – and found the work of Jessy Randall, reference librarian at the Library Company of Philadelphia and an especially helpful TEETOTALER, particularly convincing. "At a certain point in every Clover Club dinner, 'after the soup, and with the fish,' " reported Randall, "there would be several toasts drunk from the 'Loving Cup.' " Randall went on to quote from Mary R. Deacon's *The Clover Club of Philadelphia* of 1897: "The knowledge of the composition of the brew in the 'Loving Cup' is not common property. It is potent, it is strong. Those who have dipped more than once in its spring have mentioned its penetrating properties and its enervating powers. Double vision may follow two indulgences." Randall surmised that perhaps "the 'Clover Club' cocktail is related to this 'mysterious brew,' " as they call it in a poem later. "But I have no proof."

When we combine Randall's doubts with the fact that no one at the Bellevue Hotel seems to remember either the club or the cocktail – even though the establishment boasts a "Clover Room" – we wonder why no members of the Clover Club have ever commented on the story of this drink. We suspect that one evening, long ago, a few affiliates of the group offhandedly asked a bartender at the Bellevue to mix them up something new, and "Clover Club" seemed to be a good enough name for a simple enough drink. Or perhaps the bartender decided this perfectly prosaic drink didn't quite merit the flights of the picky or imaginative, and certainly not its creator's name.

COCKTAIL

GLASS	TASTE COMPLEXITY	MIXING DIFFICULTY

LOW |O━━━━━━| HIGH   LOW |━━━O━━| HIGH

DRINK ERA

OLD SCHOOL OF AMERICAN BARTENDING

Clover Club

RECIPE

2 ounces gin
1 ounce lemon juice
¼ ounce grenadine or raspberry syrup
2 teaspoons egg white

Shake with cracked ice;
strain into chilled wine goblet or cocktail glass.
Garnish with a lemon wheel.

Requiring more shaking than thought, the Clover Club is well suited to imbibers with a predilection for sweet drinks. As a general rule, this drink should be shaken for no less than 30 seconds, or else made without the egg, which adds no taste – merely texture.

For a variation, follow a recommendation from *Cocktails – How to Mix Them* of 1922: add a splash each of dry VERMOUTH and raspberry syrup, then substitute lime for the lemon juice. For a drier taste, try 1 teaspoon MARASCHINO LIQUEUR instead of a syrup.

If garnished with a mint sprig, the cocktail is called a Clover Leaf. When RUM is used instead of GIN, according to *The Old Waldorf-Astoria Bar Book*, a September Morn is made.

Similar drinks include the Ramos Gin Fizz and the Milk Punch.

F| rom the band that perfected lounge Muzak and coined the deathless phrase *Cocktail Nation*, we have the Combustible Edison. Composed of two parts BRANDY to one part CAMPARI and one part fresh lemon juice, the band's namesake drink warms the body and stimulates the spirit while putting on a fine show of shadowy blue flames dancing atop the brandy.

The Millionaire (we liked him from the moment we heard his credentials: a GIN man with the sophistication to appreciate Campari) says the hardest thing about making this drink is pouring the flaming brandy into a cocktail glass without singeing one's fingers. He quickly adds, however, that the pyrotechnics of bartending dictate that one must never be intimidated by the flame. Fortunately, the Combustible Edison's taper is the coolest of fires and is extinguished moments after hitting the brisk citrus and Campari.

Of course, some days we just don't have the energy to drag out the Bunsen burner for this drink, no matter how much we like the aroma of fervent brandy. Instead, we'll opt for the band's Edisonian: the same ingredients minus the heat – a seemingly slight change that makes this drink a true COCKTAIL. We can count on the Campari kick of the Edisonian to revive us for the evening ahead, certain that its warmer counterpart, taken as a nightcap, will welcome us home.

Before Combustible Edison released its *I, Swinger* album in 1994, The Millionaire decided the band needed a drink all its own. In a style reminiscent of the illustrious bartender Jerry Thomas, who created and showcased one of the first flaming drinks, the Blue Blazer, in the mid-19th century, Combustible Edison band members and a few loyal supporters headed to a mixology lab where they spent three exhausting nights in search of the perfect Combustible Edison drink. Having succeeded, the band published the recipe in its album notes and began a cocktail crusade, bolstered by its tour of Europe and the States. According to The Millionaire – who goes by Michael Cudahy only on official government records – we're now in the post-revolutionary stage of the Cocktail Revolution. We ourselves weren't aware the fight was over, but in our effort to qualify as optimists, we're willing to celebrate.

GLASS	TASTE COMPLEXITY	MIXING DIFFICULTY
Y	LOW ⬜⬜◯⬜⬜ HIGH	LOW ⬜⬜⬜⬜◯ HIGH
	DRINK ERA	
	THE REVIVAL OF AMERICAN DRINKING	

Combustible Edison

A versatile modern-day classic, the Combustible Edison suits nearly any evening's mood. But you'll have no flames if you fail to heat the brandy to near boiling or if you wait too long before pouring it. The spirit's flame burns quickly and appears quite faint, so remember to dim the lights – and warn guests to take their first sip with caution.

Asbestos gloves are unnecessary when flaming this drink; however, to keep mixing manageable, mix no more than two Combustible Edisons at a time. Reserve this drink for late evening and the Edisonian for the cocktail hour. The latter version will encourage the tartness of the Campari. If either drink proves too sour for some tastes, add a dash of COINTREAU.

Similar drinks include the Blue Blazer, the Jasmine, and the Negroni.

RECIPE

2 ounces brandy
1 ounce Campari
1 ounce lemon juice

Shake Campari and lemon juice with cracked ice; strain into chilled cocktail glass. Heat brandy in chafing dish. When warm, ignite the brandy and pour in a flaming stream into the cocktail glass. Variation: If the brandy is chilled and shaken rather than ignited, the drink is known as the Edisonian.

O nly a few years back, this drink was called the "stealth Martini," first by Barnaby Conrad III, author of *The Martini*, and then by its followers. Whether the name came from the Cosmo's covert kick or from its popularity among those unimpressed by the classic Martini is of little consequence now. We're just glad the cocktail crowd hasn't deemed it passé.

Some bartenders snub the Cosmopolitan, comparing it to those drinks on the short list of classic cocktails. We'll admit it lacks complexity, but few can deny this drink's appeal — nor its reliability, especially in establishments staffed by slipshod mixers. In fact, whenever unsure of a bar's integrity, we start the evening with a request for a Cosmopolitan, descendant of the Cold War's Cape Cod and respectable sibling of the Kamikaze shooter. Made with 1½ ounces of VODKA, ¾ ounce of COINTREAU, ½ ounce of lime juice, and a splash of cranberry juice, the only way a mixer can sabotage this cocktail is to substitute fake fruit for fresh.

No one seems to have bothered noting who mixed the first Cosmo, though many drink historians and bartenders agree that the gay community in Provincetown, Massachusetts, should be credited with the accomplishment. The moniker Cheryl Cook will occasionally surface, but it leads only to San Francisco, never to an actual person. Many bartenders — such as John Caine, owner of Café Mars in San Francisco and undisputed West Coast champion of this drink — partly credit the Cosmopolitan with the resurgence of the cocktail during the '70s, when FERN BARS, with their overly sweet so-called GIRL DRINKS, nearly destroyed the respectability of the bar. After all, "bounce berries" — as they're called on the East Coast — are tart treats more commonly associated with Thanksgiving than with cocktails, so adding their juice to a cocktail constituted a serious break with tradition back then.

The popularity of the Cosmopolitan quickly traveled from New England to New York and then across the country. Characters like MacGyver drink it, and Hunter S. Thompson — the self-proclaimed "mad doctor of gonzo journalism" — managed to get it cited in an affidavit used in *The People of the State of Colorado v. Hunter Stockton Thompson*. Whenever desperate for a cocktail at some endearing singles bar, we're thankful for the Cosmopolitan.

GLASS	TASTE COMPLEXITY	MIXING DIFFICULTY
▼	LOW O▬▬▬ HIGH	LOW ▬▬O▬▬ HIGH

DRINK ERA

THE DARK AGE OF AMERICAN DRINKING

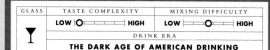

Cosmopolitan

RECIPE

1½ ounces vodka
¾ ounce Cointreau
½ ounce lime juice
1 splash cranberry juice

Shake with cracked ice;
strain into chilled cocktail glass.
Garnish with a lime wheel.

When faced with a sudden onslaught of uninvited guests around the cocktail hour, serve Cosmopolitans. A drink like this is easily adapted by home hosts on those occasions when mixing seems like too much stress and strain.

Avoid situations in which guests recite their take on the Cosmo's recipe. There are hundreds of variations, but only a few are worth mentioning and even fewer worth drinking.

With any version of the Cosmopolitan, remember that without the proper amount of lime, the drink will be too sweet. Also, avoid mixing syrups or SIMPLE SYRUP in this crisp cocktail.

Citrus-infused vodkas will allow for plenty of experimentation.

Similar drinks include the Evan, the Edisonian, and the Jasmine.

Cuba Libre

T he Cuba Libre hails from the OLD SCHOOL OF AMERICAN BARTENDING, though you cer- tainly wouldn't guess it from the drink's vapid formula – contrived to satisfy con- venience, not competence. When considering all the cocktails the world has to offer, the Cuba Libre is rarely our first choice. But it's a HIGHBALL that we've all sipped and will surely sip again, so it's worth setting the record straight: A Cuba Libre is not a RUM and Coke.

Confusion over the Cuba Libre's recipe began with the drink's earliest incarnation. Patriots aiding Cuba during the Spanish-American War – and, later, expatriates avoiding PROHIBITION – regularly mixed rum and Coca-Cola as a cocktail and a toast to this West Indies island. According to a 1965 deposition by Fausto Rodriguez – filed at the suggestion of a liquor company certain of being mentioned in the statement – the Cuba Libre was first mixed at a Cuban bar in August 1900 by a member of the U.S. Signal Corps. Surprisingly, the Cuba Libre (pronounced "KOO-buh LEE-bray") didn't strike a chord stateside until, as William Grimes points out in *Straight Up or On the Rocks*, the Andrews Sisters began performing the Trinidad tune – named for the drink's more inane ingredients, rum and Coca-Cola – around the time of World War II. But with Coke at a nickel a bottle and rum coming into vogue, it was only a matter of time before this drink rose to prominence.

Soon enough, as Charles H. Baker points out in his *Gentleman's Companion* of 1946, the Cuba Libre "caught on everywhere throughout the south ... filtered through the north and west ... carried along by the ease of its supply." In *The American Language*, H. L. Mencken writes of an early variation of the drink: "The troglodytes of western South Carolina coined *jump stiddy* for a mixture of Coca-Cola and denatured alcohol (usually drawn from automobile radiators); connoisseurs reputedly preferred the taste of what had been aged in Model-T Fords."

Whenever we consider the Cuba Libre our best option at a given bar, we remind our- selves that this drink was once viewed as exotic, with its dark syrup – made, at that time, from kola nuts and cocaine. A few American drinkers had hoped that this wonder – created by pharmacist John Pemberton of Atlanta, Georgia, in 1886 – would go on to compete with the great BITTERS of Europe. The drink, when worth drinking, contains 2 to 3 ounces of the now far from exotic soda, the juice and hull of ¼ lime, 1 ounce of rum, 2 dashes of bitters, and ½ ounce of GIN. (The last two ingredients are our own additions.) Should our order for this drink ever be questioned, we say nothing, instead reflecting on the scene in Gary Indiana's book *Gone Tomorrow* in which the main character tells of ordering a Cuba Libre: "The bar- woman, instantly hostile, stomped through her enclosure, chanting a litany of disgust that concluded with the words 'Cuba Libre' spat out with incredulity. The startling performance repelled me. I hate fools." We do, too, and we tip accordingly.

COCKTAIL

GLASS	TASTE COMPLEXITY	MIXING DIFFICULTY
	LOW |O⎯⎯⎯⎯| HIGH	LOW |O⎯⎯⎯⎯| HIGH
	DRINK ERA	
	OLD SCHOOL OF AMERICAN BARTENDING	

Cuba Libre

You'll always have one or two friends who insist that there's simply no cocktail for them. Don't despair: At some point – perhaps as they're giving their self-righteous attachment to their beverage of choice a momentary rest – you may succeed in luring them into the cocktail camp with a tasty HIGHBALL, and there's no better bait than a Cuba Libre.

Coca-Cola no longer contains exotic ingredients, but we're still convinced that the soda made in South America tastes better than that mixed elsewhere. Admittedly, we lack concrete information to support this hard-nosed view. When questioned about the matter, we merely credit the soda's recycled packaging – charming bottles complete with small scratches in the glass. Their look is as subtle and effective as a well-placed garnish.

Similar drinks include the Pedro Collins.

RECIPE

1 ounce light rum
½ ounce gin
¼ ounce lime juice
2 to 3 ounces Coca-Cola
2 dashes bitters

Pour all ingredients except soda into chilled Collins glass filled with ice. Top with cola and stir.
Garnish with a lime squeeze.
For a drink closer to the original recipe,
leave out the gin and bitters.

Daiquiri

H istory credits a gringo with creating the Daiquiri, but we dare to dispute this claim, guessing that Cubans were enjoying this cocktail long before American engineer Jennings Cox set foot on the island. Mr. Cox was sent to Daiquiri, a small town on the east coast of Cuba, by the Spanish-American Iron Co. He worked with a group of thirsty comrades that supposedly enjoyed the refreshing rum-and-lime beverage after a hard day's work, and it's said Mr. Cox named the drink after the town (some accounts, it's worth noting, also credit a Harry E. Stout with this act). *A New Century Beckons: A History of the Army and Navy Club* explains that "… Capt. Charles H. Harlow, took the ship's junior medical officer, Lucius W. Johnson, with him on a tour of the ten-year-old battlegrounds. At Daiquiri, they met Jennings Cox … who treated them to a drink he had developed to temper the fiery taste of Bacardi rum." Mr. Johnson soon introduced the drink to the Army and Navy Club in Washington, D.C. The link thus established between the Daiquiri and American national security is still celebrated in the club's Daiquiri Lounge.

Further accentuating the Daiquiri's imperialist past is the role played by the prince of presidential style himself – JFK. The Daiquiri was one of the president's preferred before-dinner drinks. This factoid, once revealed to the American public, brought the Daiquiri fame and popularity rivaled only by the Martini. Regrettably, the Daiquiri's stature – and its good name – have suffered since the emergence of strip-mall happy hours, where this drink has been promoted as a spirituous Slurpee. When making this drink, we try to follow in the footsteps of the bartender first credited with FLASH BLENDING this drink: Constantino Ribailagua – "El Rey de los Coteleros," or the Cocktail King – who mixed at El Florida when it was known as "La Catedral del Daiquiri" ("The Temple of the Daiquiri"). As David A. Embury points out in *The Fine Art of Mixing Drinks*, first published in 1948: "His limes were gently squeezed with his fingers lest even a drop of the bitter oil from the peel get into the drink; the cocktails were mixed (but not overmixed) … the stinging cold drink was strained through a fine sieve into the glass so that not one tiny piece of ice remained in it. No smallest detail was overlooked in achieving the flawless perfection of the drink."

The Daiquiri's classic recipe of a JIGGER of rum, a teaspoon of SIMPLE SYRUP, and ¾ ounce of lime juice is deceptively simple. Too much rum and the taste becomes overpowering; too much lime and it's bitter and sharp; too much sugar and you might as well toss it out. The first literary mention of the Daiquiri was in F. Scott Fitzgerald's *This Side of Paradise*, published in 1920. The novel is a fine reminder that this seemingly cathartic potion is best sipped (and mixed) with restraint: In a section of the book titled "The Devil," a character orders a double Daiquiri, but a friend changes the order to four. This act is later regretted when the old man the friend sees turns out to be a "purple zebra" – a figment of his sodden imagination.

GLASS	TASTE COMPLEXITY	MIXING DIFFICULTY
Y	LOW ⊢O━━━━━┤ HIGH	LOW ⊢━━━O━┤ HIGH

DRINK ERA

OLD SCHOOL OF AMERICAN BARTENDING

Daiquiri

RECIPE

1½ ounces light rum
¾ ounce lime juice
¼ ounce simple syrup

Shake with cracked ice;
strain into chilled cocktail glass.
Garnish with a lime wheel.

No doubt the frozen kiwi-banana Daiquiri and the watermelon-strawberry Daiquiri are superlative choices when training for a drunken balcony-to-balcony climb at a Daytona Beach hotel midway through spring break. But the odds are you're already past that – or somehow resisted such antics in the first place – and can now appreciate an unadulterated Daiquiri.

Only mildly difficult to prepare, this drink is best served ice-cold. When a dash of GRENADINE is added, it's known as a Bacardi Cocktail. If the lime is too tart, add a dash of maraschino, orgeat, or crème d'ananas. Never opt for Rose's lime juice; you'll end up with a mutated Gimlet. Always shake or flash blend the ingredients thoroughly with cracked ice.

Similar drinks include the Presidente.

W e were convinced that El Diablo – given the French and Mexican roots of its liquors – hailed from the time of Maximilian's puppet empire. In fact, we had even divined its birthplace as Mérida, known to the Spaniards as the Yucatán's *ciudad blanca*, or "white city." Surely in this town, built on Mayan ruins yet accepting of French architectural tastes, this drink had been enjoyed by people of both cultures, even if each claimed the other was the Diablo.

But alas, it was only wishful thinking. Made with a JIGGER of white or silver TEQUILA, ¾ ounce of French CRÈME DE CASSIS, and ½ ounce of lime juice topped with ginger ale, the recipe for this rogue APÉRITIF has rarely been recorded. In fact, mixologist Charles Schumann, proprietor of Schumann's in Munich, was one of the first modern-day mixers to document it in a bar book. We asked him if he knew the history of this drink, and he shattered our hopes: "Maximilian, Mérida? Ah no – an American in Los Angeles or San Francisco, not that long ago." Nowhere near as glamorous or as old as we had hoped – though we do know Trader Vic (of Mai Tai fame) was making them in the late '40s.

Nonetheless, a Diablo suits us on those evenings when we crave the spirit our gullets can never quite handle straight. With the Diablo's tequila tempered by cassis, the drink encourages stiff-necked pride while allowing for compromise. We can swallow this smooth libation, with its mild edge, without the need for a pained expression. Most bartenders, though unfamiliar with this drink, will be relieved to serve a tequila SLING, rather than indulging the bad habit of a tequila shot followed by a bite of lime. Certainly they'll jump at the opportunity to have a few patrons demonstrate acceptable tequila-related behavior, even if they do have to memorize another recipe. But warn them first: A Diablo made with too much cassis encourages daft chatter and slight tips.

GLASS	TASTE COMPLEXITY	MIXING DIFFICULTY
	LOW ═══O═══ HIGH	LOW ═O═══ HIGH
	DRINK ERA	
	YEARS OF REFORM	

Diablo

RECIPE

1½ ounces tequila
¾ ounce crème de cassis
½ ounce lime juice
Ginger ale

Stir tequila, cassis, and lime juice with cracked ice;
strain into chilled Collins glass filled with ice.
Top with ginger ale, and garnish with a lime wheel.

Serve Diablos on warm evenings when you have a hankering for the wine of Mexico. With the likes of Trader Vic calling the Diablo "a little noggin" that's "tough on your running board," we suggest measuring this drink's ingredients with care.

Diablos should be made with the most neutral of tequilas. Gold tequila, with its caramel additives and additional aging, detracts from the cassis flavor; however, if this is what you have on hand, you can mix a slightly second-rate Diablo by adding an extra dash or two of cassis. Be sure not to overdo it with the cordial, though – too much will ruin this APÉRITIF.

A zestier Diablo is mixed using ginger beer; never substitute sodas like Seven-Up in this drink.

Similar drinks include the Pedro Collins.

Years ago at the Townhouse – a nondescript bar and grill in Emeryville, California, whose patrons, at least back then, rarely knew where they were going before they got there – a classic cocktail quietly came to be. The Alchemist and his good friend Farid Dormishian, a Persian with a penchant for CHARTREUSE, were about to close up after a complacent eight-hour shift when they decided to reward themselves for a job well done.

Maybe it was the crisp fall weather and maybe it wasn't, but something made the Alchemist behave very peculiarly that evening (which by that point was well into morning). Without outside pressure – be it persuasion, coercion, or threat – the Alchemist mixed with VODKA. Although he's created plenty of drinks with this spirit, including the Mauri and the Petit Zinc, those were conceived for friends and patrons. He's a WHISKEY man, with an appreciation of GIN. Who would have imagined that, left to his own devices, he'd grab for the vodka bottle? We'd point a finger at Farid, but we know he almost always sips his Chartreuse straight.

Yet vodka was the perfect choice. In the concoction he came up with – 2 ounces of vodka with ¼ ounce of COINTREAU and ⅛ ounce of Chartreuse – the neutrality of the vodka lets this DIGESTIF's complex flavor settle back into something not everyone can appreciate. Chartreuse (the herbal, better known for the color it engendered) is subdued only slightly by the Cointreau's bittersweet orange, making for a cocktail that starts out deceptively sweet, then follows with an herbal kick. Just as your palate had to adjust to your first cocktail, your taste buds may cower when first hit with this drink. But take a second sip and reconsider: Few other cocktails will travel so well with you through life. "Never stake your reputation on it, because not everyone will like it," says the Alchemist. "It is a successful cocktail that some people really enjoy. Those who don't should learn to like it, since it reveals a person's ability to appreciate an intense flavor."

This cocktail, besides possessing a taste that's far from pedestrian, will never make the vernacular of the bar. The Alchemist may make tantalizing libations, but when it comes to naming them – well, consider this one: It's still nameless. Although we've suggested plenty of attractive handles, the Alchemist insists that none of them quite fits. For a while, the drink went by Luther, in reference to one John Luther, who ordered it often; but for whatever reason, it never stuck. We've even taken up a collection to reward whatever prodigy comes up with an epithet the Alchemist likes. So far, our money seems safe. In the meantime, we're not too concerned. Any bar that has Chartreuse is sure to have Cointreau too, and we can order this Drink Without a Name.

GLASS	TASTE COMPLEXITY	MIXING DIFFICULTY
Y	LOW ⊡━━O⊡ HIGH	LOW ⊡━━O━⊡ HIGH

DRINK ERA
THE REVIVAL OF AMERICAN DRINKING

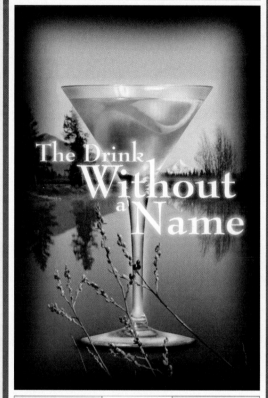

The Drink Without a Name

RECIPE

2 ounces vodka
¼ ounce Cointreau
⅛ ounce Chartreuse

Stir with cracked ice;
strain into chilled cocktail glass.
Garnish with an orange twist.

Reserve the Drink Without a Name for those ardent friends you want to impress but know you don't have to.

Contrary to popular belief, heavy foods do not deaden one's taste. Rather, they ready it for other flavors not manifest in everyday life. Only after the appropriate meal will this drink seem well chosen, and even then it helps to have crisp weather to make imbibers grateful for this cocktail's herbal kick. This drink works well as the finish to a spicy, rich repast, especially curried Indian food.

For friends still adapting to the flavor of the Drink Without a Name, dilute the cocktail by stirring it longer before straining it into a chilled cocktail glass. Also remember that the colder the libation, the smoother its taste.

Similar drinks include the **Champs Elysées** and the **Pegu**.

F irst concocted around 1732 at the State in Schuylkill fishing club in Philadelphia, Fish House Punch is said to have kicked off the club's every meeting and to have inspired several blank pages in George Washington's diary. We don't keep a diary, but we're certainly at no loss for words about this drink.

When winter's lost its charm and the months to come promise more of the same, we sip this tonic, which helps us weather any storm. Far nicer than its name, Fish House Punch manages to have a keen tropical taste while maintaining the respectability of the most venerable drinks from the northern latitudes.

Served with the bite of a true COCKTAIL – and never with a paper umbrella – Fish House Punch is so time-consuming to make that it demands to be concocted in bulk. When holed up with friends fleeing regrettable weather, we assemble our reserves of dark RUM, COGNAC, peach BRANDY, lemons, and sugar. After dissolving ¾ pound of superfine sugar in a little water, we add a whopping 24 ounces of lemon juice and almost 40 ounces more of water, give the mix a good stir, and chill it for several hours. Just before the guests become restless, we dump the brew into a sizable bowl and toss in 36 ounces of dark rum and 25 ounces of brandy, followed by a tempering 4 ounces of peach brandy. Soon enough, we forget all about the weather outdoors and sip what Fannie Merritt Farmer, in her 1896 bible of the American kitchen, *The Boston Cooking-School Book* called (as recounted in *Forbes*), a "much esteemed and highly potent punch."

We heed without fail the red flag raised by Charles H. Baker's *Gentleman's Companion* of 1946: "Warning: there are a horde of so-called Fish House punch receipts that include BÉNÉDICTINE, CURAÇAO, bourbon, and God knows what else. Eschew them." But even the fervent Mr. Baker makes alternative recommendations on the matter of which type of rum to use – Jamaican or Bacardi. His "suggestions are in no way intended as heresy, but simply indicate what substitutions, if any, are possible." Although not typically a man of compromise, Mr. Baker recommends using equal portions of Jamaican and Bacardi.

Once in 10 years, we'll come across an establishment on the East Coast that'll serve Fish House Punch. Fortunately, it's a peculiar enough concoction that if a place does serve it, the bartender or owner will be sure to let you know. Unlike the typical bar potions that are made to quiet a patron and elicit a hefty tip, Fish House Punch is made only by those who would drink it themselves and are sure to tell you why. But considering this drink's hard though subtle blow, and our intolerance for babbled tales at the bar, we'd just as soon sip it from home, safe from Mother Nature and protected from unwelcome testimonials.

GLASS	TASTE COMPLEXITY	MIXING DIFFICULTY
	LOW =O= HIGH	LOW =O= HIGH
Y	DRINK ERA	
	GOTHIC AGE OF AMERICAN DRINKING	

Fish House Punch

Serve Fish House Punch on cold evenings when you need a break from the monotony of winter. Begin preparing several hours before guests are due, because the punch must be mixed in stages and does require patience.

This drink requires a mixer of strong convictions who won't succumb to the temptation to buy cheap spirits. You'll also want to consider how you prefer to serve this drink – as a cocktail or as a punch. If you opt for the latter, a large bowl filled with attractive ice molds will suffice, and the mixer's job will be minimal. But if you'd like a more formal atmosphere, serve the drink as a cocktail.

Similar drinks include the Planter's Punch.

87

RECIPE

36 ounces dark rum
24 ounces lemon juice
25 ounces brandy
4 ounces peach brandy
¾ pound superfine sugar
40 ounces water

Dissolve sugar in a little water. Add juice and remaining water; stir. Two to three hours before serving, add spirits; refrigerate. For serving, portion punch into bowl, add ice molds to punch. Makes 30 servings.

Floridita

Always overshadowed by its younger sibling – a drink with the same name but a different nickname and a dissimilar taste – this Floridita has been forgotten for years by all but the most resolute. About the time of the Noble Experiment, rumrunners regularly journeyed from Florida to Cuba, where many American drinkers and bartenders had gone to flee the drought. One bar in particular became a common port of entry for thirsty expatriates. Originally known as La Piña de Plata ("The Silver Pineapple") in the early 1800s, this establishment became El Florida (eventually "Floridita" to its regulars) after the Spanish-American War, and was later credited with creating a handful of classic cocktails, including this one.

Still, according to William Grimes in *Straight Up or On the Rocks*, El Floridita "was just another bar until Hemingway walked in and wrapped a large paw around a sugarless frozen daiquiri, the creation of Constantino Ribailagua, a Catalonian who had begun working there in 1914." We've been assured that today, El Floridita remains an endearing bar, set in one of Havana's nicest hotels.

Less fabled and less foamy than Hemingway's drink of choice, though no less tasty, this Floridita starts out tart but ends with a chocolate finish so subtle that newcomers to this ruby-red drink always take a second sip before betraying their wonderment. Made with 1½ ounces of RUM and ½ ounce each of lime juice and sweet VERMOUTH, followed by a dash each of white CRÈME DE CACAO and GRENADINE (beware: Too much of either and this classic cocktail is ruined), this drink – shaken and served up – always makes us feel like we've won the door prize, a confidence we carry with us for the rest of the evening.

Although the ingredients for this drink can be found at just about any bar, we're always particularly impressed when a bartender has put it to memory. And if someone requests a chocolate frappé and the bartender suggests a Floridita instead, we're fans for life.

GLASS	TASTE COMPLEXITY	MIXING DIFFICULTY
▼	LOW ═══O═══ HIGH	LOW ═══════O HIGH
	DRINK ERA	
	PROHIBITION	

Floridita

The Floridita offers itself as common ground for even the most disparate of cocktail crowds. Unlike the Manhattan and the Old Fashioned, which provide the perfect backdrop for an event, the Floridita is so unusual that it actually provokes conversation.

When mixing a Floridita, shake well, and never add too much crème de cacao or grenadine. With so many ingredients, this drink often ends up unbalanced. The key to a well-made Floridita is the layering of the tastes it contains. The citrus should hit first and the cacao last. Although brown crème de cacao tastes no different from the cordial's clear version, steer clear of it unless you want a cocktail that looks like mud.

Similar drinks include the **Cosmopolitan** and the **Hemingway Daiquiri**.

RECIPE

1½ ounces light rum
½ ounce lime juice
½ ounce sweet vermouth
1 dash white crème de cacao
1 dash grenadine

Shake with cracked ice;
strain into chilled cocktail glass.
Garnish with a lime wheel.

French 75

Sipping a French 75 reminds us that while champagne hasn't always signified celebration, it has become one of life's lasting symbols: a drink raised in the hour of hope.

To toast occasions whose elements include an unknown measure of fear – such as marriage or war – we mix this cocktail with 4 ounces of champagne and ¼ ounce of GIN, the spirit that always seems to make us smarter. We add ¼ ounce each of lemon juice and COINTREAU for a rounded edge that keeps us from becoming too reflective for our own good.

Several parties claim to have christened this luscious cocktail, almost certainly named for one of the guns used by the French during World War I. *Harry's ABC of Mixing Cocktails* of 1919 suggests the first French 75 was made in 1915, but credits no one for the concoction. "Count" León Bertrand Arnaud Casenave, former owner of the French-Creole restaurant Arnaud's in New Orleans, is rumored to have given himself credit for the drink's invention a few years after that date, and Duncan MacElhone, the proprietor of Harry's New York Bar in Paris, told us his grandfather Harry undoubtedly created the recipe in the mid-'20s. Some mixologists suggest that the French 75 was first made with BRANDY, not gin, which would certainly be more in line with the tastes of the French.

An anodyne for fear, the French 75 – sans lemon and Cointreau – was reputedly sipped by French officers before they headed into battle. Enlisted men had to settle for a shot of RUM or *pinard*. Mordis Eksteins, author of *Rites of Spring*, suggests that such a disparity reminded the recruits of their "disposable status" and ultimately contributed to the widespread mutinies of 1917. Fortunately, we're told that those enlisted men who survived the war held no grudge against this drink. Upon returning to their cities and villages, they even asked for it in their local brasseries.

The Esquire Drink Book of 1956 proclaims that champagne's "restorative powers to … patients could bring a million testimonials, and its heartening influence upon the lonely soul is quite incalculable." The "gin brings a smile to the lips and a purl to the eyes" and steadiness to the mind, add the *Esquire* editors. Sadly, however, the French 75 is now as far forgotten as the Great War's promise to put an end to war itself. We ourselves request it on occasions that demand a toast – but a toast to something we haven't quite bought into – knowing that this effervescent drink will lift us out of the trenches of ennui.

GLASS	TASTE COMPLEXITY	MIXING DIFFICULTY
🍸	LOW ▭▭○▭▭ HIGH	LOW ▭▭○▭▭ HIGH
	DRINK ERA	
	OLD SCHOOL OF AMERICAN BARTENDING	

The French 75 – appropriate at any time during the day – is relatively easy to make and soothing to sip.

You may wish to experiment with slight deviations in the French 75's recipe. Up to half an ounce of Cointreau, for instance, may be added with an appealing result. The drink is occasionally mixed with an ounce of either lemon or lime juice, a dash or two of SIMPLE SYRUP, and 2 ounces of brandy. If lime juice is used, garnish with a zest of lime. A French 95 is made by substituting bourbon for the gin.

Similar drinks include the Champagne Cocktail and Kir Royal, a flute of sparkling wine with a barspoon of crème de cassis.

RECIPE

4 ounces champagne
¼ ounce gin
¼ ounce Cointreau
¼ ounce lemon juice

Shake gin, Cointreau, and lemon juice with cracked ice;
strain into chilled flute.
Top with chilled champagne, and
garnish with a lemon twist.

Frisco

R arely do we call for this drink by name, though we'll order it one way or another whenever we have a thirst for WHISKEY but not for its bite. BÉNÉDICTINE, our favorite monkish liqueur, softens the Frisco's rye without flattening its taste. The dubious status of its abbreviated handle has caused this venerable concoction to all but disappear.

Sophisticates, we're told, ordered this drink after California's gold rush in the 1850s. But back then (as many Easterners point out) the Frisco was certainly uncouth, and probably nothing more than a pony of rye with a dash of Bénédictine. We admit it's tough to imagine some newly outfitted miner having the foresight to schlepp a bottle of this fine European liqueur out West. But with the heyday of the OLD SCHOOL OF AMERICAN BARTENDING due to hit in 1897, we wouldn't be all that surprised, either.

Although partial to the sterling Frisco recipe of 2 ounces of rye, ¼ ounce of Bénédictine, and ¾ ounce of lemon juice, we remain impressed by this drink's adaptability. About the time the term *Frisco* first came under fire, bartenders began substituting bourbon for rye, in the presumed hope of appealing to the nation's gentry dwelling east of the Mississippi. By the late 1930s, *The Barman's Bible* (by Oscar Haimo, president of the International Bar Manager's Association) began giving the Frisco cocktail's recipe with this version.

In 1907, the Ladies Outdoor Art League of San Francisco started an Anti-Frisco Committee. Besides labeling the term "obnoxious," the committee declared its disgust at "poets who would sing praise to Frisco," claiming that "the person who would call San Francisco 'Frisco' would also wear diamonds to breakfast." Matters of taste aside, the committee also pointed out that there is no Frisco in California, and that such states as Alabama and Arkansas already had laid claim to the name.

Even the Fairmont, that turn-of-the-century bastille of San Fran cocktails, no longer receives requests for this drink. Sam Aronis, the establishment's beverage manager, says that's just as well, since most of the Fairmont's bartenders admittedly wouldn't know – nor would they care to know – how to mix it. We're told the term is used only by tourists and dealers nowadays. In fact, the late newspaper pundit Herb Caen made an "etymological footnote" about the word *Frisco*, noting that it's included in a list of slang terms issued by the Drug Enforcement Administration. Never in a million years would we have guessed that ordering a Frisco cocktail might get us a mixture of heroin and cocaine. So we skip the name and call out the ingredients instead – we certainly wouldn't want to be mistaken for tourists.

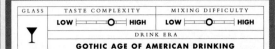

A late-evening or cold-weather cocktail, the Frisco's herbal kick may not be to everyone's taste. When making this drink, always respect the imbiber's preference in whiskey.

In the early 1990s, mixologist Charles Schumann, proprietor of a namesake bar in Munich, sweetened the Frisco's recipe with a barspoon of powdered sugar to create what he calls the Frisco Sour; see the recipes for another, more elaborate variation. If a Frisco Sour isn't sweet enough for one of your guests, don't add more sugar. Instead, opt for a dash or two of Bénédictine or add a squeeze of orange.

Similar drinks include the Blue Moon, the Rusty Nail, and the Highlander.

RECIPE

2 ounces rye
¼ ounce Bénédictine
¾ ounce lemon juice

Shake with cracked ice;
strain into chilled cocktail glass.
Garnish with a lemon wheel.

Gibson

T he not-so-evil twin of the dry Martini, the Gibson has been overlooked for years by all but its most loyal fans – the Martini's true devotees. While most drinkers down their mongrel Martini mixes of sugary syrups and WHITE LIGHTNING, fans of the Gibson sip their Martinis with gin and garnish them with pickled pearl onions. Of course, we've simplified things a bit. Twins don't have the same soul, and neither do the Gibson and the Martini. The latter, with its unctuous olive, summons up the proud libertine in an imbiber, while the Gibson lets him sit back – gnawing on the drink's crisp, clean onion – with an eye on everyone else. Made with the notoriously stiff Martini base of 2½ ounces of gin and a half ounce of dry vermouth, the Gibson subtly brings the salt brine of its garnish to the fore.

There's little consensus when it comes to the story of this drink's christening, though most agree that Charles Dana Gibson – the man who drew the comely but underfed Gibson Girl – inspired it while visiting The Players club in New York City. Some stories suggest that Mr. Gibson challenged the bartender, Charley Connolly, to improve upon the Martini's recipe. In any case, Mr. Connolly was out of olives, so he grabbed the onion jar instead. In hopes of verifying this story, we called The Players and spoke with the establishment's librarian, Raymond Wemmlinger. Although familiar with the tale, Mr. Wemmlinger could neither confirm nor deny it, though he said Mr. Gibson was indeed a member of the club from 1891 to 1903.

We buy the story, though we find some of the others more amusing. There's the tale of a card player named Gibson, in cahoots with an unnamed bar's mixers. While other card players sipped drink after drink, Gibson's winnings mounted as he sipped from a cocktail glass filled with water – marked for his benefit with a small pearl onion. Then there's Barnaby Conrad III's report from *The Martini*: "One [story] has an American ambassador named Gibson serving in London during PROHIBITION. He wished to make his English guests welcome with a good cocktail, but personally felt constrained to follow his country's laws even while abroad. So during receptions he would circulate carrying a glass of water with a cocktail onion in it." Mr. Conrad's second story comes from Steve Zell of the Occidental Grill in San Francisco: "I heard that during the '20s in Chicago there were twin sisters named Gibson who loved the Martini but hated the olives. Whenever they'd go out, they'd get the bartenders to use two pickled onions – twins for twins."

The pleasant truth about the Gibson is that we can expect to find its ingredients at any bar, though locating a bartender who understands the magic of ice and the rigors of the chilled glass isn't so easy. Of course, we're really happy just to get the drink we ordered: Six out of ten requests for a Gibson come back as a Gimlet instead.

GLASS	TASTE COMPLEXITY	MIXING DIFFICULTY
Y	LOW ⊶O⊷ HIGH	LOW ⊶O⊷ HIGH

DRINK ERA

GOLDEN AGE OF AMERICAN DRINKING

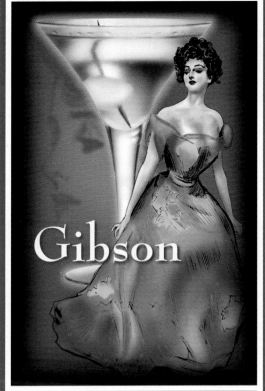

Gibson

RECIPE

2½ ounces gin
½ ounce dry vermouth

Stir with cracked ice;
strain into chilled cocktail glass.
Garnish with a cocktail onion.

Most accounts insist that the first Gibson was served with two pickled onions dropped, not skewered, into the bottom of the cocktail glass. As a general rule, one onion goes nearly unnoticed till the drink's end, two will raise an eyebrow at the first sip, and three make for a brackish bite. Oddly enough, many of the more venerable drink books list the Gibson as garnished with either a citrus twist or a cherry.

Like the Martini, the Gibson relies on slight dilution from the cracked ice, the magical third ingredient that many mixers undervalue.

Occasionally, someone will request the concoction more reminiscent of Franklin D. Roosevelt's dirty Martini: the Gibson with a hefty splash of olive brine.

Similar drinks – besides the Martini – include the Vesper and the Mauri.

Gimlet

We haven't always been gracious to the Gimlet – in fact, we once referred to this cocktail as a misdirected Daiquiri – but its diehard following has persuaded us otherwise. Our initially insolent slant on this drink was born of unrealistic expectations. Its recipe, 2¼ ounces of GIN and ¾ ounce of ROSE'S LIME JUICE, made us anticipate the citric tang of fresh fruit. But now that our taste buds know what to expect – a sour kiss followed by a syrupy-sweet finish – we've come to appreciate this drink.

Cocktail lore suggests the Gimlet was created by crafty recruits in England's Royal Navy. The men keenly combined their daily rations of gin and lime juice into a soothing tipple that would ward off scurvy. There's also been speculation that these fellows used the word *gimlet* to refer to this drink because the tool of the same name – a small device for boring, something like a corkscrew – was sent with juice containers bound for the British colonies during the late 18th century. Of course, the drink's name might also have come from that of Sir T. O. Gimlette, a Royal Navy officer and surgeon between 1879 and 1917. According to the *Dictionary of Eponyms*, the good doctor created the Gimlet as a medicinal tonic and a way to dilute gin, which he believed clouded the minds of the recruits when sipped neat.

Although well-known in the U.K., the Gimlet was rarely ordered elsewhere, and, when it did turn up, was considered an anglophilic affectation. Fortunately, Raymond Chandler came along and did for the Gimlet what Ian Fleming had done for the Martini. Chandler's chauvinistic American sleuth, Philip Marlowe, sipped Gimlets as smoothly as James Bond seduced double agents. Marlowe picked up his penchant for Gimlets from a war-scarred sot, Terry Lennox, in the 1953 novel *The Long Goodbye*. "A real Gimlet," according to Mr. Lennox, "is half gin and half Rose's lime juice, and nothing else. It beats Martinis hollow."

We're not so quick to compare the Gimlet to the Martini, since we can't imagine choosing one over the other. When we want that Everyman grounding that puts one at ease in any neighborhood bar, we order the Gimlet; if that's the last thing we're after, we take the Martini. We will concede, however, that drinkers of Gimlets are generally more interesting than the Martini's devotees: "On a bar stool a woman … was sitting alone with a pale greenish-colored drink in front of her and smoking a cigarette in a long jade holder. She had that fine-drawn intense look that is sometimes neurotic, sometimes sex-hungry, and sometimes just the result of drastic dieting," notes Marlowe just before sipping a Gimlet. "With the lime juice it has a sort of pale greenish yellowish misty look. I tasted it. It was both sweet and sharp at the same time. The woman in black watched me. Then she lifted her own glass towards me. We both drank. Then I knew hers was the same drink." We can't help thinking that even Mr. Bond would want a sip.

GLASS	TASTE COMPLEXITY	MIXING DIFFICULTY
Y	LOW ═○═══ HIGH	LOW ○═══════ HIGH
	DRINK ERA	
	GOLDEN AGE OF AMERICAN DRINKING	

Gimlet

RECIPE

2¼ ounces gin
¾ ounce Rose's lime juice

Stir with cracked ice; strain into chilled cocktail glass.
Garnish with a lime squeeze.
Variation: Add ¼ ounce more Rose's
and/or a dash of bitters.
Primary spirits like tequila, rum, and
vodka may be substituted for the gin.

The Gimlet requires no magic to mix. It's safe in the hands of a novice mixer, and when mixing for a large crowd, nothing is easier to make.

Although most commonly served up, the Gimlet can also be served ON THE ROCKS. If you'd like a more rounded Gimlet, substitute fresh lime juice for half of the Rose's lime juice. To garnish a Gimlet, squeeze a lime wedge into the drink and then drop it into the glass. If you mix a Gimlet with only fresh lime, you'll wind up with the difficult-to-pronounce Gimblet.

For a sharper Gimlet, follow Philip Marlowe's lead and add a dash of BITTERS – but only for an imbiber who needs a pick–me–up for the soul.

Similar drinks include the Daiquiri, the Pegu, and the Kamikaze.

F or a while, this crisper, more confounded rendition of an earlier classic went unnoticed, treated as a mere afterthought to the original Daiquiri. Tagged with a number instead of a name, "Daiquiri No. 3" was an easily overlooked item on Constantino Ribailagua's drink list at El Floridita, in Cuba. Of course, all that changed when an irascible (and eminently recognizable) Ernest Hemingway bellied up to the bar to order this version of the Daiquiri. The drink was renamed soon enough, earning it a popularity that would have been unlikely otherwise, owing to two sad realities of the bar: Imbibers shun grapefruit in their cocktails, and bartenders hate to squeeze it.

Although certainly not to be had at just any establishment, the Hemingway Daiquiri is still sufficiently in demand to be known – and, when sought out, found. A sugarless take on the traditional lime Daiquiri, this drink relies on maraschino liqueur as its sweetener and grapefruit juice as an accent, for an overall tart taste with a flowery finish. Served up, the Hemingway Daiquiri is best mixed with ¼ ounce of grapefruit juice, ¾ ounce of lime juice, ¼ ounce of MARASCHINO LIQUEUR, and a JIGGER of light RUM.

Debate persists as to whether the ingredients of the Hemingway Daiquiri should be shaken or FLASH BLENDED. Either method can produce the finely cracked ice we desire; however, any mention of the so-called frozen Daiquiri inevitably returns something more evocative of a Slurpee. When requesting this drink, we'll ask the mixer to take as a model the frappé described in Hemingway's *Islands in the Stream*: Thomas Hudson "was drinking one of the frozen Daiquiris with no sugar in it and as he lifted it, heavy and the glass frost-rimmed, he looked at the clear part below the frappéd top and it reminded him of the sea. The frappéed part of the drink was like the wake of a ship and the clear part was the way the water looked when the bow cut it when you were in shallow water over marl bottom. That was almost the exact color."

As a general note, though, we're not convinced that Hemingway himself was all that selective in his drinking. We're grateful for his namesake Daiquiri (as for his ABSINTHE-based Death in the Afternoon), but Hemingway himself, whose liver boasted the same rough contour as a map of Cuba, seems to have visited many a bar and eschewed few. Just as many roadside rest stops, of course, claim to have serviced Elvis. Still, we don't doubt that emulating Papa's drinking will lead directly to the fevered composition of reams of great literary work, earning for the drinker the praise of worshipful generations to come. We're just not up to trying it ourselves.

GLASS	TASTE COMPLEXITY	MIXING DIFFICULTY
🍷	LOW ⊙━━━ HIGH	LOW ⊙━━━ HIGH
	DRINK ERA	
	GOLDEN AGE OF AMERICAN DRINKING	

Hemingway Daiquiri

RECIPE

1½ ounces light rum
¼ ounce maraschino liqueur
¾ ounce lime juice
¼ ounce grapefruit juice

Shake with ice;
strain into chilled cocktail glass.
Garnish with a lime wheel.

The magic of the Hemingway Daiquiri is experienced only when it's sipped ice-cold, and to accomplish this, the drink's ingredients must be well blended. This makes the Hemingway Daiquiri a perfect candidate for flash blending.

A too-sour Hemingway Daiquiri can be salvaged with a dash of maraschino; one that's too sweet is best tossed down the drain. Procuring a bottle of Havana Club rum will improve the quality of the drink. Use ruby red grapefruit, and steer clear of the pulpy white variety. When the amount of rum is doubled, the drink becomes a Papa Doble.

Similar drinks include the Bacardi Cocktail and the Henessey Daiquiri.

Henessey Daiquiri

C hristened for an annoying patron who was bidding for attention in a certain unnamed California drinking establishment, the Henessey Daiquiri was concocted by the Alchemist a few years back to quell the loudmouthed directives emanating from this fellow, a psychologist who much preferred to practice at the bar.

Mixed with 2 ounces light RUM, ¾ ounce of lime juice, and ½ ounce of the CORDIAL Rene Niel Tangerine, this cocktail actually has a calming effect on those who make it. We find bartenders, for instance, infinitely more forgiving of our occasional uncouth lapses when we request this drink. But locating a haunt that will actually serve it – with its elusive ingredient, Rene Niel Tangerine, or some suitable substitute – can put us at the end of our tether once the craving for this cocktail hits.

A highly concentrated cordial with a low proof, Rene Niel Tangerine is made with mildly flavored spices, and tastes of the fruit for which it's named. A few years back, Moyet Cognacs of France stopped distilling its fine Rene Niel Tangerine (and, for that matter, its Rene Niel Melon) because the liqueur wasn't paying its way. As far as we can tell, no other distiller has bothered to pick up where Moyet left off, though we're still hopeful that some small concern will claim this rarely used liqueur as its niche. Although supplies are running low, we're pleased to report that a few distributors – and a few bars – have amassed a stockpile of both of these cordials. When we find ourselves at a bar without a workable substitute, we just hope for the best, which at that point is a bottle of SIMPLE SYRUP and a bowl full of tangerines. Of course, that will only happen at an establishment with a quality cook – in other words, a fine restaurant.

A while back, we were tempted to provide this drink with a creation myth all its own, but resisted, noting the wise words of Albert S. Crockett, onetime historian of the Waldorf-Astoria and the author of that establishment's bar book of 1934. "Why, you can date many American historical, society, sporting, police, and other events by those cocktails when you know the names.... But who the 'Mrs. Thompson' was, whose name was bestowed upon one of [the Waldorf bar] cocktails, frankly, I do not know."

At least we've recorded here the name and origin of this fine drink, in the absurd hope that its namesake will become as renowned as that of the Hemingway Daiquiri, instead of dropping into obscurity like the presumably well-behaved Mrs. Thompson. After all, even Ernest Hemingway was a bar rogue in his day, his foul demeanor and lousy tips forgiven only as a side effect of his fame. Should our Mr. Henessey expect any less?

GLASS	TASTE COMPLEXITY	MIXING DIFFICULTY
Y	LOW ⊢─O─────┤ HIGH	LOW ⊢───O───┤ HIGH
	DRINK ERA	
	THE REVIVAL OF AMERICAN DRINKING	

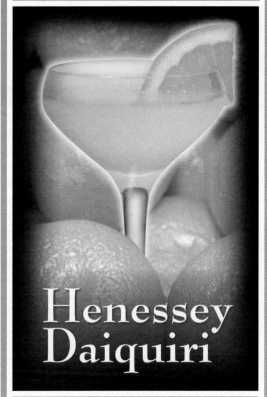

Henessey Daiquiri

RECIPE

2 ounces light rum
¾ ounce lime juice
½ ounce Rene Niel Tangerine liqueur

Shake with cracked ice;
strain into a chilled cocktail glass.
Garnish with a tangerine wheel.

Without a doubt, the most difficult aspect of making Henessey Daiquiris is to locate a bottle of Rene Niel Tangerine liqueur.

Although certainly not the ideal option, a mandarin cordial can be used instead. If that too is unavailable, mix ½ ounce fresh tangerine juice with ¼ ounce COINTREAU for each cocktail. Be certain to strain out all the tangerine pits, and reserve any stray cans of tangerines languishing in the cupboard for Jell-O creations. Be careful not to add too much of either the cordial or the substitute, which can turn a refreshing Henessey Daiquiri into an echo of that breakfast-table icon, Tang. You could substitute VODKA for the rum.

Similar drinks include the Hemingway Daiquiri and the Floridita Special.

Jack Rose

T his cocktail smacks you with a tart twinge before smoothly sliding down the gullet, swathed in sweetness. It's this mixture of pain and delight in the Jack Rose that we just can't say no to.

Mixed with 2 ounces of APPLEJACK and an ounce of lime juice, followed by half an ounce of GRENADINE, the Jack Rose combines the tang of Jersey Lightning and grenadine's sappy charm, with the lime as the bridge between the two. But it's not the Jack Rose's deep-laid taste, only hinting at apple, that attracts imbibers. It's the drink's hue – not quite red, not quite pink – that draws us to this cocktail: the precise hue of the Jacqueminot rose.

We had always assumed the Jack Rose's moniker was derived from its color, but some suggest it was named for the French general Jean-François Jacqueminot, for whom the rose is also named. Our search for a more credible account of the drink's christening led us to the Colts Neck Inn in Colts Neck, New Jersey: "The great-great-grandpa of the Laird family, the restaurant's first owner and the only distiller left making applejack, invented it," says Nelson Fastige, a Colts Neck bartender for the last 15 years. "His name was Jack, and the drink was a reddish-pink color, like the rose." This modest, straightforward tale nearly inspired us to end our quest. But just in case, we decided to give the Laird family in Scobeyville, New Jersey, a call. "The Jack Rose cocktail was not invented at the Colts Neck Inn, as some believe. Nor was it created by a Laird family ancestor," Lisa Laird-Dunn, Laird & Company's VP and a member of the family's ninth generation, told us. "One of the more colorful myths is in fact truth, not fiction.... During the late 1800s, there was a gentleman by the name of Jack Rose, from New York City. He was regarded as somewhat of a shady character, who made his living in and around City Hall and the New York courts. Mr. Rose's favorite beverage was applejack, and he consumed it mixed with lemon juice and grenadine. He became known for this cocktail – thus, it was dubbed the Jack Rose."

We certainly liked the idea that the Jack Rose was first sipped by a gangster rogue rather than a presumably well-behaved gentleman. So we called it a day and went looking for an establishment that would serve us a round of Jack Roses. Occasionally, to coax the mixer into meeting our demands, we'd quote from Ms. Laird-Dunn: "The drink became very popular in the early 1900s and remained so after the repeal of PROHIBITION. There wasn't a restaurant in New York City that did not serve the Jack Rose." To which most bartenders reply that we might consider a move.

COCKTAIL

GLASS	TASTE COMPLEXITY	MIXING DIFFICULTY
Y	LOW ═══O═══ HIGH	LOW ═O═══ HIGH

DRINK ERA

GOTHIC AGE OF AMERICAN DRINKING

RECIPE

2 ounces applejack
1 ounce lime juice
½ ounce grenadine

Shake with cracked ice;
strain into chilled cocktail glass.
Garnish with a lime wheel.

When mixed as a Jack Rose, the apple taste of the so-called BRANDY is almost completely lost. In fact, only the most sensitive palates will notice the flavor. Should someone prefer a sweeter drink, swap lemon juice for the lime juice and garnish with a lemon wheel. If you use SIMPLE SYRUP instead of grenadine, the drink is called an Applejack Sour (or, occasionally, a Jersey Sour). The cocktail glass for this drink can be FROSTED for a sweeter effect.

Some imbibers, especially WHISKEY drinkers, may make disparaging remarks about the Jack Rose's unique taste. But mention Errol Flynn sipping this drink at New York's well-known 21 Club or Humphrey Bogart drinking it at The Players restaurant in Hollywood, and we bet they'll change their tune.

Similar drinks include the Sidecar.

Jasmine

C all it an instant classic. The Jasmine has a short history, dating from a night just a few years ago when Matt Jasmine, after a shift at Chez Panisse, stopped in at the Townhouse Bar & Grill in Emeryville, California, and had the divine inspiration to ask the Alchemist to mix him up something new – specifically, "anything." It was about 10:30 on a warm summer night, and Paul tells us that at the time, he had just served that PROHIBITION classic, the Pegu, a blend of GIN, BITTERS, COINTREAU, and lime.

Not wanting to repeat himself, the Alchemist switched the sour from lime to lemon and the bitters to CAMPARI in the proper proportions. His face, as usual, betrayed little emotion. Paul, after all, prefers to keep his excitement over new discoveries hidden, lest expectations be raised too high. Not even Matt realized that a new drink had been made, let alone christened in his good name.

The Jasmine – a quarter ounce of Cointreau, ¾ ounce of lemon juice, 1½ ounces of gin, and a quarter ounce of Campari, all shaken hard over ice and served UP with a crisp zest of lemon – is a deceptive drink. For one thing, it's innocently pink. But the taste is nicely bitter and cleansing to the palate, making the Jasmine a perfect APÉRITIF. This is no heavy drinker's mainstay. One is wonderful, two are plenty, and then it's time for dinner.

The Jasmine has one drawback, though: Its looks tend to dupe unsophisticated drinkers new to Campari. Put a pink drink on the bar, and everybody wants one. They think it's a Cosmopolitan – then they make a face when they taste it. Imagine, after all, ordering a sweetly flavored juice but receiving grapefruit juice. Fortunately, a sampling of the San Francisco Bay area has adopted the Jasmine with a passion, and all devoted Campari drinkers will be grateful. The last time we had one, we saw the Alchemist pick up the Campari and look at the label. We suspect he was picturing his recipe on the back of the bottle.

GLASS	TASTE COMPLEXITY	MIXING DIFFICULTY
Y	LOW ══O══ HIGH	LOW ════O═ HIGH

Jasmine

RECIPE

1½ ounces gin
¼ ounce Cointreau
¼ ounce Campari
¾ ounce lemon juice

Shake with cracked ice;
strain into chilled cocktail glass.
Garnish with a lemon twist.

The Jasmine is easy enough to make, though careless mixers who add too much Cointreau will destroy the delicate balance between this spirit and the bitter Campari. Too much of the latter will leave your guests wondering if they've been served a misdirected Negroni, and too little will make them certain they ended up with a lackluster Delilah.

Mentally prepare your guests for drinks with complex or uncommon tastes. The tart Jasmine is a drink that closely resembles grapefruit juice both in look and in taste.

If white RUM is substituted for gin, you have the Kio.

Similar drinks include the Edisonian, the Evan, and the Negroni.

Leap Year

A fine cocktail limited more by its name than by its taste, the Leap Year cocktail seems destined to be thought of only once every four years. The dulcified cousin of the Martini, this drink is sweet without being cloying and well worth ordering whenever a Martini seems too acerbic a prospect. Far more subtle than its better-known relation, the Leap Year cocktail should be sipped slowly, and no more than one per evening, if an imbiber is to avoid the hex said to follow this drink.

Of course, Harry Craddock, the Leap Year's undisputed originator, certainly did not conceive his creation as a drink to be approached with caution. Though he openly admitted that it was "responsible for more proposals than any other cocktail that has ever been mixed," he did not acknowledge a related fact: The Leap Year is so smooth that one is easily lured into having a few too many. In the *Savoy Cocktail Book* of 1930, the 1928 Leap Year celebrations at the Savoy Hotel in London are credited with inspiring Mr. Craddock (who had been tending that busy bar) with first mixing this drink.

We recently called the American Bar at the Savoy Hotel to see if the Leap Year cocktail was still making the rounds, even if only on February 29th. Although Mr. Craddock is recalled as the "King of Cocktail Shakers" and many of his drinks still cited as mantras of mixing, his Leap Year cocktail appears nearly forgotten by the bar's clientele. In fact, upon ending our conversation with the kind Salim Khoury, who has been mixing at the Savoy for 29 years, we're not so certain this drink even survived to March 1, 1928, though we do hope the marriages it spawned were more resilient. "Of course, we promote the Leap Year cocktail every four years, and that is the extent of its popularity," says Mr. Khoury. "Some people do ask for it, but most want champagne cocktails, Bloody Marys, Sidecars, and White Ladies. We also created many others for all the different occasions."

As a general rule, never order a Leap Year cocktail by name. The bartender won't recognize the moniker, and the imbiber who orders it will seem trendy rather than tasteful. Instead, call out the ingredients: 2 ounces GIN, ½ ounce GRAND MARNIER, ½ ounce sweet VERMOUTH, and ¼ ounce lemon juice. Shake with crushed ice and pour into a FROSTED cocktail glass. We let bartenders garnish with either a lemon or an orange twist. (We're still contemplating whether or not their choice of fruit might signify some deeper design.) If they seem impressed by our request – especially the decorous use of Grand Marnier, a well-bred CORDIAL sadly besmirched by the era of shooters – we'll recount this drink's legend, with a special emphasis on its aphrodisiac powers. They tend to appreciate such words of warning, knowing that bartenders have taken the blame for more than a handful of marriages.

COCKTAIL

GLASS	TASTE COMPLEXITY	MIXING DIFFICULTY
Y	LOW ⊶O⊶ HIGH	LOW ⊶O⊶ HIGH
	DRINK ERA	
	PROHIBITION	

RECIPE

2 ounces gin
½ ounce sweet vermouth
½ ounce Grand Marnier
¼ ounce lemon juice

Shake with cracked ice;
strain into chilled cocktail glass.
Garnish with a twist of lemon or orange.

Grand Marnier is a good addition to many cocktails, if not overdone. However, this liqueur may be too sweet for some people. If so, try making their next drink with the substitution of COINTREAU for Grand Marnier. Should someone prefer an even sharper drink, add an extra dash of lemon juice or ORANGE BITTERS, such as ÂMER PICON.

Grand Marnier is a heavy cordial, so you'll need to shake this drink particularly well. If not chilled adequately – and sipped briskly – the Leap Year cocktail warms into a syrupy concoction that lets the Grand Marnier compete with the gin.

Similar drinks include the Martinez, the Elegant, and the Delilah.

Lemon Drop

Ever since renowned bartender Jerry Thomas started mixing at San Francisco's Occidental Hotel in the late 1800s, the city has claimed to be the capital of the Cocktail Nation. We've always liked San Francisco, so we won't dispute this claim. But to set the stage properly for this drink, we must delve into San Francisco's more recent, somewhat tarnished past.

In the winter of 1969, San Francisco became home to the world's first – or at least best-known – FERN BAR. The bar, Henry Africa's, pushed so-called GIRL DRINKS: mixed drinks potent enough to compete with the three-letter psychedelics of the '60s but sweet enough to mask the taste of alcohol from young adults nostalgic for the taste of pink baby aspirin and Tootsie Pops. Although we'd opt for a peyote smoothie before touching most of these drinks, there is one cocktail from the fern bars that we'll recommend – the Lemon Drop, which we suspect is named after the candy of the same name. While unabashedly sweet, this drink never went the sickly saccharin way of the offensive potations that spawned the shooters of the '80s.

With only a teaspoon of SIMPLE SYRUP, 1½ ounces of citrus-flavored VODKA, and ¾ ounce of lemon juice, the Lemon Drop maintains the edge of a cocktail when shaken with cracked ice, offering a tart respite from a hot afternoon or an over-heated bar. When reminiscing about big-haired dancing queens and electric light orchestras, we request the drink's glass FROSTED. If we're in the mood for a little imbroglio, we'll have the bartender add ¼ ounce COINTREAU and only ½ teaspoon of sugar to the drink, which inevitably susses out those bartenders who have been watching too many James Bond films. As these so-called mixologists try to convince us that we've just ordered a lemon vodka Martini, we merely smile and remind ourselves that one Lemon Drop too many only makes for a hangover – not, generally, a point well taken.

GLASS	TASTE COMPLEXITY	MIXING DIFFICULTY
Y	LOW ──O──── HIGH	LOW ────O── HIGH

DRINK ERA

DARK AGE OF AMERICAN DRINKING

LemonDrop

RECIPE

1½ ounces citrus-flavored vodka
¾ ounce lemon juice
1 teaspoon simple syrup

Shake with cracked ice;
strain into chilled cocktail glass
rimmed with sugar.
Garnish with a lemon wheel.

Lemon Drops – somewhat reminiscent of that childhood candy – are so sweet and sour that they are nearly impossible to ruin. However, more than a teaspoon of simple syrup will make this drink too syrupy. If you suspect your guest would like a sweeter Lemon Drop, sugar half the rim.

The Lemon Drop is best sipped briskly – in fact, three or four sips should finish off a 4-ounce serving. If your guests linger too long, the drink's ingredients will separate, leaving the sugar to settle at the bottom of a by-then warm glass.

Don't let your friends be caught unaware by a Lemon Drop – essentially a Daiquiri made with vodka and lemon juice. A drink mixed with vodka rarely tastes as potent as its alcohol content might suggest.

Similar drinks include the Delilah.

Maiden's Prayer

P ROHIBITION prompted a renaissance of cocktail creativity that nearly killed the fine art of mixing. As ingenuity increased, so did the number of deaths caused by foul spirits. In 1927, the early demise of nearly 12,000 imbibers was blamed on more than just a few bad olives. Forced to mix with bootleg liquor, bartenders created what they could by masking the imperfect taste of low-quality alcohol with syrups, sugars, and juices. Pussyfoots, Cubanolas, and Bosom Caressers are just a taste of what resulted. Fortunately, these cocktails died merciful deaths during the YEARS OF REFORM. However, a few – such as the Maiden's Prayer – do merit resurrection.

Light and fruity but with a sour nip, the Maiden's Prayer goes down easy on late summer afternoons. Made with equal parts GIN, light RUM, COINTREAU, and lemon juice, this drink hides any hint of a real bite behind the lemon and Cointreau. When given the option, we always request Meyer lemons, with their bitter-orange flavor, as the perfect complement to the Cointreau in this drink.

As with so many Prohibition cocktails, the creation of the Maiden's Prayer seems to have gone unnoted. Although the drink is occasionally linked to the Waldorf-Astoria, it certainly wasn't invented there. Unlike a few other well-known New York bars, the Waldorf-Astoria bar did not operate illicitly during Prohibition. To this day, the establishment offers one of its old-time barmen as an example of its comportment during the Noble Experiment: Self-respect kept bartender Joseph Taylor, who died just before repeal, from mixing at a SPEAKEASY, though he had looked forward to the day when he could mix with genuine spirits again. Johnny Brooks, the Prohibition bartender who authored *My 35 Years behind Bars* in 1954, is a much likelier candidate to be named as creator of the Maiden's Prayer, if only based on his own claim.

Nowadays, the Maiden's Prayer also goes by the name Between the Sheets (usually after drinking several). Years ago, this drink had its own discrete recipe, though it only differed significantly by one spirit – using BRANDY instead of gin. Slightly heavier and more rounded than the Maiden's Prayer, the Between the Sheets is best reserved for late-evening drinking, when we're on our way to bed. Regrettably, though, a request for either of these drinks is as strong an indication of underage drinking as an order for a Sloe Gin Fizz – but if carded, we take no offense, knowing that at this point in our lives we might as well be flattered.

GLASS	TASTE COMPLEXITY	MIXING DIFFICULTY
Y	LOW ═O═ HIGH	LOW ═O═ HIGH
	DRINK ERA	
	PROHIBITION	

Maiden's
Prayer

There are probably as many recipes for the Maiden's Prayer as years in the era of Prohibition. Shun those that are overly sweet and composed of more than five ingredients.

If an imbiber would prefer this drink less sweet, substitute lime for the lemon juice. Do not use another brand of triple sec in place of Cointreau – anything else would make a Maiden's Prayer too sweet.

After dinner – or when you're ready to start calling this drink by its more notorious name – mix it as a DIGESTIF. For romantics, add a dash of grenadine to enhance the drink's redness. For cynics who claim to want only a nightcap, add an eighth of an ounce more Cointreau.

Similar drinks include the Delilah.

RECIPE

¾ ounce gin
¾ ounce light rum
¾ ounce Cointreau
¾ ounce lemon juice

Shake with crushed ice;
strain into chilled wine goblet or cocktail glass.
Garnish with a lemon twist or a flower blossom.

Mai Tai

J ust as we never say no to watching *The African Queen*, we never turn down a Mai Tai. While we can count the number of times we've made this drink at home on two fingers, we can hardly count the times this potent concoction has gotten the best of us while we were out on the town.

We'd entertain more prejudices about the Mai Tai if only we hadn't had such fun drinking it. The irresistible irreverence of this drink always takes us from the doldrums to the tropics – and we salute Victor Bergeron, known to the world as Trader Vic, for creating this drink before he'd even visited the tropics.

By most accounts, Vic whipped up the first Mai Tai in 1944 at his Hinky Dink's restaurant in Emeryville, just over the bridge from San Francisco, and for doubters, Trader Vic himself tried to set the record straight in his bartender's guide of 1947: "There has been a lot of conversation over the beginning of the Mai Tai.... I originated the Mai Tai. Many others have claimed credit.... The drink was never introduced by me into Tahiti except informally through our good friends, Eastham and Carrie Guild.... Anybody who says I didn't create this drink is a dirty stinker." Trader Vic goes on to write that his two friends who had been visiting from Tahiti requested something special from the bar, so he grabbed the Jamaican RUM, a lime, CURAÇAO, ORGEAT, and rock candy syrup, and concocted the Mai Tai prototype.

Just as Trader Vic tempered Polynesian cuisine to the tastes of North Americans, we've taken the liberty of altering his drink recipe slightly. In a shaker, we combine 2½ ounces dark Jamaican rum – either Appleton or Myers's – ½ ounce curaçao, ¾ ounce fresh lime juice, and a splash of orgeat, followed by another splash of either SIMPLE SYRUP or GRENADINE, depending on the color we're after. When strained and served in a tall, frosted glass filled with shaved ice, this drink always brings warm tropical thoughts to mind, even when we're in the midst of a blizzard. Some bartenders say using a fine orange LIQUEUR in a Mai Tai is a little like slathering Mrs. Butterworth's syrup on a crepe. To us, that view is only a telltale sign that the mixer is using some modern-day recipe with far too many ingredients. The Mai Tai, after all, is nothing more than a dressed-up Daiquiri. Fortunately, nearly all recipes for the Mai Tai are sweet enough that if a bartender screws up, we're unlikely to notice. By the second or third round, the bartender may even have us shouting Tahitian phrases like "Mai Tai – Roa Ae!" – which means "Out of this world – the best!" – just as Carrie Guild first did years ago.

GLASS	TASTE COMPLEXITY	MIXING DIFFICULTY
⬺	LOW ⊢─○─┤ HIGH	LOW ⊢──○─┤ HIGH
	DRINK ERA	
	YEARS OF REFORM	

RECIPE

2½ ounces dark rum
¾ ounce lime juice
½ ounce curaçao
1 splash grenadine or simple syrup
1 splash orgeat

Shake with cracked ice; strain into chilled wine goblet
or Collins glass filled with ice. Top with ½ ounce dark
rum. Garnish with a paper umbrella or
a cherry and a flower blossom.

Sip the Mai Tai to toast the Everyman of cocktails, the late Trader Vic. Although it's impossible to ruin the taste of this drink, you could go wrong with the garnish. An attractive paper umbrella is really all the Mai Tai needs, so resist the temptation to overdo it with a fruit-bowl topping that looks like some over-the-top prop from a cruise ship.

Because Jamaican rum is heavy-bodied and you are already using either simple syrup or grenadine, there is no need to splurge for Cointreau. Any curaçao will work nicely in this drink. If you suspect your guests will expect a layered look, shake the rum, lime juice, and curaçao first; then strain the drink into its glass before adding a splash of grenadine.

Similar drinks include the Planter's Punch.

Manhattan

H ailing from a time when the Dow was less than 200, the Dodgers were in Brooklyn, and a joint was still your local bar, the Manhattan held court when the cocktail was *de rigueur*. It gave the blue bloods a chance to slug back a bit of WHISKEY.

On the East Coast, you're likely to get rye whiskey; in Kentucky and parts further west, expect bourbon. We take our Manhattans with four parts bourbon and one part sweet VERMOUTH, shaken over ice and poured through a strainer. Occasionally, as with other vermouth cocktails, we'll take them DRY or PERFECT. Let the vermouth take the edge off the bourbon, but never let it compromise the flavor. Wise bartenders add a dash or two of BITTERS to this concoction, which otherwise can be overly sweet.

The origin of the Manhattan is almost undisputed. There are two widely held versions of its creation, both tied to New York's Manhattan Club. The earliest tale of this drink's nativity dates back to William J. Tilden's election as New York's governor in 1874. Winston Churchill's American mother hosted the victory celebration, and a forgotten bartender invented the Manhattan there, naming the drink after the club. The other story credits Supreme Court judge Charles Henry Truax with instigating the drink's invention several years later. According to *The Dictionary of American Food and Drink*, Mr. Truax asked a Manhattan Club bartender to mix him up a new drink, his doctor having instructed him to lay off the Martinis to lose weight. There's one more account we'll mention on the slight chance that it's true: A New York bartender named Black invented the drink and named it after the island.

Although we generally abstain from Manhattans during the summer, we soak them up with a vengeance after Labor Day. During the fall, you'll find us at a certain zinc-capped bar, sipping this aesthetic creation from a cocktail glass, getting our ass kicked (in the most genteel fashion) by dose after dose of true Kentucky sour mash. If you're paying attention, you may note that we don't become cleverer with each round, as we would with Martinis; instead, we become louder and slightly more petulant. And then you'll see us catch ourselves, take in our environs, and decide that the one we're drinking is the evening's last.

GLASS	TASTE COMPLEXITY	MIXING DIFFICULTY
Y	LOW ═══O═══ HIGH	LOW ═══O═══ HIGH

DRINK ERA

GOLDEN AGE OF AMERICAN DRINKING

Manhattan

RECIPE

2 ounces rye
½ ounce sweet vermouth
1 to 2 dashes Angostura bitters (optional)

Stir with cracked ice;
strain into chilled cocktail glass.
Garnish with a maraschino cherry.

The Manhattan's sound recipe base has provided a starting point for a hundred other drinks.

Typically, the Manhattan is served sweet and garnished with a maraschino cherry. When made correctly, the vermouth and bitters only accent the whiskey's flavor. A dry Manhattan calls for French vermouth instead of Italian; garnish it with a twist. A perfect Manhattan, however, calls for ¼ ounce each of sweet and dry vermouth. It's garnished with a twist.

A dash of a cordial like COINTREAU, BYRRH, or KÜMMEL will make a Manhattan more complex in taste.

An Uptown Manhattan is a perfect Manhattan with a splash of lemon juice. The Sidney is a dry Manhattan with a dash of ORANGE BITTERS and a splash of CHARTREUSE.

Similar drinks include the Rob Roy.

Margarita

F ew classic cocktails have had to contend with as many base influences as the Margarita. The drink has been so besmirched that few recognize it for what it is: a genuine cocktail dating back to the early '30s, not some lemon Slurpee designed for poolside guzzling at Club Med. Despite its degradation by corporate restaurant chains, the Margarita still enjoys our respect when we're seeking respite from life's doldrums.

The Margarita almost certainly hails from Mexico, and is revered by gringos whose weak gullets are menaced by straight TEQUILA, the exotic spirit of leisure. But when it comes to the Margarita's history, we hate to be overly specific, knowing there are far too many claims from far too many people regarding the circumstances of its creation for us rightly to favor one over another. Granted, there are a few contenders worth noting, if only for entertainment's sake. Their tales usually mention the year 1930 and a supposed beauty named, not surprisingly, Margarita. There's Doña Bertha, proprietor of Bertita's Bar in Tasca; Pancho Morales of Tommy's Place in Juárez; Daniel Negrete, a bartender who stopped by and may have mixed the drink at the Garcí Crespo Hotel in Puebla; an unnamed bartender in Mexico City; and Margarita Sames, who might have made the drink at home while living in Acapulco. But if we had to put money on the drink's origin, we'd pick some old-time mixer from the Caliente Race Track bar in Tijuana and leave it at that.

On principle and out of deep respect for this drink, we never order it frozen, though we may let a careful bartender FLASH BLEND it. For us, a proper Margarita requires the juice of half a lemon and half a lime, 1½ ounces of tequila, and ¾ ounce of COINTREAU shaken in a shaker full of ice. We always request that the rim of the glass be moistened with a lime and then dusted with fine kosher salt. Although we prefer small flecks of ice in our Margaritas, we certainly don't balk when they're served ON THE ROCKS. On Cinco de Mayo, we let the salt and tequila from a few Margaritas transport us to Mexico during its heyday in 1862, just after the Mexican defeat of the French at Puebla la Heroica. As we conjure up an image of the French troops – naively proffering baguettes as sop for the people of Puebla – we vow to defend the Margarita from mini-mall madness. But first we'll need another, to bolster *el coraje*.

GLASS	TASTE COMPLEXITY	MIXING DIFFICULTY
🍷	LOW ⊢─O───┤ HIGH	LOW ⊢──O──┤ HIGH
	DRINK ERA	
	PROHIBITION	

Margarita

RECIPE

1½ ounces tequila
¾ ounce Cointreau
½ ounce lemon juice
½ ounce lime juice

Shake with cracked ice;
strain into chilled wine goblet or cocktail glass
with kosher salt on its rim.
Garnish with a lime wheel.

A properly concocted Margarita lets the imbiber taste the tequila. Of course, depending on a guest's experience with tequila, the amount of spirit needed in a drink will vary.

When mixing a Margarita to be served on the rocks, double the amount of fruit juice. If you've inadvertently purchased mescal (which comes with a senselessly murdered worm) and not tequila, do not purée the poor creature – it adds only protein to the drink.

When salting the rim of a glass, moisten the rim with a lime garnish, then dip it in fine kosher salt, and garnish with a lime. If you start your party before noon, add fruit to your Margaritas. Although we're partial to strawberries and bananas, just about any fruit would be appropriate.

Similar drinks include the Daiquiri.

Martini

O n days when we're feeling especially mortal and set adrift from the American dream, we order a Martini in hope of a spiritual revival. As libertine Bob Shacochis wrote, "I know I'm not going to live forever, and neither are you, but until my furlough here on earth is revoked, I should like to elbow aside the established pieties and raise my Martini glass in salute to the moral arts of pleasure."

No other cocktail has come to symbolize so much. "Generally, the Martini signifies absolute decadence," wrote James Villas in a 1973 *Esquire* article. "Specifically it means a bitter, medicinal-tasting beverage. It stands for everything from phony bourgeois values and social snobbery to jaded alcoholism and latent masochism." But an impartial view of the Martini is absurd.

The origin of the Martini is as debatable as that of the cocktail. Lowell Edmunds' fine tome, *The Silver Bullet: The Martini in American Civilization*, suggests that the name *Martini* has much to do with the confusion regarding the drink's origin. The Martinez – arguably a Martini incognito – first appeared in O. H. Byron's *Modern Bartender's Guide* of 1884, reports Mr. Edmunds. In 1862, bartender Jerry Thomas included a "Gin Cocktail" that resembled the Martini in his *Bon Vivant's Companion*. By the book's 1887 edition, he had renamed the drink the Martinez and claimed credit for its creation. According to legend, a traveler wandered into the San Francisco Occidental Hotel bar before taking a ferry to Martinez, and Mr. Thomas mixed him the first Martinez. The people of Martinez, however, say the traveler was on his way to San Fran from their now defunct Julio's Bar. Bartender Julio Richelieu mixed the drink as change for a gold nugget used to buy a bottle of WHISKEY.

Before the '20s, America's expatriates took the Martini overseas; in 1929 Hemingway made the drink famous for its refining effect in *A Farewell to Arms*. Amid the throes of World War I, protagonist Frederic Henry said, "I had never tasted anything so cool and clean. They made me feel civilized." By the '30s, the Martini had become an icon of American culture. But if you plan to remember anything of the drink's past, note that a dry Martini was wet by today's standards. Before the War to End All Wars, a DRY Martini was 2 parts GIN to 1 part VERMOUTH. Today, the ratio has grown to a ridiculous 25 to 1. "The affliction that is cutting down the productive time in the office and destroying the benign temper of most of the bartenders is the thing called the *very* dry Martini. It is a mass madness, a cult, a frenzy, a body of folklore, a mystique…," wrote C. B. Palmer of *The New York Times* in 1952. When in need of a Martini as a reminder of our potential – and that the American dream carries a lot of baggage – we order an ice-cold medium Martini at the best bar we can afford, knowing that the bartender will appreciate our sensibility and that the occasional snickers from the bench will only improve our character.

GLASS	TASTE COMPLEXITY	MIXING DIFFICULTY
Y	LOW ═══○═══ HIGH	LOW ═══○═══ HIGH
	DRINK ERA	
	GOTHIC AGE OF AMERICAN DRINKING	

Martini

RECIPE

3 ounces gin
½ ounce dry vermouth

Stir with cracked ice; strain into chilled cocktail glass. Garnish with a lemon twist or an olive. For a wet Martini mix 1¼ ounces gin and 1¼ ounces dry vermouth, and for a sweet Martini try 2¼ ounces gin and ¾ ounce sweet vermouth. A black olive makes it a Buckeye, and if an onion is used, it's a Gibson. A Martini with a dash of scotch is "smoky," and one with a splash of olive brine is "dirty."

Preparing a palatable Martini requires a unique style and masterful technique. First, completely fill the mixing vessel with the freshest, coldest ice available. The container can be glass, silver, or stainless steel, but it must hold 16 ounces. Pour ½ ounce dry vermouth into the vessel in a circular motion, so that as much vermouth as possible touches the ice. Next, strain the vermouth from the container. Whatever liquid stays on the surface of the ice will be enough for one or two Martinis.

Add 3 ounces of your favorite gin. With a BAR-SPOON, stir in a clockwise motion, agitating the ice against the gin. If the ice and the gin are moving at the same speed, you are not succeeding. Lastly, strain the liquid into a chilled cocktail glass. Garnish with a lemon twist or a stuffed olive.

Similar drinks include the Martinez.

Milk Punch

Not as innocent as it sounds, Milk Punch is more than occasionally blamed for the woes of New Orleans natives, come the city's renowned annual celebration for imported oafs. This early-morning eye-opener and late-night DIGESTIF blurs the tourist's day and night into one long week that is only barely endured by the locals, who insist Milk Punch is to be sipped only before noon.

About as difficult to make as spiked coffee, the recipe for Milk Punch has few who'll claim it as their own. Anglophiles are quick to point to the English syllabub (a euphemism for Egg Nog, as far as we're concerned), but others insist it could only be a thoroughly American predecessor to the milkshake. Still another explanation of the drink's origins can be found in the research of Caroline Moore: "Aphra Behn is ... in many ways a typical good-humored, impecunious, hedonistic professional scribbler from that convivially cutthroat literary world," wrote Ms. Moore for Times Newspapers Ltd. in 1993. "An ex-spy; the prolific author of 20 or so lively but sprawling plays; the inventor of Milk Punch; a poet with a pleasantly undemanding line in erotic pastoral…"

When we reflect on the Southern legend that Milk Punch cools the mind while inspiring the body, we see no reason why Ms. Behn shouldn't be credited with the feat of creating this drink. We order our Milk Punch with equal parts bourbon and milk, half a teaspoon of dark RUM, and a tablespoon of SIMPLE SYRUP, the whole being shaken fiercely with ice and served straight-faced. Admittedly, that last requirement limits our bar options, leaving only establishments east of the Mississippi – the closer to the City of Sin, the better – as places to get a proper Milk Punch. New Orleans adopted Milk Punch wholeheartedly back in the 19th century – around the same time the steamy town's French Market began serving breakfast feasts with the allure of five-course dinners – and *Breakfast, Luncheon, and Tea* of 1875 reported that the mixed drink, when hot, is "an admirable remedy for a bad cold if taken in the first stages," though most wisely before bed.

Of course, Keith Peyrefitte – on staff for the last 22 years at Brennan's, the New Orleans restaurant credited with reviving breakfast feasts back in the early '50s – will tell you the only patrons even mildly concerned with the drink's medicinal qualities are those who order it with low-fat milk. The rest – and, as it happens, the majority – are after the lazy Southern breakfast, with Milk Punch only as a digestive tonic. "Milk Punch isn't an overly special drink – it's almost mundane," Mr. Peyrefitte told us. "But it's the most popular drink in the morning on any day of the year. If you want to try it in this town, though, take it from a local: Skip Mardi Gras and come on down for the jazz fest."

COCKTAIL

Milk Punch

There are plenty of recipe deviations that suit the Milk Punch nicely, but adding ice cream to the mix is certainly not one of them (though regretfully the most common).

One tasty option is to substitute a dash of vanilla for the rum. Swapping BRANDY for whiskey makes a Tiger's Milk; adding 2½ ounces of rum and 1½ ounces of brandy makes it a Bull's Milk. Any of these versions, as well as the original, can be served hot.

True devotees of the Milk Punch will demand fresh milk – which brings to mind James Gordon Bennett, an American newspaper tycoon who, around 1877, built a yacht with a padded room for an Alderney cow so he could have fresh milk for his Milk Punch.

Similar drinks include the Tom and Jerry and the Ramos Gin Fizz.

RECIPE

3 ounces bourbon
3 ounces milk
½ teaspoon dark rum
1 tablespoon simple syrup
Nutmeg

Shake liquids with cracked ice;
strain into chilled tumbler or highball glass.
Dust with nutmeg.

Mint Julep

W e sip this fine bourbon and mint elixir on Derby Day only if we are at least 10 miles from the track. As far as we're concerned, the Kentucky Derby is slowly slaying this classic with its sorry, fake concoction shot from drink guns and served to revelers certain to find the mint syrup distasteful, if not noxious. Hunter S. Thompson – never one to pass judgment quickly – called the Derby a scene of "decadent and depraved … people, most of them staggering drunk." Even the Kentucky Derby Museum's curator, Candace Perry, won't defend the event, noting that with 140,000 people ordering more than 100,000 Mint Juleps and 100,000 hot dogs, the cheapening of the julep was a foregone conclusion.

For us, this softens the blow only slightly. The Mint Julep has been vilified by a worldwide populace. But contrary to the jaundiced press reports that appear every year at race time, the Mint Julep is a fine libation when properly made: namely, with 3 ounces of bourbon, 6 sprigs of mint, 2 tablespoons of SIMPLE SYRUP, and shaved ice. Basic ingredients aside, this simple concoction is mired in mixing dicta promulgated around the turn of the century by the South's gentry in hopes of uprooting the Mint Julep from its working-class heritage. The racetrack's clubhouse began mixing juleps circa 1875 out of convenience – the mint was right out back, and the bourbon well stocked within.

Of course, none of this touches on the Mint Julep's actual origins. Although the drink is indelibly linked to Kentucky, debate persists as to whether it was first made there. Several other states, among them Maryland, Pennsylvania, and Mississippi, lay claim to the Mint Julep, and we're obliged in good conscience to mention the stance adopted by most Virginians: Not only did they once own Bourbon County, whence bourbon hails, they were the first to sip it in a julep. Richard B. Harwell penned a treatise on the matter in 1975: "Clearly the Mint Julep originated in the northern Virginia tidewater, spread soon to Maryland, and eventually all along the seaboard and even to transmontane Kentucky."

We suspect that's how Mr. Harwell would account for the infamous night in 1842 when Charles Dickens argued the merits of a particular julep with Washington Irving in a Baltimore hotel. "It was quite an enchanted julep," Dickens wrote, "my memory never saw [Irving] afterwards otherwise than as bending over it, with his straw, with an attempted air of gravity…." We often emulate this air of gravity, and when annoyed by bartenders selling Mint Julep mixing myths, we'll mention that Samuel Pepys, an English government official, was drinking juleps in the 1660s. If we're on our first Mint Julep, we'll feel properly embarrassed by our own outburst, but console ourselves with the words of William Grimes: "If the mark of a great cocktail is the number of arguments it can provoke and the number of unbreakable rules it generates, the Mint Julep may be America's preeminent classic, edging out the Martini in a photo finish."

GLASS	TASTE COMPLEXITY	MIXING DIFFICULTY
	LOW ○━━ HIGH	LOW ━━○ HIGH

DRINK ERA

GOLDEN AGE OF AMERICAN DRINKING

Mint Julep

RECIPE

3 ounces bourbon
6 sprigs mint
2 to 4 tablespoons simple syrup

Mix 3 ounces bourbon, 6 sprigs of mint, and 2 to 4
tablespoons simple syrup in a pint glass. Add three pieces
of ice and muddle for about a minute. Let stand for
several minutes. Strain into glass filled with shaved ice.
Top with soda water and a mint sprig. For a mintier
version, remove the three pieces of ice, leave the mint, and
pour all ingredients into the glass followed by fresh ice.

The Mint Julep is a simple, relaxing drink to mix, complicated only by tradition. Always remember one overriding dictum for this drink, as set out by Alben Barkley, a Kentucky-born statesman: "A Mint Julep is not the product of a formula."

So-called purists will mix the mint and the sugar the night before a gathering. In theory, this allows the mint to further release its essence. In reality, it gives the sugar enough time to dominate.

Some guests will counsel that a Mint Julep should always be served in a pewter cup and with Irish linen, because touching the glass with the bare hand will disturb the frost. Ignore them if you like, confident that with a little bravura and practice, your mixing traditions will rise above such chatter.

Similar drinks include the Mojito.

Mojito

T he balmy, mambo-dancing, cocktail-sipping halcyon days of Cuba are long gone. We never find today's Hemingways on Havana's terraces. But that sweet bygone era of Mafia-supported elegance has bequeathed us the Mojito, a cooling, effervescent libation.

The Mojito was born in Cuba during this century's teen years. Simple enough and old enough to be claimed as the creation of more than a few bartenders, this classic is most closely tied to Cuba's famous La Bodeguita del Medio bar. This establishment's bartenders worked hard to popularize the drink during the '30s and '40s – often resorting to name-dropping, most notably that of Ernest Hemingway. Their efforts paid off. Soon popular with Havana's hipsters, the Mojito lifted fresh mint out of its bit part as a mere cocktail garnish. An easy blend of sugar, mint leaves, lime juice, RUM, ice, and soda water (strictly in that order), a Mojito (pronounced "moe-HEE-toe") is served in a tall glass sparkling with bubbles and greenery, garnished with a sprig of mint on top.

It's such an elegant, cosmopolitan drink that few would guess it takes a miniature baseball bat to mix it. The first step in Mojito creation is to use this tool to MUDDLE – crush together – the mint leaves and the SIMPLE SYRUP to release mint oil into the mixture. The other key to a successful Mojito is to allow half of your squeezed lime to bob in the mixture. The oils from the rind add a faint bitterness that – take our word for it – is the essence of this drink. Its detractors, though few, are quick to point out that "Mojito" is really just a fancy name for a rum COLLINS mixed with mint.

As we sit, chewing on mint leaves after finishing a Mojito or two, we often recall one of the drink's greatest charms, and its only liability: While it is one of the rare cocktails that actually improves the odor of one's breath, we occasionally walk away from the experience with bits of flora conspicuously stuck to our front teeth.

GLASS	TASTE COMPLEXITY	MIXING DIFFICULTY
	LOW ⊢─O──⊣ HIGH	LOW ⊢───O⊣ HIGH
	DRINK ERA	
	OLD SCHOOL OF AMERICAN BARTENDING	

Mojito

You may not have the chance to escape to a warmer climate during the winter, but with a Mojito in hand, even on the coldest nights, you won't miss it.

Whenever possible, use red-veined mint in your Mojitos, and the freshest chilled soda water you can find. When muddling, take care not to pulverize the mint or to rip it into small shreds. The amount of rum and sugar can vary greatly; just note that the drink's unique aspect comes from leaving the hull in it. The soothing subtlety of the Mojito derives from the mint and citrus juice. It may be served with either a straw or a swizzle stick.

Similar drinks include the Pedro Collins.

RECIPE

2 to 3 ounces light rum
1 lime
½ ounce simple syrup
8 to 10 mint sprigs
Soda water

Place sugar, mint, and a splash of soda water in chilled 16-ounce glass. Lightly muddle until sugar dissolves and you smell the mint. Squeeze both halves of lime into the glass, leaving one hull in the mixture. Add rum, stir, and fill with ice. Top with soda water; garnish with a mint sprig.

Monkey Gland

O ccasionally we contemplate our fragile constitutions and mull over our prospects of finding the elixir of life. We comfort ourselves with the sanguine cocktail that tastes far better than its name – the Monkey Gland – suggests.

Typically, we avoid drinks referencing glands of any kind, but we can rarely resist this beverage. This nearly forgotten placebo of the '20s and '30s was once mockingly credited with unnatural restorative powers. Made with 1½ ounces of GIN, 1½ ounces of orange juice, a dash of ANIS, and ¼ ounce GRENADINE, the Monkey Gland's name comes from the work of the Russian doctor Serge Voronoff, director of experimental surgery at the Laboratory of Physiology of the Collège de France. Shaken with cracked ice and served UP, the drink makes us think we feel better, even if we really don't. When drinking this classic, however, we never discuss its namesake. Somehow the thought of poor, pathetic monkeys forced to pony up their sex glands to even more pathetic humans hoping to prolong their own lives puts our appetites on hold. And that's before we consider the tedious operation itself, in which slices of the monkeys' testes are grafted to the inside of a patient's scrotum. But the good doctor insisted that his grafts did the trick, as reported by Times Newspapers Ltd.: " 'Like my old rams, they become young in their gait, full of vitality and energy.' A 65-year-old man even required a second graft after two years, having been 'over-prodigal of the vital energy supplied by his first one.' "

Most drink historians agree that Harry MacElhone, then proprietor of Harry's New York Bar in Paris, first mixed this drink. His grandson Duncan, who now runs the establishment, assures us this is indeed the case, though he adds that these days, the patrons requesting this classic are few. "We've always served popular cocktails," he told us. "But times have changed. The Germans are a cocktail nation. But it's amazing how the Brits have gone awry. The French never go out – they don't have the chip on their shoulders like they did 15 years ago. But some people are again developing an interest in gastronomy. They are reverting back to the classic." Although the recipe devised by Mr. MacElhone's grandfather innocently calls for anis, we suspect that ABSINTHE was poured. Patrick Gavin Duffy suggested mixing the drink with BÉNÉDICTINE instead of anis, in his 1934 *Official Mixer's Manual*. Many mixers followed suit (or forgot about the drink) until Charles Schumann, proprietor of Schumann's in Munich, published the recipe in his 1995 *American Bar* with PERNOD in its place.

A serious APÉRITIF with an eye-opening bite, the Monkey Gland can be ordered at most well-stocked bars. We never expect a bartender to recognize the drink by name, but with its simple recipe and common ingredients, we've been able to order it by slowly spouting its formula. In fact, we abstain from mentioning its name, though we will occasionally toast the poor simians who gave their lives – and more – to inspire this creation.

GLASS	TASTE COMPLEXITY	MIXING DIFFICULTY
Y	LOW ═══○═══ HIGH	LOW ═══○═══ HIGH
	DRINK ERA	
	PROHIBITION	

Monkey Gland

RECIPE

1½ ounces gin
1½ ounces orange juice
1 dash anis
¼ ounce grenadine

Shake with cracked ice;
strain into chilled cocktail glass.
Garnish with an orange twist.

Before serving a COCKTAIL that calls for an absinthe substitute, make sure guests appreciate anis, the predominant flavor in black licorice. If they do, there are three methods for infusing a drink with this LIQUEUR:

The first is to add the liqueur before shaking or stirring the drink, which allows for a hint of anis. The next method is used with unchilled glasses. Fill each vessel with ice, and top with ½ ounce of the liqueur – swirl, and then toss out the ice. You'll be left with enough liqueur to affect only the cocktail's finish. Most will note the anis accent only as an afterthought. If the glasses are chilled, add a drop of liqueur to each, and swirl. Toss the liquid out and then portion the drink, producing an effect much like the method above, except that the liqueur will not be as diluted.

Similar drinks include the Sazerac.

Moscow Mule

A strange creature with a mild bite, the Moscow Mule owes more to stateside hucksterism than to its pre-perestroika namesake. After World War II, Americans were intrigued by one of their more notorious allies, and some went so far as to suggest that the Moscow Mule, made with the WHITE WHISKEY most associated with Russia, was meant as a heady olive branch. Although we'd like to encourage such claims of good will, we must stick to the true tale of this ersatz classic of a mixed drink.

Made with 2 ounces of VODKA and an ounce of lime juice topped with 4 ounces of ginger beer, the Moscow Mule was a marketing ploy by John G. Martin of Heublein Inc., an East Coast distributor of food and spirits. The drink managed to become a national favorite in just a few years, though Martin's decision to buy a vodka distiller – that spirit being practically unknown in the States during the '30s – nearly got him fired. The vodka in question was Smirnov, first made by a family of the same name. When the family became the official purveyor of vodka to the court of Nicholas II, the Bolsheviks were less than understanding, and in 1918 the faction turned the distillery into a garage. The family recipe made it to France and eventually into the hands of Martin, anglicized name and all. Several years later, the purchase became known as "Martin's folly," and to save face, Martin hit the road with the vodka in tow. While in Hollywood, he dined at the Cock 'n' Bull, then owned by Jack Morgan, a fine restaurateur who was losing money fast trying to sell the ginger beer he made on the side. Morgan had a friend who was also experiencing business troubles; she was trying to offload mugs made in a copper factory. The three sat down and concocted the Moscow Mule – to be sold in a copper cup embossed with a kicking mule, a warning of its bite.

During the Korean War, when the *New York Daily News* ran a front-page photo of bartenders parading down city streets with banners declaring, "We can do without the Moscow Mule," Heublein explained that Smirnoff had cut any ties with those nasty Commies long before. The Yanks bought the story – and the spirit – and as James Brady shows, the Moscow Mule was soon associated with the innocence of youth: "…we were 21 or 22 and sure we would always be young," he wrote in the *Washingtonian*. "We drove up the Shirley Highway to Washington weekends to chase girls, which it was okay to call them then … and drink Manhattans and a new vodka drink called a Moscow Mule. And when you look back on it now, it seems as wonderful and yet unreal as an MGM musical."

Older, perhaps wiser, and not terribly worried about the Reds, we admit to liking this mixed drink more for its story than for its taste. Any bartender at any bar can make it well, and we'll even take it with ginger ale in place of ginger beer, though we always skip the cucumber peel. Besides, it serves as a pleasant reminder of how long it's been since that whole Sputnik incident.

COCKTAIL

GLASS	TASTE COMPLEXITY	MIXING DIFFICULTY
▮	LOW ⊢─○───┤ HIGH	LOW ○────┤ HIGH
	DRINK ERA	
	YEARS OF REFORM	

Moscow Mule

RECIPE

2 ounces vodka
1 ounce lime juice
4 ounces ginger beer

Stir vodka and juice together well in chilled Collins
glass. Add fresh cracked ice and a swizzle stick;
top with chilled ginger beer.
Garnish with a lime squeeze.

"There is only one vodka left," Peter the Great, former czar of Russia, supposedly wrote to his wife from Paris. "I don't know what to do." We would have suggested mixing the vodka in Moscow Mules to make it last longer.

As easily made for one as for twelve, the Moscow Mule garners interest whether served at a cocktail soiree or an after-game bash. It is also safe in the hands of the novice mixer. Store the drink's vodka in the freezer and chill its soda to make certain that the drink will be cold.

Ginger ale may be substituted, though be warned: it'll be palatable, but far from memorable. If you must use this soda, add a few dashes of Angostura BITTERS or an extra squeeze of lime to give it an edge.

Similar drinks include the Pimm's Cup.

129

Negroni

There's no fence-sitting when it comes to this cocktail, made with one of the brightest of BITTERS: Either you love it or you hate it. As a most efficient APÉRITIF, this ruddy libation is just what we want when needing a little color in our cheeks and a spring in our step. The heads-up CAMPARI taste makes our throats tingle and our minds determined.

The recipe for what was first called the Camparinete cocktail – 1 ounce of GIN, 1 ounce of Campari, 1 ounce of sweet VERMOUTH – has been around for a while, maybe as long as a hundred years. Most people – including those working for the Italian company Campari – can't quite recall when it first surfaced. Some say the Caffe Giacosa in Italy is its birthplace; others insist that no one in particular should receive credit for its simple recipe, an inspiring standby at outdoor cafés for years. There is, however, a general consensus that during the 1950s, Campari decided the drink should be called a Negroni to avoid confusion with all the other Campari cocktails – most of which were also being called Camparinetes. As always, though, there are dissenters. Some insist that the name Negroni is at least tenuously tied to Count Camillo Negroni, a Florentine aristocrat from the '20s who supposedly frequented numerous bars in Italy. From what we're told, the count ordered this drink so often that bartenders of the day began to call the drink by his name.

The name change hasn't fazed this drink's fanatical following. For them, Negroni is synonymous with Campari, and Campari remains, as one chronicler wrote, "beautiful and sparkling red, with a taste and smell that made it impossible to guess its origin; it was like the 24 carats, the four quarterings of nobility." When mixed with the proper quantity of gin and garnished with an orange wheel to soften the spirit's bite, a Negroni gives its drinker sense enough to know that such rankings rarely matter and that their value is only relative.

GLASS	TASTE COMPLEXITY	MIXING DIFFICULTY
	LOW ⊢━━━O━━⊣ HIGH	LOW ⊢━━O━━━⊣ HIGH
Y	DRINK ERA	
	GOLDEN AGE OF AMERICAN DRINKING	

Negroni

RECIPE

1 ounce gin
1 ounce sweet vermouth
1 ounce Campari

Shake with cracked ice;
strain into chilled cocktail glass.
Garnish with an orange wheel.

The Negroni isn't for the fainthearted or conservative in spirit. Serve those guests intimidated by the bitterness of this drink a Negroni in a COLLINS glass filled with cracked ice and topped with soda water. Even fanatics of the drink will appreciate this version of the Negroni on a midsummer afternoon.

A hard-hitting apéritif, the Negroni should be followed by dinner or hors d'oeuvres. The drink is best finished with a small orange wheel, squeezed and then dropped into the glass. The sweetness of the juice completes the drink, making it truly Italian. The use of a lemon twist in a Negroni, though common, fails to buffer the extremely bitter characteristics of this drink.

Similar drinks include the Jasmine, the Americano, and the Edisonian.

Nicky Finn

We've yet to come across someone brave enough to order this drink by name from anyone but the closest of friends. In fact, this fine cocktail faces near-extinction due to a name too similar to that of a death wish.

Made with typically benign ingredients – equal parts BRANDY, COINTREAU, and lemon juice, followed by a dash of the mildly toxic-tasting PERNOD – the Nicky Finn is admittedly a drink feistier than most. But on late nights when we're after a second wind, there's nothing better, though there are plenty worse (the most notable of which is the notorious Mickey Finn – a poisonous bar concoction that keeps the Nicky Finn from getting its due respect).

We've never been able to trace its origins, though William Grimes' *Straight Up or On the Rocks* suggests that the recipe was created in 1946 by Nicky Quattrociocchi, one-time owner of the now-defunct El Borracho restaurant in New York. We're not surprised that Mr. Quattrociocchi didn't christen the drink solely after himself. But just as most people don't name their children Satan – a moniker that does work for a drink or two – there are abundant reasons not to attach "Finn" to a cocktail name that rhymes with "Mickey."

We won't belabor the point, assuming that Mr. Quattrociocchi had the best intentions. After all, what stalwart mixer would want his drink tied to the Mickey Finn, a drugged drink used to send ill-behaved patrons through the door or to the grave? Some sources suggest that one of the more notable saloonkeepers of Chicago's Whiskey Row, a seamy district during the 1870s, created the drink to complement his efforts as a pickpocket. In *The Vocabulary of the Drinking Chamber*, H. L. Mencken does credit the Chicago mixer – not surprisingly said to have been named Mickey Finn – for operating "a college for pickpockets," pointing out that "the patrons of the place were a somewhat mischievous lot, and not infrequently Finn had to go to the aid of his bouncer … but the work was laborious, and Finn longed for something sneakier and slicker." Newspaper pundit Herb Caen dedicated a chapter of his 1953 book *Don't Call It Frisco* to his experience with the drink. "Its effects are almost immediate, and so violent," he wrote, "that they have caused countless fatalities. In the state of California, it is a felony to administer a Mickey. It is also a felony to commit murder, but people are still being murdered." Caen gave this account: "[T]he poison – for it is – was invented on the Barbary Coast, circa 1870, by a discredited Scotch chemist named Michael Finn. Finn, supposedly a fugitive from justice in Scotland, worked as a bartender on the Coast, and soon became known as a fine source of manpower for ship captains whose crews had deserted to the gold fields." Since the '20s, bartenders of the most reputable dives have translated requests for Mickey Finns to orders for a double. But not trusting our luck, our diction, or our bartenders' hearing, we always call out the ingredients for a Nicky.

GLASS	TASTE COMPLEXITY	MIXING DIFFICULTY
Y	LOW ─────O──── HIGH	LOW ───O──── HIGH

DRINK ERA
YEARS OF REFORM

RECIPE

1 ounce brandy
1 ounce Cointreau
1 ounce lemon juice
1 dash Pernod

Shake with cracked ice;
strain into chilled cocktail glass.
Garnish with a maraschino cherry or a lemon twist.

For any Nicky Finn to be well received, it should be served during the late evening, when guests are beginning to look long in the face and longingly at the door. If you're wanting to start the evening with an APÉRITIF cocktail, mix up a few batches of Sidecars – a classic that calls for nearly all the ingredients of the Nicky Finn but in very different proportions.

The Nicky Finn allows for much leeway in the way of garnishes. For hopelessly somber types, twist a lemon zest over the glass and then drop it into the drink. Guests who go for novelty will appreciate the same thing done with the rarely used orange peel. Imbibers who insist on eating their drink garnishes will demand the use of maraschino cherries.

Similar drinks include the Sazerac and the Monkey Gland.

Old Fashioned

We can never quite resist an Old Fashioned, though the name of this WHISKEY drink still conjures up images of a church bingo game. This drink offers the sophisticated connoisseur a chance to indulge the senses and rekindle long-lost memories. Old-fashioned, yes, but certainly not weak, it's strong enough to cut through any lingering thoughts of a bad day.

First, we combine a teaspoon of sugar with a splash of water and two dashes of Angostura BITTERS in the bottom of a large tumbler, then we toss in a maraschino cherry and an orange wedge. After muddling these ingredients until their juices start to disperse, we add 2 ounces of WHISKEY, then fill it with ice and give it a good stir.

We often contemplate this drink's supposed birth more than a hundred years ago, whether bourbon or rye was first used, and whether others along the way found it as soothing around the winter holidays as we do. Charles Browne, author of the 1939 *Gun Club Drink Book*, goes as far as to suggest that the Old Fashioned was probably the first American cocktail. We don't quite buy it, falling back as always on *The Old Waldorf-Astoria Bar Book* of 1934, which credits Colonel James E. Pepper, proprietor of the once-celebrated Old 1776 bourbon, for introducing – or at least inspiring – the Old Fashioned at that bar. The colonel was a member of the blue-blooded Pendennis Club in Louisville, where a young bartender mixed it first. Of course, that's only one version of the drink's story. Those familiar with the Whiskey Rebellion of 1794 – which ensued after Uncle Sam tried to enforce an excise tax in western Pennsylvania – insist that the region's rye whiskey producers fled to Kentucky with the Old Fashioned recipe in tow. We try to remain neutral on the matter, and – like *The Old Waldorf-Astoria Bar Book* – tell the drink's tale, but make a nonpartisan call for "whiskey" in the recipe.

Whether mixed with rye or bourbon, the first sip of an Old Fashioned makes the throat come alive, and we smile as the home fire burns inside us ever so boldly. At some point, though, the drink is transformed from the brimstone and fire of whiskey to a bouquet of cherry and oranges suspended gently over our taste buds. The Old Fashioned, with its layered taste, is an open invitation for both the whiskey lover and the froufrou cocktail drinker. It's frilly but disciplined; our cocktail compadres compare it to a good old-fashioned spanking.

GLASS	TASTE COMPLEXITY	MIXING DIFFICULTY
	LOW ⊢─O───┤ HIGH	LOW ⊢───O─┤ HIGH
	DRINK ERA	
	GOTHIC AGE OF AMERICAN DRINKING	

The **Old Fashioned** cocktail provides an adequate test of mixing skills for a host. Versatile and simple to make, this drink lets hosts relax and guests feel special.

When catering to the requests of guests, keep in mind that varying the amount of bitters and sugar allows for flexibility with this drink. Another option is to add a dash of an orange liqueur such as CURAÇAO or COINTREAU.

Old Fashioned aficionados may bicker with you about whether this drink should be made with SIMPLE SYRUP or with a sugar cube. From the imbiber's perspective, simple syrup sweetens the whole drink, while an adequately muddled sugar cube sweetens primarily the last few sips.

Similar drinks include the **Manhattan**.

135

RECIPE

2 ounces whiskey
2 dashes Angostura bitters
1 teaspoon sugar
Splash soda water

In chilled Old Fashioned glass, muddle sugar, bitters,
orange wheel, and maraschino cherry
until sugar is dissolved. Add whiskey and ice, and stir.
Optional: Garnish with a lemon twist.

Pegu

G eorge Orwell, a British colonial police officer in Burma during the '20s and later a writer after Big Brother, observed that the past belongs to those who control the present. When it comes to the nearly forgotten Pegu cocktail, few words could ring more true.

Between the '20s and the '40s, not many exotic mixes were as sought after as this stimulating drink, which hails from the Pegu Club, located in a small town of nearly the same name. The bar was about 50 miles outside Rangoon, the capital of Burma – the country we refuse to call Myanmar. According to Harry Craddock's *Savoy Cocktail Book* of 1930, people traveled the world round, asking everyone for this simple but rejuvenating drink. About 15 years later, around the time that Orwell pointed out Big Brother's attentiveness in his classic *1984* – and Burma gained its so-called independence – the Pegu vanished.

Fortunately for us, though, the Pegu is more than mildly in resurgence, meaning that this inspiring GIN APÉRITIF has been successfully ordered at most bars and dining establishments we frequent. With 1½ ounces of gin, ½ ounce of COINTREAU, ½ ounce of lime juice, and a few dashes of Angostura BITTERS, all shaken with ice and strained into a chilled cocktail glass, the Pegu makes for a pungent drink that stimulates the senses and soothes all else during the first few rounds. Old-time bartenders occasionally tossed in a dash or two of orange bitters in hopes, we're told, of smoothing the disposition of their early-evening clientele.

Although we can rarely stomach more than one or two of these cocktails, it's just as well. The Pegu's composition tends to make us surly; so, for the sake of those around us, we never overindulge. Instead, we let this drink organize our thoughts into smart, laconic streams that seem to flow as smoothly as chants from the temples in the jungle.

GLASS	TASTE COMPLEXITY	MIXING DIFFICULTY
Y	LOW ⊢──O──┤ HIGH	LOW ⊢──O──┤ HIGH
	DRINK ERA	
	GOLDEN AGE OF AMERICAN DRINKING	

137

Pegu

RECIPE

1½ ounces gin
½ ounce Cointreau
½ ounce lime juice
2 dashes Angostura bitters

Stir with cracked ice;
strain into chilled cocktail glass.
Garnish with a lime twist.

If your friends are wavering in their feelings toward Angostura bitters, they'll be decided after a Pegu. Few other cocktails highlight this bitter so well.

The amount of bitters can be varied for different colors and tastes in this afternoon apéritif. A dash adds an accent, while a splash lets the bitters dominate. The Pegu must be shaken well to adequately disperse the bitters. If you have added too much bitters or desire a fruitier taste, add a squeeze of lime. Some older recipes for the Pegu call for a dash each of Angostura and orange bitters.

But even without bitters, the Pegu is worthy. With Cointreau, citrus juice, and gin – three of the easiest ingredients to mix with – few drinks are easier to make.

Similar drinks include the Jasmine and the Kamikaze.

Petit Zinc

Nearly a Paul Harrington original, the Petit Zinc was ordered vaguely by an American at the Townhouse Bar & Grill in Emeryville, California, several years back. Having just returned from an extended stay in France, the patron could only recall what he thought – but could not swear – were the drink's name and ingredients. Unable to find a recipe for a drink by this name, the Alchemist collected the known facts – the Petit Zinc is a VODKA drink that tastes of bittersweet orange and brings to mind fond thoughts of places you'd rather be – and from there, he improvised.

By relying on color and base, the most advanced mixologist can decipher the basic properties of a cocktail. But without knowing a drink's classic proportions, a bartender must rely on trial and error to mix the drink right. After a few taste tests by the returning American, the liquid gained his approval and our general cheer. The final mix – 1 ounce of vodka, ½ ounce of COINTREAU, ½ ounce of sweet VERMOUTH, and ½ ounce of freshly squeezed Seville oranges, shaken and poured into a chilled cocktail glass garnished with an orange wheel – was surprisingly similar to the unassuming Bronx. But unlike the Bronx, whose gin and dry vermouth leave imbibers satisfied with everyday life, the Petit Zinc reminds them that the grass is always greener elsewhere.

As we sip this cocktail, we imagine the diminutive zinc bars and rooftops of Paris, bracing ourselves for that inevitable time when we're harshly accused of bastardizing some classic French concoction with an American version. We take solace, though, in the thought that if the French can elevate Jerry Lewis and Sharon Stone to the rank of *haute culture*, we can surely be permitted to add vodka to Cointreau.

GLASS	TASTE COMPLEXITY	MIXING DIFFICULTY
Y	LOW ⊶⊙⊶ HIGH	LOW ⊶⊶⊙⊶ HIGH

DRINK ERA

REVIVAL OF AMERICAN DRINKING

Petit Zinc

RECIPE

1 ounce vodka
½ ounce Cointreau
½ ounce sweet vermouth
½ ounce orange juice

Shake with cracked ice;
strain into chilled cocktail glass.
Garnish with an orange wheel or a maraschino cherry.

For those vodka-drinking friends you'd like to introduce to gin, start with the Petit Zinc and follow with a Bronx.

Although best suited for cool evenings, a Petit Zinc can be served either before or after meals. When coupled with sweet vermouth, Cointreau can dominate a drink, so exercise restraint when pouring this ingredient in the Petit Zinc. If you'd like to experiment with the drink, try citrus-flavored vodkas.

The Petit Zinc is also a lesson in approximating drinks. Imbibers often forget a cocktail's name and ingredient proportions; however, most will recall its color and primary taste. These two clues are all you need to mix a drink that can spark a guest's memory, or at least remind them of the time when the drink was first enjoyed – typically during a vacation.

Similar to the Drink Without a Name.

139

Picon-Limón

T he forgotten footnote to a FIZZ, the Picon-Limón was first graciously noted by Charles H. Baker during his meanderings up and down the Andes in the late '40s. A fine bit of exotica mixed with French spirits, this drink cools the body but not the appetite, and reminds us of the debt owed to Mr. Baker, a cocktail connoisseur who filled volume after volume with drink recipes and miscellany of the bar.

Mr. Baker was a man who noticed subtleties, including the fact that the "1950 Christmas catalogue of no less a pillar of conservatism than Sears, Roebuck & Company featured a doll-house equipped with a built-in bar." We suspect this knack for detail is what drew him to the Picon-Limón, a drink whose bold ingredients are hidden behind a smooth taste that's nothing like its parts. A well-measured Picon-Limón is mixed with 1½ ounces of AMER PICON, ½ ounce CRÈME DE CASSIS - or really good GRENADINE - and ½ ounce ROSE'S LIME JUICE in an ice-filled glass topped with soda water. When made with grenadine, the drink is a burnt-orange color with a candy-red cast, while the much-favored cassis gives the Picon-Limón a slightly purple hue, depending on the light and the swirl of the glass.

Invented by an artist, the Picon-Limón hails from Buenos Aires and was discovered at a cocktail party hosted by Pepe Ezyguirre. "Sculptor Lagos, probably the best in all of Argentina, gave us this receipt...." reported Mr. Baker in his *South American Gentleman's Companion* of 1951. Occasionally given to excessive fawning, as perhaps in the instance of the now little-known Lagos, Mr. Baker has often built expectations too high. But with the Picon-Limón, he is a realist: "This Picon-Limón is not included here with any idea that it will sweep our fair country from Maine to California.... Some of your international travelers may like it enough to list on your own home-bar wine-card. Certainly, it's simple enough to do." And with that we agree, pleased that we can make it at home or order it out, just as long as the bar stocks cassis and Picon and we're quick with the recipe and the tip.

We'll only sip one or two of these drinks, though. The Picon-Limón's acidic nature agitates the stomach if food doesn't follow soon, and impressed as we are with the recipes of Mr. Baker, we certainly wouldn't want to need one of his so-called Latin preventions against a pained stomach: "Not a few of the *Caballeros* we locked glasses with in South America believe in a little carefully-planned pre-drink strategy, both to lessen liquor's prompt bite – and to modify the gruesome challenge of mornings-after, chiefly by pre-lining the stomach with a mild liquid priming-coat of some variety," wrote Mr. Baker, before suggesting "that old job of swallowing a spoon or two of medically proper olive oil an hour or so before the bout, and maybe another pair half an hour later." Instead, we opt for up-front common sense, and sip less than three Picon-Limóns at a sitting – grateful and confident that we'll never nurse a grudge against this fine fizz.

GLASS	TASTE COMPLEXITY		MIXING DIFFICULTY	
	LOW ⊢━━O━⊣ HIGH		LOW ⊢O━━━⊣ HIGH	
	DRINK ERA			
	YEARS OF REFORM			

Picon Limón

RECIPE

1½ ounces Amer Picon
½ ounce crème de cassis or grenadine
½ ounce Rose's lime juice
Soda water

Stir first three ingredients with cracked ice;
strain into chilled 16-ounce glass.
Top with soda water, and
garnish with a lemon twist.

Refreshing and light, the Picon-Limón saves flagging appetites, especially in high humidity.

Charles H. Baker suggests occasionally using ¼ ounce of lemon juice instead of Rose's lime juice for a drier taste.

There is a significant taste difference between a Picon–Limón made with grenadine and one made with cassis. The latter makes for a more attractive and complex drink. The earlier it is, and the warmer the day, the drier you should make this drink. If serving this fizz at the height of the day, replace any Rose's with fresh lemon juice. But on late afternoons, engulfed in still air, opt for the Picon–Limón with Rose's and crème de cassis.

Similar drinks include the Vermouth Cassis and the Pimm's Cup.

141

◆►◄ COCKTAIL ◄►◆

Picon Punch

T he French created it and the Italians refined it. But we won't split hairs over the lineage of this refreshing spritzer, which always makes us a little nostalgic for an Old World we never knew.

Back in 1837, a Frenchman named Gaëtan Picon was living in Philippeville, Belgium, when he first created AMER PICON, a bitter orange cordial that does wonders for the appetite and works well as a stomachic. By the turn of the century, Mr. Picon moved back to his native land and began mass production of Amer Picon. Finding it too acerbic a spirit on its own, many imbibers began mixing what became known as the Picon Punch: 1½ ounces of Amer Picon and a dash of GRENADINE, served in a tumbler filled with fresh ice and chilled soda water. The Italians went on to perfect the technique for adding grenadine to this drink. Following their recipe – as we always do – we first swirl a dash of grenadine in a glass, so that it just coats the vessel. We then ice the glass, add Amer Picon, and top with soda water. For occasions when the heart or spirit needs particular comfort, a BRANDY float is added.

On warm weekend afternoons, we often find ourselves huddled around a bar with a Picon Punch in hand. Fortunately, we've always found a Little Italy in any town where we've looked. With its soothing strength, the Picon Punch is certain not to let us lose our head after a few, though we've decided that this drink does entertain some of the more endearing characters of the bar. For the most part, these folks seem to have certain peculiarities when it comes to the details of this drink. We wouldn't call their habits strange or especially unsettling, but we have noted that a few demand their punches in a tulip-shaped glass without ice, while others take the brandy float only on days of bad weather involving wind gusts. Still others skip the brandy altogether and go particularly light on the grenadine. But regardless, they are all intriguing enough to make us order a second round and stay on into the early evening.

GLASS	TASTE COMPLEXITY	MIXING DIFFICULTY
	LOW ⊢━━O━━┤ HIGH	LOW ⊢━O━━━┤ HIGH
	DRINK ERA	
	GOTHIC AGE OF AMERICAN DRINKING	

Picon Punch

RECIPE

1½ ounces Amer Picon
1 dash grenadine
Soda water
Float of brandy

Coat inside of chilled 16-ounce glass with grenadine.
Add Amer Picon and ice;
top with soda water, and stir.
Float brandy, and garnish with a lemon twist.

Called the drink of bartenders, the Picon Punch can be made quickly and easily. It also affords a host a drink or two without impacting said host's productivity.

If the occasion calls for a pungent bitter, serve this drink in a 6-ounce Irish coffee glass, which most emphasizes the spirit. The much taller COLLINS glass, which allows for more ice and soda, will produce a lighter-tasting Picon Punch. If the drink is too bitter for particular guests, suggest they try the Picon-Limón.

For some imbibers, a splash of lemon juice better balances the grenadine's sweetness. In the evenings, the drink can be served as a traditional cocktail by omitting the soda water and adding a splash of lemon juice before shaking, then straining the mix into a chilled cocktail glass.

Similar drinks include the Edisonian.

T his peculiar spring quaff, with its brash-looking but subtle-tasting cucumber garnish, gets as close to health food as anything we'd care to recommend. A delicious whistle-wetter, the drink suggests at least a partial mental leap from JUNIPER to ginseng with its hardy serving of PIMM'S No. 1 – a tawny gin sling that first catered to the posh corners of the West End and then courtside Wimbledon.

We request our Pimm's Cups topped with ginger ale and served over ice, garnished with a squeeze of lemon and a sliver of cucumber. Those with a penchant for hard-edged poisons may be disappointed by the drink's refreshing fruit flavor, but the Pimm's Cup is not without zing. The blend of citrus, cucumber, and gin smacks of the good earth – though, as most Martini drinkers will point out, the taste can be reminiscent of dirt. However, it's worth noting that the blue bloods of England, who typically steer clear of muck, have rarely complained about this drink since its inception in the late 19th century.

Most drink historians agree that the creation of the Pimm's Cup followed closely on the heels of the invention of Pimm's No. 1 in 1840. First mixed as a digestive tonic by James Pimm, this concoction – made with numerous herbs and QUININE – was initially served only at Mr. Pimm's oyster bar in the financial district of London. Many establishments of the day mixed house spirits to serve with cordials, brandies, and juices as "cups," in reference to the tankards in which they were sold. However, few of these tonics became as popular as that of Mr. Pimm. Within 20 years, Mr. Pimm began distributing his drink. By the '20s, Pimm's was being sold throughout England. According to *Grossman's Guide to Wines, Spirits, and Beer*, Pimm's was exported to England's many colonies, making it as far as the officer's mess of General Gordon in Khartoum, the capital of Sudan. After World War II, the Pimm's company expanded its product line, adding Pimm's Nos. 2 through 6. Each version used a base other than gin – 2 through 5 were scotch, BRANDY, RUM, and rye, respectively. Other than the original Pimm's, only No. 6, mixed with VODKA, is still made. No. 1 boasts of being made to James Pimm's original recipe, a secret known only to six people. However, we began to doubt this upon discovering that the liquor now includes caramel coloring.

We enjoy Pimm's Cups while watching those three-day-long cricket matches, which usually involve the English getting their cheeks thrashed by a former colony. At a low PROOF, Pimm's has less kick than most spirits, so we can drink it for the entire test series – the equivalent of watching a double-header with extra innings and no hits. Only chess is better for crowd excitement. If guests still accuse us of being anglophiles, we remind them that though the English continue to sip Pimm's, former British colonies like India have claimed this drink as their victory toast after cricket matches. Based on game results from the last 20 years, these colonials have been drinking Pimm's more often than anyone in England.

GLASS	TASTE COMPLEXITY	MIXING DIFFICULTY
▮	LOW ═O═ HIGH	LOW ═O═ HIGH
	DRINK ERA	
	GOLDEN AGE OF AMERICAN DRINKING	

Nearly a premixed drink – and certainly the closest we'd come to suggesting one – Pimm's No. 1 requires only the addition of a soda and a garnish to make a tasty libation.

The Pimm's Cup is traditionally mixed with lemon soda. However, this mildly sweet, carbonated beverage is difficult to find in the States, though quite common in England. As a substitute, use ginger ale – not lemonade, as some old-time drink books suggest. Seven-Up or soda water may be substituted for a drink less interesting in taste. If Seven-Up is used, the drink is called the Pimm's Rangoon.

More than a mere garnish, the cucumber tempers the bitter flavor of Pimm's. The skin of the cucumber can be left or removed from the fruit for this drink.

Similar drinks include the Picon Punch.

RECIPE

2 ounces Pimm's No. 1
3 ounces ginger ale
Cucumber

Pour Pimm's into chilled pint glass; fill with ice.
Top with chilled ginger ale.
Garnish with a lemon wheel
and a cucumber slice.

Pink Gin

W ith all its bourgeois baggage, the Pink Gin is the English equivalent of the Yank's Martini. Bold and biting, it takes the banal – GIN and BITTERS – and makes it distinctive. But unlike the Martini, this classic cocktail suffers from a pathetically prosaic name that occasionally opens it up to disparaging remarks.

Fortunately, the Pink Gin's taste rises above its name, though its past is another matter. The Pink Gin has the Royal Navy to thank for its well-dispersed recipe, and as proof that anything can be justified, these fine imperialists sipped Mother's ruin as a stomachic while sailing the seas. We doubt it was the 3 ounces of gin that calmed the waters, but rather the Angostura bitters.

Well-documented legend has it that Dr. Johann Gottlieb Benjamin Siegert, a surgeon for the Prussian army at the battle of Waterloo, invented the bitters in 1824 for a military hospital at Angostura, Venezuela. When added to gin, these lurid orange-colored bitters – now made in Trinidad, by appointment to Her Majesty – blend into a soothing salmon hue. But the Pink Gin wasn't for everyone. Those on the Royal Navy's lower decks drank RUM, while only the officers in the wardrooms sipped Pink Gins. Of course, that's why it's none too surprising that this cocktail was wasting away in the upper crust of white-bread establishments until Ian Fleming started sipping it between interviews about a certain secret agent. In no way do we mean to imply that Mr. Fleming did not frequent those bars – we're just certain that most of his readers did not. But before too long, the Pink Gin was beginning to be sipped by those without breeding. Soon enough, even typical Englishmen could be spotted imbibing Pink Gins while waiting for their invites to the Queen's tea party.

True devotees of the Pink Gin mix the cocktail with Plymouth, not London, gin. According to John Ayto, the lexicographer who scribed *The Diner's Dictionary*, the Royal Navy may have preferred Plymouth, "since it is fuller in flavor" than London's Dry gin. Regrettably, we've never been able to verify this critique. For a fact, it's impossible to buy a bottle of Plymouth in the States, and we've heard reports that obtaining it elsewhere isn't much easier. But we are certain that drinking more than one or two Pink Gins mixed without Plymouth makes the drinker belligerent at best. "Plymouth gin differs from its peers (described, in most cases meaninglessly, as London gins) in that it is softer, less assertive, less pepper-pungent, with an earthier, more gently spicy style," wrote Andrew Jefford for the *Evening Standard* back in 1993. "In some ways it seems restrained and decorously naval, tasted alongside flamboyant wide-boy London rivals." If ever in the mood for a fight, we order a London Pink Gin and ask a few Englishmen how many dashes of Angostura should go into it, knowing there'll be no agreement, but there will be amusement galore.

GLASS	TASTE COMPLEXITY	MIXING DIFFICULTY
⍋	LOW ═══○═══ HIGH	LOW ═○═══ HIGH

DRINK ERA

GOTHIC AGE OF AMERICAN DRINKING

Pink Gin

RECIPE

3 ounces gin
2 dashes Angostura bitters

Shake with cracked ice;
strain into chilled cocktail glass.
Garnish with a lemon twist or a lime squeeze.

A biting bracer, the Pink Gin quickly whets the appetite, sending guests off soon enough in search of sustenance.

In fact, the Pink Gin is not a drink to linger over long – it's the cocktail equivalent of a slap in the face.

The key to making a Pink Gin is serving it ice-cold. Imbibers who cherish the taste of gin will appreciate it if the bitters are merely swirled in the chilled cocktail glass, and then shaken or flicked out before 3 ounces of chilled gin is poured into the glass. If you suspect that guests might find this drink too strong, serve it on the rocks, adding tonic water to taste with plenty of lime juice.

Similar drinks include the dry Martini, the Astoria, and the Gibson.

Pisco Sour

A ny self-respecting Chilean will politely and firmly deny it, but the BRANDY called PISCO – the pith of the Pisco Sour – is originally from Peru, where it's been a staple of the economy and of local *joie de vivre* since the 16th century. It wasn't until the '30s, when Chile's President Riesco trademarked the term, that Chile deviously appropriated the spirit. The origin of the Pisco Sour – a powerful, tart libation popular in both countries – is an even greater point of contention. Chilean pisco producers claim it was developed in the '20s and '30s, when American and European steamship passengers on their way to San Francisco would lay over in the port of Coquimbo. In trying to extract some tangible benefit from the local spirits, they may have been inspired by the trendy Whiskey Sour. Peruvians, of course, claim the port of Pisco, Peru, is the correct setting for this tale. In this matter, cool-headed objectivity from anyone with Peruvian or Chilean loyalties – as in the vexed question of the rightful ownership of the northern part of Chile – is rare.

Whenever we sip this zesty libation, we're reminded why it's such a coveted item. Like good GIN cocktails, it has the curious quality of loosening people's tongues while sharpening their wits. We're told that the wife of Alain Touraine, a French social scientist with Latin American interests, likes to serve this drink at the start of an evening to ensure a smooth, easy rapport among guests. Some even say pisco has hallucinogenic properties. While we can't prove that, we agree that it makes for a good party. Some of the secret lies in a deceptively sweet, tangy taste that masks a strong dose of liquor.

The Pisco Sour is typically served by well-to-do city dwellers, especially in the hot season around Christmas, when summer vacation begins and spirits run high. It is, however, common throughout the year and across class lines, and is as much the cocktail of choice for Lima's mining magnates as for provincial *huasos* (the Chilean take on the cowboy). Regrettably, most bars in the U.S. and Europe fail to stock pisco, though A. J. Liebling documented its arrival in the States more than 100 years ago in his 1952 biography of journalist Colonel John R. Stingo, *The Honest Rainmaker.* "It was said New York had not before ever seen or heard of the insidious concoction which in its time had caused the unseating of South American governments and women to set world's records in various and interesting fields of activity. In early San Francisco, where the punch first made its North American appearance in 1856, the police allowed but one drink per person in 24 hours, it's that propulsive."

To counter today's lack of interest in this fine spirit stateside, we often pack our own, in hopes of getting a Pisco Sour mixed while at our favored establishments. Sweet and innocent as a velvet hammer, this drink has a potency and versatility that are sure to get things rolling. If we're unable to chivy a bartender into making this drink, it at least translates well into cocktail parties at home.

GLASS	TASTE COMPLEXITY		MIXING DIFFICULTY	
🍷	LOW ▭▭O▭▭ HIGH		LOW ▭▭O▭▭ HIGH	

DRINK ERA

GOTHIC AGE OF AMERICAN DRINKING

Pisco Sour

RECIPE

2 ounces pisco
1 ounce lemon juice
½ ounce simple syrup
1 dash bitters
1 dollop egg white

Shake with cracked ice;
strain into chilled champagne flute.
Optional: Garnish with a lemon twist or a mint sprig.

To entice drinkers who prefer the gentlest of cocktail fare, mix a traditional Pisco Sour minus the bitters and pour it into a tall glass. Top with ginger ale, and if a garnish is desired, add a lemon twist or a sprig of mint. Refreshing and inoffensive, this version is an especially good thirst quencher.

For the sweet tooth, add a teaspoon of pineapple juice to the mix, but note that South Americans may take offense at this addition. For those imbibers seeking a more potent drink, add a dash of scotch to the mixing tin before shaking.

In a sour, egg white makes for a frothy head, so FLASH BLENDING any such drink is an especially good idea.

Similar drinks include the Maiden's Prayer and the Caipirinha.

Planter's Punch

T his classic drink barely hits the definition of "punch." In fact, *Esquire* called it a cocktail in its listing of the best drinks of 1934. Regrettably, though, the Planter's Punch now has the stature of a melted Popsicle, thanks to distillers set on using its good name for spiked lemonades made from ersatz fruit juices and chalky mixes more likely to be sold in a six-pack than a respectable bar. Nonetheless, when concocted with care and what we consider the classic formula, the Planter's Punch is a fine tropical libation that rests easy on the tongue.

Made with 2 ounces dark RUM, 1 ounce lemon juice, and a dash of both orange juice and SIMPLE SYRUP shaken with cracked ice and strained into a FROSTED wine glass filled with ice, this drink's simple and forgiving recipe can be trusted to even the most novice mixer. *The Bon Vivant's Companion* of 1933 credits "Jerry Thomas, the Juniper Olympus of the bar and the presiding deity" at the Planter's Hotel in St. Louis around 1840, with the creation of this drink. "His very name is synonymous with quality in the lexicon of mixed drinks, and remember that he was inexorable as the Medes and Persians in his principle that no excellent drink can be made out of anything but excellent materials." Though we wholeheartedly agree with George A. Zabriskie, who wrote those words, on the latter point, we can't quite buy into a tropical tipple that hails from the Midwest. Instead, we side with Charles Browne's *Gun Club Drink Book* of 1939: "The Planter's Punch ... gets its name because it has been drunk by the sugar planters in Jamaica for over a hundred years. Unfortunately, like a Mint Julep, it is made in a hundred different ways and seems to reflect the idiosyncrasies of the various bartenders."

Although partial to what seems to be the oldest, most basic recipe, we never turn down a Planter's Punch whose mixer has followed the one hard and fast rule of this drink, as first set to paper by Charles H. Baker: "Get decent, well-aged rum." Second-rate rum in a Planter's Punch will only be disguised by the fruit juices for roughly five seconds, after which the imbiber is left with an overpowering raw spirit that should have been left in wood casks for another eight years.

The charm of the Planter's Punch is its refreshing mellowness – not to be interpreted as sweetness. The drink's smoothness is especially comforting on warm afternoons or early evenings in overheated bars. It's also a fine reminder that rums are best called by country, not color – and for the Planter's Punch, we honor heritage and order Jamaican.

Planter's Punch

Unlike most modern tropical drinks, the Planter's Punch doesn't mask the distillation's taste with sweet syrups. Instead, it's a smooth mixed drink that subtly suggests it's time for dinner, or perhaps a late lunch.

Distilled from sugarcane, rum is inherently sweet; therefore, sweeteners are rarely needed for this drink. If a guest finds the rum too strong, try a dash more of orange juice.

Soda water may be used to top off this drink, though it's best served as a traditional cocktail. Add a dash or so of BITTERS to the drinks of those who consider this tipple too sweet.

Similar drinks include the Pedro Collins, the Mai Tai, and the Rum Julep.

151

RECIPE

2 ounces dark rum
1 ounce lemon juice
1 dash orange juice
1 dash simple syrup

Shake with cracked ice;
strain into large wine goblet filled with ice.
Garnish with a lemon twist.

Ramos Gin Fizz

T o disrespect this drink, call it a gin FIZZ – as though it's been around forever, as though it could have been mixed by anyone from anywhere. But bear its reality in mind: This great classic could only have come from New Orleans – and for that reason, we flinch only slightly when we hear it called the New Orleans Fizz.

The latter moniker smacks of a Johnny-come-lately without the balls to put his name behind a product too similar to the archetype. We agree that the ORANGE-FLOWER WATER of the Ramos Gin Fizz is the wonder-working ingredient of this drink; however, we're not about to concede that three to four drops of this potion – or any other, for that matter – is enough to separate it from the fizz named after the city.

But the name notwithstanding, we seem to come across this creamy drink in only a handful of establishments, most of which are well situated in our favorite city of sin and noted for their brunch cuisine. The Ramos Gin Fizz might have fared better had it not been for that awkward time known as PROHIBITION, when the Ramos brothers of New Orleans were forced to close their establishments' doors. But as Charles H. Baker points out in his *Gentleman's Companion* of 1946, the world might never have known the original recipe for this drink had the brothers Ramos not been "in a fit of generous aberration" brought on by the "ridiculous drouth of the Prohibition era." According to Baker and other historians of mixology, the brothers (especially Henry, the actual creator of the drink) tried their darnedest to keep the recipe a secret, from its inception in 1888 until the late '20s – when, in retaliation against the Feds and out of sympathy for their friends, they let the more elusive ingredients slip out. Since then, the recipe for the Ramos Gin Fizz has passed through more than a few hands, but the trademark for its name resides with the Fairmont Hotel, formerly the Roosevelt Hotel, in New Orleans.

Whenever sipping Ramos Gin Fizzes, we make newcomers guess the drink's ingredients after only a brief sampling of the tipple. No one has ever suspected the orange-flower water, and only a few have guessed the egg white. In anticipation of a light brunch, we shake 1½ ounces of GIN, ½ ounce of lemon juice, three dashes of flower water, a teaspoon of SIMPLE SYRUP, an egg white, and 2 ounces of cream until they become a rich mixture, which we pour into a large wine goblet and top with soda water. If we're especially wanting warmer spring weather, we'll add a dash of vanilla extract and garnish with a flower blossom.

As we sip the dulcifying froth that's always so picture-perfect, we see how Mr. Baker came to write that "the Ramos Fizz has long been synonymous with the finest in all the New Orleans art" and that "the formula, like any history dealing with the dead arts, should be engraved on the tablets of history."

GLASS	TASTE COMPLEXITY	MIXING DIFFICULTY
▼	LOW ⊢─O───┤ HIGH	LOW ⊢────O─┤ HIGH

GOLDEN AGE OF AMERICAN DRINKING

Ramos Gin Fizz

1½ ounces gin
½ ounce lemon juice
3 to 4 drops orange–flower water
1 teaspoon simple syrup
2 ounces cream
1 egg white
Soda water

Place in blender with a scoop of cracked ice; flash blend for 15 to 30 seconds. Pour mixture into wine goblet, and top with soda water. Garnish with a small flower blossom.

"What happens ... when it never comes the way you want it?" asked Lizabeth Scott in the 1947 movie *Dead Reckoning.* "What do you do? Go on singing songs and drinking Ramos Gin Fizzes." Sounds fine to us, especially for those days when you start imagining yourself as a tortured character in a flick noir. If you've noticed yourself brooding self-indulgently about universal corruption and its relation to your own illusory integrity, it's high time to alter your drinking protocol: Wake up mid-morning. Go outdoors. Put eggs in your cocktail.

To make the Golden Fizz, use the yolk of one egg. For the Royal Fizz, use an entire egg. Just keep in mind that this drink – as any mixed with egg – calls for mechanical blending.

Similar drinks include the Bee's Kiss.

◆◆◆ COCKTAIL ◆◆◆

W e'll try to keep this one short, knowing that if you've paused on this PICK-ME-UP, you're probably in no mood for a drink. But on the off chance you're in a weakened state, we really must mention that the Bloody Mary was first made with GIN, not VODKA, and was christened the Red Snapper. We wouldn't bet our lives on this factoid, though after the holidays we'd certainly consider betting our siblings'.

In fact, the only verity we really have on the Red Snapper is that this mixed drink does wonders for self-inflicted illnesses, particularly those brought on by the occasional bad Martini olive or maraschino cherry. We can also make a good case that the Bloody Mary has no direct ties to dear Mary Tudor, Mary I of England and Ireland – best remembered for her nickname, "Bloody Mary," and the mess she made with the Protestants.

Mixed with 2 ounces of gin, 4 ounces of tomato juice, the juice of half a lemon, and a few shakes of salt and pepper, followed by a splash of Worcestershire sauce (pronounced "what's-this-here-sauce") and then Tabasco, the Red Snapper always manages to keep our stomachs weighted down and our spirits high. We also count sipping any drink with a celery stalk in it as fair penance for past instances of poor judgment.

After one or two Snappers, we're ready to defend the heritage of this fine concoction. According to the story we like, Ferdinand Petiot, a bartender at Harry's New York Bar in Paris, concocted a blend of tomato juice, a clear spirit, and seasonings sometime in the early '20s. There is substantiated speculation – most notably confirmed by Duncan MacElhone, the current proprietor of the bar and a grandson of Harry – that the Bloody Mary was first made with gin, a spirit far more popular then than now. Nonetheless, the Parisians were unimpressed, and Mr. Petiot emigrated to the States, where he manned the St. Regis Hotel bar during the mid-'30s. According to Mr. MacElhone, the name Red Snapper was used until the '50s, when vodka – thanks in part to the efforts of Smirnoff – came into vogue. Again, it's worth noting that during the OLD SCHOOL OF AMERICAN BARTENDING, right on through to the early '40s, WHITE WHISKEY was almost unheard of in the States.

Origins aside, we second Hemingway when summing up the merits of the Bloody Mary. In a 1947 letter, our favorite bad boy of the cocktail world wrote that after he introduced this drink to Hong Kong in 1941, it "did more than any other single factor except the Japanese Army to precipitate the Fall of that Crown Colony." We keep that last bit of information in mind for those expected occasions when some presumptuous bartender second-guesses our order and swaps vodka for gin. If it tastes like tomato juice with spices but no spunk, we send it back – knowing that downing the spirit you can't really taste before day's end is a far worse fate than a spat with a bartender.

GLASS	TASTE COMPLEXITY	MIXING DIFFICULTY
🍷	LOW ═══O═══ HIGH	LOW ═══O═══ HIGH
	DRINK ERA	
	PROHIBITION	

RECIPE

2 ounces gin
4 ounces tomato juice
½ ounce lemon juice
1 to 2 pinches salt and pepper
2 to 3 dashes Worcestershire sauce
2 to 3 drops Tabasco sauce

Shake first four ingredients with cracked ice;
strain into chilled 16–ounce glass filled with ice.
Stir in Worcestershire, Tabasco, salt, and pepper.
Garnish with a celery stalk and a lemon wheel.

Old-school bartenders insist that drinks like the Red Snapper be imbibed only before noon, while most modern-day mixers will serve it late into the night. Because "morning" is a relative time that often bleeds into the afternoon, we'd serve it any time before four, but after that, we have to side with the old-timers: If you're still needing a pick-me-up by then, admit defeat and head for bed.

Mixing any more than three Red Snappers dictates making a batch in a pitcher. Fortunately, Red Snapper mix is like a good stew: It only gets better with time. If you'd like, make it the night before.

As far as the garnish goes, a celery stalk and lemon wheel will suffice. The unbecoming habit of using more than two garnishes is only proof of a greedy gut.

Similar drinks include the Caesar, Bloody Mary, and the Bullshot.

Rob Roy

W | hen all else fails, we turn to the Rob Roy. We can count on this drink, with its simple recipe and subtle kick, to give any day a happy ending.

Two ounces of scotch and half an ounce of sweet VERMOUTH, stirred and poured through a strainer, with more than an occasional dash of BITTERS — a bartender would have to be a real louse to mess this one up. Merely a Manhattan made with a different WHISKEY, the Rob Roy is an obvious drink variation that managed to attract its own following, much as the Gibson did in spite of the Martini. A Manhattan, of course, is still a Manhattan whether made with bourbon or rye, but make it with scotch and suddenly you have a novel cocktail — one that H. L. Mencken credits to enterprising bartenders. We're not quite so sold on that enterprising bartender bit. Rather, we suspect the mixer decided to borrow a recipe, then added the banality that a drink made with scotch ought to be — or at least sound — fierce. William Grimes, in *Straight Up or On the Rocks*, suggests that the name was inspired by a play called, not surprisingly, *Rob Roy*.

If a greenhorn tries to slide us a Roy Rogers, a GRENADINE-and-Coke concoction reminiscent of cough syrup, we politely send it back and request a whiskey ON THE ROCKS, which is only slightly easier to make than a Rob Roy. If we think the bartender has been around the block, we'll contemplate ordering our favorite variation on the Rob Roy, the Santiago Scotch Plaid — perfect for those days when subtlety has lost its charm. Delivered with all the ambiguity of a Presbyterian sermon, the Santiago Scotch Plaid leaves no doubt you're drinking heads-up scotch, with just a tinge of dry vermouth, bitters, and a twist of lemon. A Chilean friend says the drink was created during the early 19th century by a Scottish general who married a Mapuche (a Chilean native) and fought against the Spanish army to free her people. After battle, they drank this cocktail, mixed with the blood of their opponents. Reason enough for us to wash down this drink with a Rob Roy.

During the summer, we may take our Rob Roys on the rocks. In the winter, though, they're always up. By the time we've finished our second Rob Roy (or even our first Scotch Plaid), we're feeling ferocious again, and after the third, we're ready to head into battle, naked under our kilts.

GLASS	TASTE COMPLEXITY	MIXING DIFFICULTY
▼	LOW ══O══ HIGH	LOW ══O══ HIGH

DRINK ERA

GOLDEN AGE OF AMERICAN DRINKING

Rob Roy

RECIPE

2 ounces scotch
½ ounce sweet vermouth
1 dash Angostura bitters (optional)

Stir with cracked ice;
strain into chilled cocktail glass.
Garnish with a lemon twist or a maraschino cherry.

The key to this drink is not to make mixing it any harder than it ought to be. Forgiving in its measurements, the Rob Roy is an especially good drink for a novice host to start with.

If you wish to experiment with this drink, first vary the amount of vermouth. For a drier Rob Roy, mix with French vermouth, not sweet. Those hesitant about their ability to balance the ingredients in this drink should reach for the Angostura bitters.

The ideal day to serve Rob Roys is Bobbie Burns Day – January 25, the holiday to commemorate the birth of 18th-century poet and Scotsman Robert Burns. Add a dash of DRAMBUIE to the drink and you have the Bobbie Burns, the perfect accompaniment to haggis.

Similar drinks include the Highland and the Highlander.

Satan's Whiskers

F orgotten since the late '30s, the Satan's Whiskers soothes the savage at twilight. A rich DIGESTIF with a distracting taste whose ingredients are always enjoyed though rarely identified, this cocktail reminds imbibers that not all behavior is becoming. In *The Cocktail: The Influence of Spirits on the American Psyche*, Joseph Lanza went so far as to interpret the cocktail hour as "a ceremonial disunion of man from beast." We don't quite buy that, but when we sip this drink, the idea does have appeal.

The Satan's Whiskers also satisfies our bent for incidental dramatics. As if its name weren't inviting enough to well-mannered rogues, this drink has two versions: straight and curled. When properly made, both recipes balance ¾ ounce of GIN, ¾ ounce each of sweet and dry VERMOUTH, ½ ounce of orange juice, and a dash of ORANGE BITTERS. Add ½ ounce of GRAND MARNIER and the whiskers are straight; add ½ ounce of CURAÇAO and they're curled.

We contend that the "curled" Satan's Whiskers is the more diabolical, but most bartenders insist that's not the case, maintaining that the first Satan's Whiskers was made with Grand Marnier and that somewhere along the way, a bartender ran out of the LIQUEUR. Rather than disappoint, the mixer improvised and used orange curaçao, a cordial of similar (but lighter) taste and color. We sip our Satan's Whiskers curled if it's still light outside and straight if it's not.

Inevitably, we end up contemplating how such a nice drink could have been saddled with such a portentous name. We'd blame the Temperance Society, but with Ambrose Bierce, Master of the Macabre and all-around cynical wag, defining TEETOTALER as "one who abstains from strong drink, sometimes totally, sometimes tolerably totally" in *The Devil's Dictionary* of 1911, who's to say that someone like him didn't name the drink out of spite?

Nonetheless, a request for Satan's Whiskers – straight or curled – works well to instill dread in most bartenders, though we're not sure whether it's the name or the recipe that does the trick. We're most inclined to order it by name around Halloween, or on full-moon evenings at bars displaying the image of the ever fulsome Elvira. Once served, we'll recite from Richard Cavendish's *The Black Arts*, as recounted in Mr. Lanza's *The Cocktail*: "Some medieval alchemists thought that alcohol was a form of the quintessence, the pure fifth element of which the heavens are made."

GLASS	TASTE COMPLEXITY	MIXING DIFFICULTY
Y	LOW ⊢━O━┤ HIGH	LOW ⊢━━O┤ HIGH

DRINK ERA

GOLDEN AGE OF AMERICAN DRINKING

A Satan's Whiskers tastes swell whenever it is sipped, whether under a full moon or an impish spell, so don't reserve this drink for Halloween.

Evenhandedness will be paramount in keeping this cocktail balanced. Pouring measurements of less than an ounce isn't easy; any twitch will alter the amount.

A Satan's Whiskers is most difficult to make for one or two people. The perfect batch size would be for five guests, since you'd simply measure a PONY of nearly all of the ingredients. Because the Satan's Whiskers is a hearty DIGESTIF, start the evening by serving the Bronx, a bare-boned Satan's Whiskers.

Similar drinks include the Delilah.

RECIPE

¾ ounce gin
¾ ounce dry vermouth
¾ ounce sweet vermouth
½ ounce orange juice
½ ounce Grand Marnier
1 dash orange bitters

Shake with cracked ice; strain into chilled cocktail glass. Garnish with an orange twist. For a Satan's Whiskers curled, substitute curaçao for Grand Marnier.

Sazerac

D ixieland jazz, Tabasco sauce, *A Streetcar Named Desire*, blackened anything – we've always liked New Orleans. But it was only after we had our first Sazerac, New Orleans' most famous cocktail, that we truly forgave that steamy Southern city for hosting an annual celebration for drunken lunkheads.

Southern legend traces the Sazerac to an eponymous bar, opened in 1859, where drinks were mixed from Sazerac-de-Forge et Fils COGNAC and New Orleans' own Peychaud's BITTERS, delivered straight and often to the Sazerac Coffee House from the Antoine Peychaud apothecary three blocks away. John B. Schiller, the initial owner of the Sazerac, named the bar after the BRANDY, which he sold on the side.

Early on, Mr. Schiller asked his friend Antoine to develop a drink recipe that incorporated both the brandy and the bitters into a medicinal tonic good enough to be enjoyed without the excuse of illness. Some say that what resulted – the initial iteration of the Sazerac – was the country's first COCKTAIL. Eleven years later, Mr. Schiller's bookkeeper, Thomas H. Handy, took over the business, changing the establishment's name and the drink's recipe. The coffee house became the Sazerac House, and the revised libation now reflected the craze for ABSINTHE that had swept the city following the French-Algerian war. The new Sazerac also mirrored the shift in local tastes toward WHISKEYS and away from brandy. Few doubt that Mr. Handy was first to swap the spirits; however, some – presumably those with loyalties to other establishments – say another mixer, perhaps Leon Lamothe, a well-known New Orleans bartender of the day, should be credited with the addition of absinthe to the drink.

During the heyday of the Sazerac, the mixture of rye whiskey, BITTERS, and sugar would have derived its anis scent from real absinthe (now forbidden because of its reputation as addictive and mania-inducing). Today we pour our shaken rye, sugar, and bitters into a chilled glass just touched by an absinthe substitute, such as PERNOD, Ricard, or, preferably, the local brand, HERBSAINT.

If we find a patient bartender who can master the traditional Sazerac, a full-bodied drink with layered flavors of rye and anis and the bite of bitters, we'll order the smoother variation of the standard, requesting the substitution of Barbados or Cuban RUM for rye. Only slightly more sensitive to mixing mishaps, this version of the drink is better suited to summer's afternoon heat. And whenever we have a foolish urge to head to New Orleans for Mardi Gras, we do what most wise people would: have a Sazerac and wait it out.

GLASS	TASTE COMPLEXITY	MIXING DIFFICULTY
	LOW ═══O═ HIGH	LOW ═O═══ HIGH

Steer clear of prepackaged Sazerac mixes. Like other mixes, they're best saved for bomb shelters.

You'll need to size up a guest quickly before serving a Sazerac. Anis is an unexpectedly complex flavor when mixed in a cocktail. Just a drop adds a rich herbal blanket to anything you serve.

Most people will enjoy the traditional Sazerac recipe; however, a Sazerac made with Barbados rum instead of whiskey is often better received by those trying the drink for the first time. If you opt for this variation, garnish with an orange twist. Substituting bourbon for rye is another mixing option.

Similar drinks include the Monkey Gland and the Nicky Finn.

RECIPE

2 ounces rye
3 dashes Peychaud's bitters
1 splash Herbsaint

Coat the inside of chilled
Old Fashioned glass with Herbsaint,
turning the glass to coat it evenly and thoroughly.
Shake rye and bitters with cracked ice;
strain into prepared glass.
Optional: Garnish with a lemon twist.

Scofflaw

T his WHISKEY cocktail used to be as bad as it sounds. Imbibers sipped it throughout PROHIBITION as they publicly thumbed their noses at the Volstead Act. Of course, they initially did this from a licit overseas establishment, Harry's New York Bar in Paris, where the drink was first concocted for wistful expatriates unwilling to admit they missed the States. Although these Americans brought the Scofflaw's recipe home soon after its invention, it seems this classic concoction's popularity didn't outlast the Noble Experiment.

Made with 1½ ounces each of Canadian WHISKEY and dry VERMOUTH, ½ ounce lemon juice, a hearty dash of GRENADINE, and another of ORANGE BITTERS, the Scofflaw's exacting recipe tests a mixer's patience and skill. Notable for its easy-to-swallow flavor, this cocktail is also associated with an important semantic innovation. "I was 5 when my grandfather died," Duncan MacElhone, the current proprietor of Harry's, told us. "I didn't know him that well. Men of that age and those years didn't get involved with children, but he did have a sense of humor – always trying to name his drinks and those created by his staff after what was going on in world events, which is how the Scofflaw came to be. Roosevelt spelled backward is another of Harry's cocktails."

In *The American Language*, H. L. Mencken, our favorite quotable drinker and preferred reference on our native tongue, explained that the word *scofflaw* can be traced to a contest kicked off in 1924. An article in the *Boston Herald* of January 16, 1924, reported that a local contest to coin a term for the lawless imbiber of illicit drink drew more than 25,000 entries, finally netting Henry Irving Dale and Miss Kate L. Butler $200 for their submission: "scofflaw." News of the word's acceptance traveled west quickly. By January 24, the *Chicago Tribune* was reporting: "Hardly has Boston added to the gaiety of nations by adding to *Webster's Dictionary* the opprobrious term of 'scoff-law,' when Jock, the genial manager of Harry's Bar in Paris, yesterday invented the Scoff-Law Cocktail, and it has already become exceedingly popular among American Prohibition dodgers." Even if the drink did come after the word, they were only days apart.

The word *scofflaw* has gone on to designate habitual or flagrant traffic breaches and other equally unintriguing violations. But alas, the Scofflaw cocktail – with its now archaic moniker – is best ordered by its ingredients and not by its name. On the few occasions when we have ordered it as the Scofflaw, bartenders shot us that long, annoyed look that implies we're high-maintenance clientele. When we've politely recited the recipe and waived the use of the hard-to-find orange bitters, we've been pleased to receive the Scofflaw, the subtle APÉRITIF that fares well in any season and reminds us not to judge all drinks by their names.

GLASS	TASTE COMPLEXITY	MIXING DIFFICULTY
Y	LOW ═══O═══ HIGH	LOW ═══O═══ HIGH
	DRINK ERA	
	PROHIBITION	

Scofflaw

RECIPE

1½ ounces Canadian whiskey
1½ ounces dry vermouth
½ ounce lemon juice
1 dash grenadine
1 dash orange bitters

Stir with cracked ice;
strain into chilled cocktail glass.
Garnish with a lemon wheel.

The Scofflaw cocktail is one of the best preserved drinks from the Noble Experiment, though there are a few variations on its recipe. Patrick Gavin Duffy, in his 1934 *Official Mixer's Manual*, suggests mixing the drink with any reputable rye whiskey, not necessarily Canadian. Although a seemingly slight change, the use of rye whiskey usually makes for a stronger-tasting drink and may not be to the liking of sweet-toothed imbibers.

A dollop of GRENADINE can be added to the drink after mixing to give the Scofflaw a layered look. Be careful not to add too much of this syrup, which could ruin the drink's balance.

Similar drinks include the Sazerac, the Whiskey Sour, and the Petit Zinc.

T wo parts strong, one part sweet, and one part sour: These are the golden proportions of the classic cocktail, the Pythagorean formula of bibulous bliss. If you make the strong parts BRANDY, the sweet part COINTREAU, and the sour part fresh-squeezed lemon, shake it all vigorously over ice, and serve it up with a twist, be prepared to be transported back to the days before VODKA arrived on the scene and ruined almost everything. And if you can make a brilliant Sidecar, you can make many a classic cocktail.

The Sidecar has been in full resurgence recently, meaning that versions both execrable and sublime have appeared in the bars we frequent. Out on the town, it's easy to tell if a bartender knows his or her trade by watching one prepare this libation. A neatly sugar-coated rim, a pale opacity, a biting chill off the glass, and a tartness that makes it impossible to tell where the lemon leaves off and the Cointreau begins – these are signs that you've got a live one. If you see your bartender reach for the sweet-and-sour mix, though, you're flat out of luck.

One advantage of developing an attachment to this drink is that you have at least a ten percent chance of getting one at any non-dive bar – and the odds are improving, though the quality isn't. "This cocktail is the most perfect example I know of a magnificent drink gone wrong," explained David A. Embury in *The Fine Art of Mixing Drinks*. "It was invented by a friend of mine at a bar in Paris during World War I and was named after a motorcycle sidecar in which the good captain customarily was driven to and from the little bistro where the drink was born and christened." Mr. Embury doesn't name his friend, so we can only wonder if Harry, of Harry's New York Bar in Paris, had first mixed the drink, as is quietly rumored. But even Harry's grandson, Duncan MacElhone, seems unsure, merely mentioning that "the history of the Sidecar is most confusing." So we've decided our energy's better spent researching the Sidecar's recipe instead of its past.

Few drinks boast as many variations as the Sidecar. When feeling overwhelmed by our options, we recall a bit of common sense first presented by Mr. Embury: The Sidecar is essentially a Daiquiri made with brandy and lemon in place of RUM and lime. From there, we mix – partial, as always, to this drink's classic proportions.

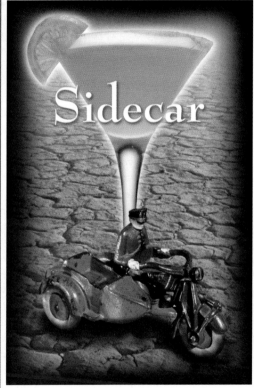

Sidecar

RECIPE

1½ ounces cognac
¾ ounce Cointreau
¾ ounce lemon juice

Shake with cracked ice;
strain into chilled cocktail glass.
Garnish with a lemon wheel.

Given its due diligence, the Sidecar can be made well by even the most inexperienced of mixers. The drink's recipe also lends itself to any other primary spirit. When apple brandy is substituted, the drink becomes the Apple Cart.

Catching up with the growing wine trade, California has recently begun to produce some very fine brandies. These brandies, though not aged as long as the very best COGNACS, show many distinct qualities that make them perfect for delicious cocktails like the Sidecar. Such distillers as Carneros Alambic Distillery, Germain Robin, and Clear Creek Distillers (Oregon) are producing spectacular spirits that you should sample the next time you're thinking of this classic.

Similar drinks include the Newton's Special and the Jack Rose.

Stinger

T his postprandial cocktail was once the oft-ordered "stengah" of turn-of-the-century watering holes. Let common sense explain how the Stinger got its name, but be advised that one poorly made will leave a mark far worse than a sting.

Always a bit leery of drinks made with CRÈME DE MENTHE, we had let this one pass us by for years. Perhaps the aversion came from Life Savers candy of the same flavor; we tried it once, and fed the dog the one-off from every package after that. But one evening a few years ago – perhaps in perverse nostalgia for that now-extinct candy flavor – we ordered a Stinger, whose ½ ounce of white crème de menthe was well-tempered by 2 ounces of BRANDY. We felt a cool gust of mint wrapped in the smoothness of good brandy.

It was a serendipitous discovery. There was a time when even Somerset Maugham, who was typically busy promoting GIN drinks, ordered this classic cocktail. Evelyn Waugh, the eccentric writer who palled around with Ian Fleming, claimed it as his signature drink.

We think of Mr. Waugh whenever we order this cocktail, knowing we'll need pluck to face down the snickers that are bound to follow our request. When legendary explorer and infamous English grouch Wilfred Thesiger heard tell of Mr. Waugh's favored drink, he sniffed, "Just the sort of affectation he would have."

When challenged, we quote the great no-frills bartender of the '20s and '30s, Patrick Gavin Duffy, who included the Stinger in his tome *The Official Mixer's Manual*. Having "rejected all those [recipes] not in the best tradition," Mr. Duffy included only those "wholesome and well concocted," not "the follies which the enactment of the 18th Amendment produced.... The youth and many adults ... took to the 'SPEAKEASY,' and gilded cabarets and the orgies which followed became more and more wild until finally those well-meaning persons who brought Prohibition on became alarmed and sought Repeal as eagerly as they had, two decades before, clamored for the 'Dry Law.'"

If we spy a bartender grabbing a bottle of the green crème de menthe instead of the white, we put a stop to our order right away. Using the garish green cordial for a Stinger can mean only one thing: The bartender's never rightly made it – or any drink like it – before. So we insist that that bottle rest until Saint Paddy's Day, when we're sure that bartender will find plenty of unsavory uses for it.

GLASS	TASTE COMPLEXITY		MIXING DIFFICULTY	
Y	LOW ═O═══ HIGH		LOW ═O═══ HIGH	
	DRINK ERA			
	GOLDEN AGE OF AMERICAN DRINKING			

RECIPE

2 ounces brandy
½ ounce white crème de menthe

Stir with cracked ice;
strain into chilled cocktail glass.
Garnish with mint sprigs and
serve with a glass of ice water.

Save the Stinger as your ace in the hole for late-night occasions when guests are wanting more, and the APÉRITIF cocktail has long run its course.

With the heavily flavored cordials of today, it's best to go very light on crème de menthe, rather than strictly following any recipe for the Stinger. Each guest's taste will vary, and after two sips they'll be able to tell you if they would prefer more or less of the cordial.

The delicate balance of any cocktail, once disrupted by an overdose of sweet (or any accent), is hard to correct. Practice the dictum "less is more," knowing that more can always be added.

Serve the Stinger with the traditional glass of water. The cold water, which shouldn't be carbonated, keeps a Stinger from tasting too heavy.

Similar drinks include the Bee's Kiss.

Tom Collins

C hances are you've already met the Collins boys. These tall troopers returned from the war as popular summer SLINGS to be ordered at any watering hole, reputable or otherwise.

The senior sibling – the Tom Collins – is made with 2 ounces of GIN, 1 ounce of lemon juice, and a teaspoon of SIMPLE SYRUP topped with soda water. Tom is the overbearing patriarch of the Collins family, which makes us sympathize with the other brother – the nearly forgotten John Collins, once made with Holland gin but now mixed with bourbon.

We've heard that the Tom Collins was named for its creator, who in turn named the John Collins after his brother. We can't argue with the common-sense appeal of this explanation, though we're not quite sold on it. As far as the Tom Collins goes, we suspect the name has more to do with the original sweet gin used, known as Old Tom gin. Collins? Well, maybe that was the bartender's surname.

Nowadays, nearly all bars pour English dry gin as a base for the Tom Collins. The original John Collins was made with the overly flavorful Holland gin, which accounted for earlier confusion over the difference between the two siblings. However, since Holland gin is often difficult to come by, English dry gin is an occasional – though incorrect – substitute, leaving a few bartenders insisting that a Tom Collins and a John Collins are identical twins. The accepted and "correct" recipe for the John Collins, as far as we're concerned, now replaces the gin with the whiskey. But whenever ordering a Collins, we always say the drink's name and call out the ingredients, too, just to be certain that we and the bartender are acquainted with the same Tom and John.

By the '50s, the Collins boys had – as some would say – married down, shedding much of these drinks' original postwar seriousness and mixing with the likes of VODKA. Soon the family expanded to include numerous cousins, like Pedro, Sandy, Mike, Brandy, and Jack, with the Singapore Sling not far behind. At this point, it's probably worth confessing that we're really not sure after which war the first Collins was created – some have proposed the Civil War, while others say it was World War I. With such a simple drink recipe, though, we can't help but believe it was concocted sooner rather than later.

On those warm late nights when we're tempted to call up Mom and Pop or some old friend for advice and comfort, we order a Tom Collins instead, knowing it's far too late to ring anyone's phone. The soothing simplicity of a Collins, with its notable citrus tang, always seems to send our mind in the right direction. So, in our typical fashion, we'll sip a drink or two and piece together the sensible thing to do.

GLASS	TASTE COMPLEXITY	MIXING DIFFICULTY
	LOW O━━━━ HIGH	LOW ━━O━ HIGH

DRINK ERA
GOTHIC AGE OF AMERICAN DRINKING

RECIPE

2 ounces gin
1 ounce lemon juice
1 teaspoon simple syrup
Soda water

Shake with cracked ice;
strain into chilled Collins glass filled with ice.
Top with soda.
Garnish with a maraschino cherry and an orange wheel.

The Collins family is large enough that there's a drink for every day of the week, thanks to the number of spirits available.

Always serve a Collins in its namesake glass or in a chimney glass, either of which holds up to 14 ounces. Their narrow design retains the effervescence of the drink. To help maintain the fizz of a Collins, use chilled soda, and never stir the drink for more than three seconds in order to minimize the release of carbon dioxide into the water.

Don't be tempted by prefab Collins mixes. These citrus-flavored concoctions are no better than carbonated Kool-Aid and are certainly not suited for cocktails.

On the East Coast, garnish with a cherry and an orange wheel, but use a cherry and a lime wheel out west.

Similar drinks include the Mojito.

Tom and Jerry

T his tepid nightcap has nothing to do with the cat-and-mouse antics that hit the big screen in the early '40s. In fact, the drink goes back to the days before Tom and Jerry were even a cat and a mouse – long before the 1931 cartoon, when the tricky rascals were a blonde and a brunette – all the way back to the racy account (on paper, not celluloid) of two rowdy Regency rogues in Pierce Egan's 1821 *Life in London*, "The Day and Night Scenes of Jerry Hawthorn, Esq., and his elegant friend Corinthian Tom, accompanied by Bob Logic, the Oxonian, in their Rambles and Sprees through the Metropolis."

Creamier and more heavy-hitting than Egg Nog (the middle-aged black sheep of the bar), the Tom and Jerry is the perfect reminder that we're only obliged to be good until the holidays, not necessarily through them. Although labor-intensive and loathed by most bartenders, we still like this drink's comforting taste and its broad-gauge use of distillations. Made with just about any ardent spirit – bourbon, rye, or BRANDY and RUM – this hot grog can be mixed in a batch with 1 egg, 1 teaspoon superfine sugar, and milk or water. On especially cold winter nights, we diligently separate the egg yolks from the whites, then beat the yolks thin and the whites thick before mixing them with sugar. Into each toasty glass we add a few dollops of the egg mix, then stir in 1½ ounces of rye, bourbon, or brandy, and then ¾ ounce of rum. We top ours with hot – not boiled – milk, and add warm water only to the cups of our weight-watching friends before dusting all the drinks with nutmeg.

Whenever our taste for this drink is questioned, we quote from *The Savoy Cocktail Book* of 1933: "The Tom and Jerry was invented by Professor Jerry Thomas – rise please – over 70 years ago, in the days when New York was the scene of the soundest drinking on earth. The Tom and Jerry and the Blue Blazer – the latter a powerful concoction of burning whiskey and boiling water – were the greatest cold weather beverages of that era."

As we sip Tom and Jerrys, we're reminded how grateful we are for the words of Mr. Egan, who wrote our favorite treatise on pugilism, calling the sport "the sweet science of bruising." According to underground London publisher John Camden Hotten of the mid-1800s, who rarely turned away a banned book, Egan's *Life in London* "was *the* book – *the* literature – of that period, the one work which many elderly gentlemen still remember far away in the distance of their youth. A tedious – and by some will be considered an absurd – composition….These were the last days of coarse caricatures, of duelling, and of the glorious three-bottle system after dinner." The book *Life in London* is now long forgotten, perhaps still stashed in the stacks of old libraries or on the shelves of nearly dead relatives. Having seen the book, we're not so bothered that it has nearly disappeared, so long as the drink and its namesake slang for loutish though endearing behavior – "Tom-and-Jerrying" – live on.

GLASS	TASTE COMPLEXITY	MIXING DIFFICULTY
🍷	LOW ⊶━━━━ HIGH	LOW ━━━⊷ HIGH
	DRINK ERA	
	GOTHIC AGE OF AMERICAN DRINKING	

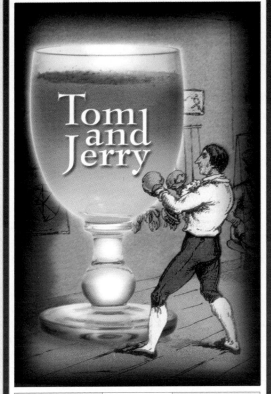

RECIPE

1½ ounces bourbon, rye, or brandy
¾ ounce rum
1 egg, chilled
1 teaspoon superfine sugar
1 dash allspice
Milk or water

Stir egg yolk, spirits, sugar, and spice in warmed mug or wine goblet; mix thoroughly. Whip egg white until it stiffens; stir into mixture. Add hot milk or water to taste, and serve. Garnish with grated nutmeg

When planning a winter holiday, keep the Tom and Jerry in mind, noting the words of Trader Vic: "A 'Thomas and Jeremiah' is as much a part of our Thanksgiving and Christmas as the noble bird itself, and it's a tradition to be honored by the best possible drink you can make." And if you come across those kitschy ceramic mugs with "Tom" and "Jerry" painted on them – the drink's traditional serving containers – by all means use them.

Vary the proportion of light and dark spirits to the tastes of your guests. But only emphasize one, so the drink will have an interesting edge. The Tom and Jerry can also be made with just one spirit, though this version tastes most like Egg Nog. Top the mix with either hot water or hot milk, or a mix of the two (most folks prefer the latter variation).

Similar drinks include Egg Nog.

Vesper

A refined aphrodisiac that's smoother than a Martini, the Vesper has a cool sting that lasts late into the night. Named by James Bond not for the canonical hour but for the favored femme fatale of *Casino Royale*, double agent Vesper Lynd, this cocktail gives its imbiber a captivating glow, particularly notable when surrounded by banal drinkers of the Martini.

In Ian Fleming's 1953 *Casino Royale*, Mr. Bond boasted of his high hopes for this drink. "The Vesper," he said. "It sounds perfect and it's very appropriate to the violet hour when my cocktail will now be drunk all over the world." But the drink never made it that far. Vesper killed herself, and Mr. Bond never sipped that cocktail again, though such fine establishments as the Rainbow Room in New York and numerous Ritz-Carltons are doing their best to revive it.

Notoriously particular about his drinks, Mr. Bond ordered Vespers with precision: "In a deep champagne goblet....Three measures of Gordon's, one of VODKA, half a measure of Kina LILLET. Shake it very well until it's ice-cold, then add a large thin slice of lemon-peel." We actually prefer mixologist Dale Degroff's take on the Vesper, as bartenders too easily influenced by the presumed habits of Agent 007 tend to be heavy-handed with the vodka. At the Rainbow Room, Mr. Degroff's bartenders never skimp on the Vesper's GIN, which is decidedly Gordon's London Dry. They garnish with an orange peel to better highlight the blonde Lillet, and serve the drink in a traditional cocktail glass.

No one – not even Gilberto Preti, the Vesper's inventor and London's renowned mixologist – is certain why the drink's recipe demanded vodka, though presumably the fair maiden's Russian sympathies had something to do with it. But as Mr. Degroff points out, the vodka probably wouldn't be missed if ignored: "Let's face it – vodka is an odorless, tasteless liquid." Nonetheless, we leave the Vesper's tradition and key ingredients intact.

Thanks to the sugarcoated espionage of the movie *Casino Royale* – which completely sidesteps both Vesper's drink and her suicide – there are thousands of James Bond fans who, never having read the book, believe the Vesper is the "James Bond Martini." Mr. Bond sipped several renderings of the Martini, including one involving Roquefort cheese. So we leave nothing to chance and always use the drink's given name. Of course, had the drink been named after one of Mr. Bond's more knavish sirens – say, Pussy Galore – we might handle things differently.

We never have just one Vesper, though we don't doubt its power, which nearly got the best of Mr. Bond when he almost proposed to the ill-fated Vesper. "Like all harsh, cold men," wrote Mr. Fleming of Her Majesty's spy, "he was easily tipped over into sentiment." When drinking Vespers, we keep that in mind.

GLASS	TASTE COMPLEXITY	MIXING DIFFICULTY
Y	LOW ══O══ HIGH	LOW ══O══ HIGH
	DRINK ERA	
	ERA OF THE RAT PACK	

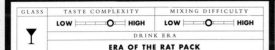

Vesper

RECIPE

2 ounces gin
1 ounce vodka
½ ounce Lillet blonde

Stir with cracked ice;
strain into chilled cocktail glass.
Garnish with an orange wheel.

We usually steer clear of James Bond's 13 commandments (as laid out by Ian Fleming), but there's one rule we follow: "See the brand-name on the bottle." We are, however, uncertain what to make of the decree, "Don't waste your time on women who wear a bracelet on their left ankle."

Easy to make, the Vesper is best varied by the amount of Lillet used. For more citrus flavor, snap an orange zest in the drink. For a slight show, break the twist over an open flame before dropping it into a Vesper. Certain to appeal to pyromaniacs – and to Mr. Bond himself – a drink with this functional garnish is rarely resisted.

Similar drinks include the Martini, the Martinez, and the Leap Year.

Ward Eight

T he ravages of natural selection have left us with only a few dozen recipes unspoiled by the meddlings of time. Selective breeding by liquor companies and society's fickle tastes have created many concoctions that are best avoided. But just as Darwin came across the Galápagos Islands, we've discovered a classic cocktail that's survived unaltered – the Ward Eight.

Back in 1898, mixologist Tom Hussion joined Boston's downtown Locke-Ober Café. For a little perspective on this fine establishment, we quote from Ogden Nash: "A trip to Boston without visiting Locke-Ober is like a trip to Agra without visiting the Taj Mahal." According to Lance Barbakow, manager of the modern-day Locke-Ober, Mr. Hussion attracted a loyal crowd at the bar, particularly members of the Hendrick's Club, the political organization of Democrat Martin Lomasney. In the fall of that year, Lomasney was vying to be the representative from Ward Eight in the Massachusetts General Court. The night before the election, a group of Hendrick's Club cronies collected at the bar and requested that Mr. Hussion create a new drink to toast the next day's hoped-for victory. Well aware of his customers' staid desires, no matter how wildly expressed, Hussion merely added a teaspoon of GRENA-DINE to a WHISKEY sour (three parts bourbon to one part each orange and lemon juice) and christened it the Ward Eight.

One sad irony, though: Lomasney, an ardent prohibitionist, did win the election, and when the drought hit, helped dry out the Boston area. The owner of the Locke-Ober – who begrudgingly honored PROHIBITION – closed the bar area of the establishment until the early 1950s, when the Ward Eight returned with little of its history intact. Most imbibers by that time merely assumed the name stemmed from the belief that too many iterations of this drink would send you to the eighth ward of the hospital – i.e., the nuthouse. To confuse matters even further, a whiskey sour with grenadine had surfaced elsewhere in the country, though under the name Scottish Guard's Cocktail. The Ward Eight did at least weather Prohibition well, and in 1934, the drink was deemed one of the best cocktails of the year by *Esquire*.

We credit the grenadine with this drink's longevity and its noted ability to put its imbiber in the winner's circle. The whiskey, first tempered by the orange juice and then teased by the lemon, improves confidence but slights one's disposition. A teaspoon of grenadine is just enough to soften the whiskey's bite – along with any cheekiness brought on by victory or drink.

COCKTAIL

GLASS	TASTE COMPLEXITY	MIXING DIFFICULTY
Y	LOW ⊙ HIGH	LOW ⊙ HIGH
	DRINK ERA	
	GOLDEN AGE OF AMERICAN DRINKING	

RECIPE

2 ounces bourbon
½ ounce lemon juice
½ ounce orange juice
1 teaspoon grenadine

Shake with cracked ice;
strain into chilled cocktail glass.
Garnish with a lemon wheel.

Most grenadine brands today come about as close to the original flavor of their classic predecessors as a Miata does to the style of the Austin-Healey.

Grenadine syrup – originally made from sweetened pomegranate juice – used to add more than just a rosy glow and a sweet finish to a drink. Modern grenadine may share the same sanguine color as yesterday's brands, but it adds little to a drink.

Whenever possible, use French grenadine, which is much drier than other types. If high-quality grenadine is unavailable, use the syrup only as coloring and sweetener, not as a flavor enhancer. If you desire an added dimension in your cocktail, try substituting another syrup, such as raspberry, strawberry, or cassis.

Similar drinks include the Whiskey Sour.

Zombie

O n occasions when we need to break the bonds of banality, we order a Zombie without guilt and without regard for the bartender's sneer. With a name drawn from the root of the West African Kongo word for *fetish*, the Zombie rouses us to contemplate bacchanalian behavior without threatening us with unwise inspiration.

There have been hundreds of resurrections of the Zombie's recipe. Some include COGNAC, while others are enlivened by apricot BRANDY. All, however, require RUM, the presumed source of the drink's sorcery. Best made with 1½ ounces of brown rum, ¾ ounce each of Jamaican dark rum, light rum, pineapple juice, and papaya juice, and an ounce of lime juice, followed by a float of 151-PROOF Demerara rum, the Zombie goes down far too smoothly considering all that it contains. We're far from certain which version came first and who might have made it. Most reports point to Ernest Raymond Beaumont-Gannt, an enterprising fellow who changed his name to Don Beach after opening the Hollywood restaurant Don the Beachcomber in the late '30s. During the same decade and in the same restaurant – so the story goes – Mr. Beach greeted a patron still suffering from the alcohol-based indiscretions of the night before. In hopes of curing the man's hangover, he mixed a drink that seemed to lift the imbiber's spirits. Returning to the bar later, the man was asked how he had liked the drink, to which he replied that it had transformed him into a member of the living dead. From that remark came the drink's name.

There's another creation story that we much prefer. "A Zombie … has been called back from the Spirit World, labours without pay, without food, without complaint, in a weird sort of spirit bondage," wrote Charles H. Baker in 1946. "Christopher Clark, from a five months' stay in Cap Haitian, … brought back … this Zombie cocktail, claiming that it will put the spirits to work for you, but whether they or ourselves are in bondage is something for each man to decide according to occasion and the needs thereof." Mr. Baker goes on to explain that the original Zombie's recipe was recorded in 1935: "The high-proof, so-called Zombie known to most bar men did not raise its dizzy head until two years, or better, later."

But there is a third notable creation tale for this mixed drink: "At the 1939 World's Fair in Flushing, New York, the supertechnologized 'world of tomorrow' stood before thousands of patrons," wrote Joseph Lanza in *The Cocktail: The Influence of Spirits on the American Psyche*. "But anyone looking for a high-tech escape from streamlined excess had only to take refuge in the Hurricane Bar, where a new cocktail was introduced to the world: the Zombie." We truly doubt there's much refuge to be found in a Zombie. But when we contemplate drinks of the same ilk – particularly the Viscous Virgin and the Missionary's Downfall, both created by Don Beach of Don the Beachcomber fame – we're convinced that sipping one every now and again really can't be all that bad. Unless, of course, we want it to be.

GLASS	TASTE COMPLEXITY	MIXING DIFFICULTY
	LOW ═══○═══ HIGH	LOW ═══○═══ HIGH
	DRINK ERA	
	YEARS OF REFORM	

Zombie

The Zombie's recipe is complicated to remember, but impossible to ruin. Follow the base recipe and alter it as you see fit, confident that such a sweet drink won't reflect poorly on your skills.

Just as the Planter's Punch isn't really a punch, the Zombie isn't really a cocktail. So if the convenience of punch would better suit the size of your gathering, serve it as such.

For a crowd pleaser, dim the room's lights and float 151 Demerara rum on top of the punch. Have the crowd stand back, then light the high-proof liquor with a fireplace matchstick. (Anything shorter and you'll burn the hair off your knuckles.) Don't assume there's no flame just because you can't see one: Make certain that the flame has gone out before serving or allowing your guests to take a taste.

Similar drinks include the Singapore Sling.

RECIPE

1½ ounces brown rum
¾ ounce Jamaican dark rum
¾ ounce light rum
¾ ounce pineapple juice
¾ ounce papaya juice
1 ounce lime juice
¼ ounce simple syrup

Shake with ice; strain into chilled tumbler or hurricane glass. Garnish with a pineapple wheel and a cherry. Float Demerara rum and sprinkle powdered sugar on top.

THREE

Drink Recipes

GIN
BASE

ABBEY

TASTE COMPLEXITY		MIXING DIFFICULTY
LOW ===O=== HIGH	Y	LOW ===O=== HIGH

2 ounces gin
1 dash sweet vermouth
1 ounce orange juice
1 dash Angostura bitters

Shake with cracked ice;
strain into chilled cocktail glass.
Garnish with a maraschino cherry.

• AVIATION •

TASTE COMPLEXITY		MIXING DIFFICULTY
LOW =O=== HIGH	Y	LOW ===O=== HIGH

1½ ounces gin
½ ounce maraschino liqueur
¾ ounce lemon juice

Shake with cracked ice;
strain into chilled cocktail glass.
Garnish with a maraschino cherry
or a lemon twist.

ALEXANDER

TASTE COMPLEXITY		MIXING DIFFICULTY
LOW O=== HIGH	♦	LOW O=== HIGH

¾ ounce gin
¾ ounce crème de cacao
¾ ounce cream

Shake with cracked ice;
strain into chilled snifter.
Grate nutmeg on top.

BEE'S KNEES

TASTE COMPLEXITY		MIXING DIFFICULTY
LOW =O=== HIGH	Y	LOW ===O=== HIGH

2 ounces gin
½ ounce lime juice
1 barspoon honey

Shake with cracked ice;
strain into chilled cocktail glass.
Garnish with a lemon wheel.

• ASTORIA •

TASTE COMPLEXITY		MIXING DIFFICULTY
LOW ===O=== HIGH	Y	LOW ===O=== HIGH

2 ounces gin
½ ounce dry vermouth
1 dash orange bitters

Shake with cracked ice;
strain into chilled cocktail glass.
Garnish with a twist of
orange or lemon.

BEL-AIRE

TASTE COMPLEXITY		MIXING DIFFICULTY
LOW =O=== HIGH	Y	LOW O=== HIGH

1 ounce gin
1 ounce sweet vermouth
2 dashes curaçao

Shake with crushed ice;
strain into chilled cocktail glass.
Garnish with an orange twist.

BENNETT

TASTE COMPLEXITY		MIXING DIFFICULTY
LOW ⊢━━O━━⊣ HIGH	Y	LOW ⊢━O━━━⊣ HIGH

2 ounces gin
½ ounce lime juice
2 dashes Angostura bitters
½ teaspoon simple syrup

Shake with crushed ice;
strain into chilled cocktail glass.
Garnish with a lime squeeze.

BLUE DEVIL

TASTE COMPLEXITY		MIXING DIFFICULTY
LOW O━━━━⊣ HIGH	Y	LOW ⊢━━O━━⊣ HIGH

2 ounces gin
½ ounce maraschino liqueur
½ ounce lime juice
1 dash blue vegetable coloring

Shake with cracked ice;
strain into chilled cocktail glass.
Garnish with a maraschino cherry.

BERMUDA

TASTE COMPLEXITY		MIXING DIFFICULTY
LOW ⊢O━━━━⊣ HIGH	Y	LOW O━━━━⊣ HIGH

1½ ounces gin
½ ounce peach brandy
½ ounce lemon juice
2 dashes orange juice
1 dash grenadine

Shake with crushed ice;
strain into chilled cocktail glass.
Garnish with a maraschino cherry.

BLUE FLYER COCKTAIL (BLUE TRAIN)

TASTE COMPLEXITY		MIXING DIFFICULTY
LOW O━━━━⊣ HIGH	Y	LOW O━━━━⊣ HIGH

2 ounces gin
½ ounce Cointreau
½ ounce lime juice
1 dash blue vegetable coloring

Shake with cracked ice;
strain into chilled cocktail glass.
Garnish with a lemon twist.

BITTER

TASTE COMPLEXITY		MIXING DIFFICULTY
LOW ⊢━━━━O HIGH	Y	LOW ⊢━━━O━⊣ HIGH

1½ ounces gin
½ ounce green Chartreuse
½ ounce lemon juice
1 dash Pernod

Shake with cracked ice;
strain into chilled cocktail glass.
Garnish with a lemon twist.

* BRONX *

TASTE COMPLEXITY		MIXING DIFFICULTY
LOW ⊢━━━O━⊣ HIGH	Y	LOW ⊢━━━O━⊣ HIGH

1 ounce gin
½ ounce sweet vermouth
½ ounce dry vermouth
1 ounce orange juice

Shake with cracked ice;
strain into chilled cocktail glass.
Garnish with a maraschino cherry
or an orange wheel.

BRONX RIVER

TASTE COMPLEXITY		MIXING DIFFICULTY
LOW ⊢—O—⊣ HIGH		LOW ⊢—O—⊣ HIGH

2 ounces gin
½ ounce sweet vermouth
¼ ounce lemon juice
1 dash simple syrup

Shake with cracked ice;
strain into chilled cocktail glass.
Garnish with a lemon wheel.

* CLOVER CLUB *

TASTE COMPLEXITY		MIXING DIFFICULTY
LOW O—⊣ HIGH		LOW ⊢—O—⊣ HIGH

2 ounces gin
1 ounce lemon juice
¼ ounce grenadine or raspberry syrup
2 teaspoons egg white

Shake with cracked ice;
strain into chilled
wine goblet or cocktail glass.
Garnish with a lemon wheel.

BRONX TERRACE

TASTE COMPLEXITY		MIXING DIFFICULTY
LOW ⊢—O—⊣ HIGH		LOW ⊢—O—⊣ HIGH

1½ ounces gin
¾ ounce dry vermouth
¾ ounce lime juice

Shake with cracked ice;
strain into chilled cocktail glass.
Garnish with a lime twist.

COCKNEY

TASTE COMPLEXITY		MIXING DIFFICULTY
LOW ⊢—O—⊣ HIGH		LOW ⊢—O—⊣ HIGH

¾ ounce gin
½ teaspoon lemon juice
½ teaspoon simple syrup
Champagne

Shake gin, lemon, and simple syrup
with cracked ice;
strain into chilled cocktail glass.
Top with chilled champagne, and
garnish with a lemon twist.

CHINATOWN

TASTE COMPLEXITY		MIXING DIFFICULTY
LOW ⊢—————O HIGH		LOW ⊢—O—⊣ HIGH

¾ ounce gin
¾ ounce dry vermouth
¾ ounce sweet vermouth
1 dash brandy

Shake with cracked ice;
strain into chilled cocktail glass.
Garnish with a lemon twist
or a maraschino cherry.

DELILAH

TASTE COMPLEXITY		MIXING DIFFICULTY
LOW O—⊣ HIGH		LOW ⊢—O—⊣ HIGH

1½ ounces gin
¾ ounce Cointreau
¾ ounce lemon juice

Shake with cracked ice;
strain into chilled cocktail glass.
Garnish with lemon squeeze.

DO BE CAREFUL

TASTE COMPLEXITY	MIXING DIFFICULTY
LOW ⊶——— HIGH	LOW ——⊙—— HIGH

1½ ounces gin
¾ ounce Cointreau
¾ ounce lemon juice
1 dash grenadine

Shake with fine ice;
strain into chilled cocktail glass.
Garnish with a maraschino cherry.

DUPLEX

TASTE COMPLEXITY	MIXING DIFFICULTY
LOW ——⊙— HIGH	LOW —⊙—— HIGH

1½ ounces gin
¼ ounce sweet vermouth
¼ ounce dry vermouth
¼ ounce lemon juice
2 dashes orange bitters

Shake with cracked ice;
strain into chilled cocktail glass.
Garnish with a lemon twist.

183

DOM

TASTE COMPLEXITY	MIXING DIFFICULTY
LOW ———⊙ HIGH	LOW ——⊙— HIGH

1½ ounces gin
½ ounce orange juice
1 drop Bénédictine

Shake with cracked ice;
strain into chilled cocktail glass.
Garnish with an orange twist.

ELEGANT, NUMBER ONE

TASTE COMPLEXITY	MIXING DIFFICULTY
LOW ———⊙ HIGH	LOW ——⊙— HIGH

1½ ounces gin
¾ ounce dry vermouth
1 dash Grand Marnier

Stir with cracked ice;
strain into chilled cocktail glass.
Garnish with a lemon squeeze.

DOUBLE DRY MARTINI

TASTE COMPLEXITY	MIXING DIFFICULTY
LOW ——⊙— HIGH	LOW ——⊙— HIGH

2 ounces gin
¼ ounce fino sherry

Stir with cracked ice;
strain into chilled cocktail glass.
Garnish with a lemon twist.

EMERALD MARTINI

TASTE COMPLEXITY	MIXING DIFFICULTY
LOW ———⊙ HIGH	LOW ———⊙ HIGH

1½ ounces gin
½ ounce dry vermouth
1 dash Chartreuse

Stir with cracked ice;
strain into chilled cocktail glass.
Garnish with a lemon twist.

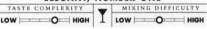

GENEVER

TASTE COMPLEXITY		MIXING DIFFICULTY
LOW ⊩——————O⊣ HIGH		LOW ⊩——O⊣—————⊣ HIGH

2 ounces Genever gin
2 dashes Angostura bitters

Shake with cracked ice;
strain into chilled cocktail glass.
Garnish with a twist or nothing at all.

GIN & BITTERS

TASTE COMPLEXITY		MIXING DIFFICULTY
LOW ⊩——————O⊣ HIGH		LOW ⊩O⊣—————————⊣ HIGH

2 ounces gin
Angostura bitters to taste

Shake with cracked ice;
strain into chilled cocktail glass.
Garnish with a lemon twist.

• GIBSON •

TASTE COMPLEXITY		MIXING DIFFICULTY
LOW ⊩——O⊣————⊣ HIGH		LOW ⊩———O⊣———⊣ HIGH

2½ ounces gin
½ ounce dry vermouth

Stir with cracked ice;
strain into chilled cocktail glass.
Garnish with a cocktail onion.

GIN BUCK

TASTE COMPLEXITY		MIXING DIFFICULTY
LOW ⊩—O⊣————⊣ HIGH		LOW ⊩O⊣—————————⊣ HIGH

1½ ounces gin
2 quarter sections of lime
Ginger ale

Muddle lime with its hull in chilled highball
glass; add cracked ice and gin.
Stir and top with ginger ale.

• GIMLET •

TASTE COMPLEXITY		MIXING DIFFICULTY
LOW ⊩—O⊣—————⊣ HIGH		LOW ⊩O⊣—————————⊣ HIGH

2¼ ounces gin
¾ ounce Rose's lime juice

Stir with cracked ice;
strain into chilled cocktail glass.
Garnish with a lime squeeze.
Variations: Add ¼ ounce more Rose's and/or
a dash of bitters. Primary spirits
like tequila, rum, and vodka
may be substituted for the gin.

GIN FIZZ

TASTE COMPLEXITY		MIXING DIFFICULTY
LOW ⊩—O⊣—————⊣ HIGH		LOW ⊩—O⊣—————⊣ HIGH

2 ounces gin
1 ounce lemon juice
½ ounce simple syrup
Soda water

Shake gin, juice, and syrup with cracked ice;
strain into chilled wine glass.
Top with chilled soda water, and
garnish with a lemon twist.

GIN RICKEY

TASTE COMPLEXITY		MIXING DIFFICULTY	
LOW	HIGH	LOW	HIGH

1½ ounces gin
¾ ounce lime juice
Soda water

Shake gin and juice with cracked ice;
strain into chilled Collins glass
filled with ice. Top with soda water, and
garnish with a lime squeeze.

* LEAP YEAR *

TASTE COMPLEXITY		MIXING DIFFICULTY	
LOW	HIGH	LOW	HIGH

2 ounces gin
½ ounce sweet vermouth
½ ounce Grand Marnier
¼ ounce lemon juice

Shake with cracked ice,
strain into chilled cocktail glass.
Garnish with a twist of
lemon or orange.

JACK DEMPSEY

TASTE COMPLEXITY		MIXING DIFFICULTY	
LOW	HIGH	LOW	HIGH

1 ounce gin
½ ounce light rum
¾ ounce lemon juice
¼ ounce simple syrup

Shake with cracked ice;
strain into chilled cocktail glass.
Garnish with a lemon wheel.

LONDON FOG

TASTE COMPLEXITY		MIXING DIFFICULTY	
LOW	HIGH	LOW	HIGH

2 ounces gin
¼ ounce Pernod

Shake with cracked ice;
strain into chilled wine glass
packed with shaved ice.

* JASMINE *

TASTE COMPLEXITY		MIXING DIFFICULTY	
LOW	HIGH	LOW	HIGH

1½ ounces gin
¼ ounce Cointreau
¼ ounce Campari
¾ ounce lemon juice

Shake with cracked ice;
strain into chilled cocktail glass.
Garnish with a lemon twist.

A Paul Harrington original

* MAIDEN'S PRAYER (BETWEEN THE SHEETS) *

TASTE COMPLEXITY		MIXING DIFFICULTY	
LOW	HIGH	LOW	HIGH

¾ ounce gin
¾ ounce light rum
¾ ounce Cointreau
¾ ounce lemon juice

Shake with crushed ice;
strain into chilled
wine goblet or cocktail glass.
Garnish with a lemon twist
or a flower blossom.

MARTINEZ

TASTE COMPLEXITY		MIXING DIFFICULTY
LOW ⊢───O───┤ HIGH	Y	LOW ⊢────O─┤ HIGH

1 ounce gin
¾ ounce dry vermouth
¼ ounce Cointreau
2 dashes Angostura bitters

Shake with cracked ice;
strain into chilled cocktail glass.
Garnish with a lemon twist.

* MARTINI (DRY) *

TASTE COMPLEXITY		MIXING DIFFICULTY
LOW ⊢────O─┤ HIGH	Y	LOW ⊢────O─┤ HIGH

3 ounces gin
½ ounce dry vermouth

Stir with cracked ice;
strain into chilled cocktail glass.
Garnish with a lemon twist or an olive.

MARTINI (CLASSIC)

TASTE COMPLEXITY		MIXING DIFFICULTY
LOW ⊢───O───┤ HIGH	Y	LOW ⊢────O─┤ HIGH

2 ounces gin
½ ounce dry vermouth

Stir with cracked ice;
strain into chilled cocktail glass.
Garnish with an olive.

MARTINI (PERFECT)

2 ounces gin
½ ounce sweet vermouth
½ ounce dry vermouth
1 dash orange bitters

Stir with cracked ice,
strain into chilled cocktail glass.
Garnish with a lemon twist.

MARTINI (DIRTY)

2½ ounces gin
½ ounce olive brine
1 dash dry vermouth

Stir with cracked ice;
strain into chilled cocktail glass.
Garnish with an olive.

MARTINI (WET)

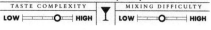

1¼ ounces gin
1¼ ounces dry vermouth

Stir with cracked ice;
strain into chilled cocktail glass.
Garnish with a lemon twist or an olive.

MISTER MANHATTAN

TASTE COMPLEXITY		MIXING DIFFICULTY
LOW ⊢⊢O⊢⊢ HIGH	Y	LOW ⊢⊢⊢⊢O HIGH

1½ ounces gin
¼ ounce lemon juice
½ ounce orange juice
1 teaspoon sugar
4 mint leaves

Crush sugar with a dash of charged water in
mixing glass; muddle with mint leaves.
Add remaining ingredients. Shake with
cracked ice; strain into chilled cocktail glass.
Garnish with a mint sprig.

MULE

TASTE COMPLEXITY		MIXING DIFFICULTY
LOW O⊢⊢⊢ HIGH	Y	LOW ⊢O⊢⊢ HIGH

1 ounce gin
¾ ounce crème de cassis
¾ ounce lemon juice

Shake with cracked ice;
strain into chilled cocktail glass.
Garnish with a lemon squeeze.

187

MOLLY PICON

TASTE COMPLEXITY		MIXING DIFFICULTY
LOW ⊢⊢⊢O HIGH	Y	LOW ⊢⊢⊢O HIGH

1 ounce gin
1 ounce Amer Picon
1 ounce sweet vermouth

Shake with cracked ice;
strain into chilled cocktail glass.
Garnish with a lemon twist.

THE OLD WALDORF'S LAST

TASTE COMPLEXITY		MIXING DIFFICULTY
LOW ⊢⊢O⊢⊢ HIGH	Y	LOW ⊢O⊢⊢ HIGH

1 ounce gin
1 ounce curaçao
1 ounce cream

Shake with cracked ice;
strain into chilled cocktail glass.
Garnish with an orange wheel.

* MONKEY GLAND *

TASTE COMPLEXITY		MIXING DIFFICULTY
LOW ⊢⊢⊢O HIGH	Y	LOW ⊢⊢O⊢ HIGH

1½ ounces gin
1½ ounces orange juice
1 dash anis
¼ ounce grenadine

Shake with cracked ice;
strain into chilled cocktail glass.
Garnish with an orange twist.

ONE SPOT

TASTE COMPLEXITY		MIXING DIFFICULTY
LOW ⊢⊢⊢O HIGH	Y	LOW ⊢⊢O⊢ HIGH

2 ounces gin
½ ounce Pernod
¼ ounce lemon juice
2 drops Angostura bitters

Shake with cracked ice;
strain into chilled cocktail glass.
Garnish with a lemon twist.

OPERA

TASTE COMPLEXITY		MIXING DIFFICULTY
LOW ⟜O⟜ HIGH		LOW ⟜O⟜ HIGH

2 ounces gin
½ ounce Dubonnet
¼ ounce maraschino liqueur
1 dash orange bitters

Shake with cracked ice;
strain into chilled cocktail glass.
Garnish with a lemon twist.

* PEGU *

TASTE COMPLEXITY		MIXING DIFFICULTY
LOW ⟜O⟜ HIGH		LOW ⟜O⟜ HIGH

1½ ounces gin
½ ounce Cointreau
½ ounce lime juice
2 dashes Angostura bitters

Stir with cracked ice;
strain into chilled cocktail glass.
Garnish with a lime twist.

ORANGE BLOOM

TASTE COMPLEXITY		MIXING DIFFICULTY
LOW O⟜ HIGH		LOW O⟜ HIGH

1½ ounces gin
½ ounce Cointreau
1 ounce orange juice

Shake with cracked ice;
strain into a cocktail glass.
Garnish with an orange wheel.

PENDENNIS

TASTE COMPLEXITY		MIXING DIFFICULTY
LOW ⟜O⟜ HIGH		LOW ⟜O⟜ HIGH

1½ ounces gin
½ ounce apricot brandy
½ ounce lime juice
1 dash Peychaud's bitters

Shake with cracked ice;
strain into chilled cocktail glass.
Garnish with a lime wheel.

ORANGE BLOSSOM

TASTE COMPLEXITY		MIXING DIFFICULTY
LOW O⟜ HIGH		LOW ⟜O⟜ HIGH

1½ ounces gin
1¾ ounces orange juice
1 dash orange flower water

Shake with cracked ice;
strain into chilled cocktail glass.
Garnish with an orange wheel.

* PINK GIN *

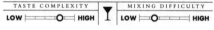

TASTE COMPLEXITY		MIXING DIFFICULTY
LOW ⟜O⟜ HIGH		LOW ⟜O⟜ HIGH

3 ounces gin
2 dashes Angostura bitters

Shake with cracked ice;
strain into chilled cocktail glass.
Garnish with a lemon twist
or a lime squeeze.

PINK ROSE

TASTE COMPLEXITY		MIXING DIFFICULTY
LOW ◦━━━━ HIGH		LOW ━━◦━━ HIGH

1 ounce gin
¼ ounce grenadine
½ ounce lemon juice
1 teaspoon cream
1 egg white

Shake with cracked ice;
strain into chilled cocktail glass.
Garnish with a lemon squeeze.

SATAN'S WHISKERS (CURLED)

TASTE COMPLEXITY		MIXING DIFFICULTY
LOW ━◦━━ HIGH		LOW ━━━◦━ HIGH

¾ ounce gin
¾ ounce dry vermouth
¾ ounce sweet vermouth
½ ounce orange juice
½ ounce orange curaçao
1 dash orange bitters

189

Shake with cracked ice;
strain into chilled cocktail glass.
Garnish with an orange twist.

QUEEN ELIZABETH

TASTE COMPLEXITY		MIXING DIFFICULTY
LOW ━━━◦ HIGH		LOW ━━━◦ HIGH

2 ounces gin
¼ ounce Cointreau
½ ounce lemon juice
1 dash Pernod

Shake with cracked ice;
strain into chilled cocktail glass.
Garnish with a lemon twist.

* SATAN'S WHISKERS (STRAIGHT) *

TASTE COMPLEXITY		MIXING DIFFICULTY
LOW ━━━◦ HIGH		LOW ━━━◦ HIGH

¾ ounce gin
¾ ounce dry vermouth
¾ ounce sweet vermouth
½ ounce orange juice
½ ounce Grand Marnier
1 dash orange bitters

Shake with cracked ice;
strain into chilled cocktail glass.
Garnish with an orange twist.

* RED SNAPPER *

TASTE COMPLEXITY		MIXING DIFFICULTY
LOW ━━◦━━ HIGH		LOW ━━◦━━ HIGH

2 ounces gin
4 ounces tomato juice
½ ounce lemon juice
1 to 2 pinches salt and pepper
2 to 3 dashes Worcestershire sauce
2 to 3 drops Tabasco sauce

Shake first four ingredients with cracked ice;
strain into chilled 16-ounce glass filled with ice.
Stir in Worcestershire, Tabasco, salt and pepper.
Garnish with a celery stalk and a lemon wheel.

SAVOY

TASTE COMPLEXITY		MIXING DIFFICULTY
LOW ━━━◦ HIGH		LOW ━◦━━ HIGH

1½ ounces gin
½ ounce dry vermouth
2 dashes Dubonnet

Stir with cracked ice;
strain into chilled cocktail glass.
Garnish with an orange twist.

Inspired by The Savoy Cocktail Book, *1930*

SAVOY HOTEL SPECIAL

TASTE COMPLEXITY	MIXING DIFFICULTY
LOW ⊢──○── HIGH	LOW ⊢───○── HIGH

2 ounces gin
½ ounce dry vermouth
2 dashes grenadine
1 dash Pernod

Stir with cracked ice;
strain into chilled cocktail glass.
Garnish with a lemon twist.

Inspired by The Savoy Cocktail Book, *1930*

SENSATION

TASTE COMPLEXITY	MIXING DIFFICULTY
LOW ⊢─○─── HIGH	LOW ⊢───○── HIGH

1½ ounces gin
¼ ounce maraschino liqueur
½ ounce lemon juice
3 mint sprigs

Shake with cracked ice;
strain into chilled cocktail glass.
Garnish with a mint sprig.

TEXAS FIZZ

TASTE COMPLEXITY	MIXING DIFFICULTY
LOW ⊢─○─── HIGH	LOW ⊢─○──── HIGH

1 ounce gin
½ ounce orange juice
¼ ounce lemon juice
¼ ounce grenadine
Soda water

Shake gin, juices, and grenadine with
cracked ice; strain into chilled wine glass.
Top with soda water, and
garnish with a lemon twist and
a maraschino cherry.

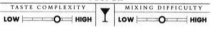

• TOM COLLINS •

TASTE COMPLEXITY	MIXING DIFFICULTY
LOW ○───── HIGH	LOW ⊢───○── HIGH

2 ounces gin
1 ounce lemon juice
1 teaspoon simple syrup
Soda water

Shake with cracked ice;
strain into chilled Collins glass filled with ice.
Top with soda water.
Garnish with a maraschino cherry and
orange wheel.

• VESPER •

TASTE COMPLEXITY	MIXING DIFFICULTY
LOW ⊢───○── HIGH	LOW ⊢──○─── HIGH

2 ounces gin
1 ounce vodka
½ ounce Lillet blonde

Stir with cracked ice;
strain into chilled cocktail glass.
Garnish with an orange wheel.

ZAZA

TASTE COMPLEXITY	MIXING DIFFICULTY
LOW ⊢──○─── HIGH	LOW ⊢─○──── HIGH

1½ ounces gin
1½ ounces Dubonnet Rouge

Shake with cracked ice;
strain into chilled cocktail glass.
Garnish with a lemon twist.

ADELLE SPECIAL

TASTE COMPLEXITY		MIXING DIFFICULTY
LOW ⊢━O━━━┤ HIGH		LOW ⊢━━O━━┤ HIGH

1½ ounces scotch
1 ounce orange curaçao

Stir with cracked ice;
strain into chilled tumbler filled with ice.
Garnish with a lemon or an orange twist.

APPETIZER

TASTE COMPLEXITY		MIXING DIFFICULTY
LOW ⊢━━━O━┤ HIGH		LOW ⊢━━O━━┤ HIGH

2 ounces rye
3 dashes Cointreau
2 dashes Peychaud's bitters
1 orange
1 lemon

Shake with the hull of an orange and a
lemon with cracked ice;
strain into chilled cocktail glass.
Garnish with a lemon twist.

AFFINITY

TASTE COMPLEXITY		MIXING DIFFICULTY
LOW ⊢━━━O━┤ HIGH		LOW ⊢━O━━━┤ HIGH

¾ ounce scotch
¾ ounce dry vermouth
¾ ounce sweet vermouth
2 dashes Angostura bitters

Shake with cracked ice;
strain into chilled cocktail glass.
Garnish with a lemon twist.

BIANCO

TASTE COMPLEXITY		MIXING DIFFICULTY
LOW ⊢━━━O━┤ HIGH		LOW ⊢━O━━━┤ HIGH

2 ounces bourbon
1 ounce dry vermouth
2 dashes Angostura bitters

Shake with cracked ice;
strain into chilled cocktail glass.
Garnish with a lemon twist.

ALGONQUIN

TASTE COMPLEXITY		MIXING DIFFICULTY
LOW ⊢━O━━━┤ HIGH		LOW ⊢O━━━━┤ HIGH

2 ounces rye
1 ounce dry vermouth
1 ounce pineapple juice

Shake with cracked ice;
strain into chilled cocktail glass.
Garnish with a maraschino cherry.
This drink is sometimes referred to
as the Adirondack Special or the Florida.

BLARNEY

TASTE COMPLEXITY		MIXING DIFFICULTY
LOW ⊢━━O━━┤ HIGH		LOW ⊢━━O━━┤ HIGH

2 ounces Irish whiskey
1 ounce sweet vermouth

Stir with cracked ice;
strain into chilled cocktail glass.
Garnish with a maraschino cherry.

* BLUE BLAZER *

TASTE COMPLEXITY		MIXING DIFFICULTY
LOW ▭▭▭O▭ HIGH		LOW ▭▭▭▭▭O HIGH

4 ounces scotch
4 ounces boiling water
2 teaspoons honey or 2 sugar cubes

For the flaming version of the Blue Blazer,
use 16-ounce mixing tins
or Pyrex pitchers with hefty handles.
Mix 2 teaspoons honey with 4 ounces
water; boil the mixture. (If sugar cubes
are used, drop into the drink right
before serving.) Simmer 4 ounces scotch
in a chafing dish; ignite.
Once the water-and-honey mixture
and the whiskey are ready, pour each
into a mixing container.
Place a fire-resistant covering over
the mixing area and dim the lights.
Pour from one container into
the other until the flame burns out.
Portion the drinks into two thick cut-glass
tumblers that won't crack from the heat.
Let the Blazer cool slightly before drinking.
For a short cut, follow the above
instructions but don't ignite
the concoction or dim the lights.

BLUE MOON

TASTE COMPLEXITY		MIXING DIFFICULTY
LOW ▭▭O▭ HIGH	Y	LOW ▭▭O▭ HIGH

1½ ounces rye
¼ ounce Bénédictine
Ginger ale

Stir rye and Bénédictine with cracked ice;
strain into chilled cocktail glass.
Top with ginger ale, and
garnish with a lemon twist.

BOBBY BURNS

TASTE COMPLEXITY		MIXING DIFFICULTY
LOW ▭▭▭O▭ HIGH	Y	LOW ▭▭O▭ HIGH

1 ounce scotch
1 ounce sweet vermouth
3 dashes Bénédictine

Shake with cracked ice;
strain into chilled cocktail glass.
Garnish with a lemon twist.

BORDEVER

TASTE COMPLEXITY		MIXING DIFFICULTY
LOW ▭O▭▭ HIGH	Y	LOW O▭▭▭ HIGH

1½ ounces bourbon
1 ounce chilled ginger ale

Shake with cracked ice;
strain into chilled cocktail glass.
Garnish with a lemon squeeze.

BOURBON SQUASH

TASTE COMPLEXITY		MIXING DIFFICULTY
LOW O▭▭▭ HIGH		LOW ▭▭▭O▭ HIGH

2½ ounces bourbon
1 ounce orange juice
½ ounce lemon juice
1 teaspoon simple syrup

Squeeze citrus juices into a pint glass, and
drop in hulls. Add simple syrup, and pack the
glass with shaved ice. Add whiskey, and stir.
Serve with a cocktail straw.

WHISKEY
BASE

BRAINSTORM

TASTE COMPLEXITY	MIXING DIFFICULTY
LOW ——O—— HIGH	LOW ——O—— HIGH

2 ounces Irish whiskey
2 dashes Bénédictine
2 dashes dry vermouth

Shake with cracked ice;
strain into chilled cocktail glass.
Garnish with an orange twist.

CASSIS

TASTE COMPLEXITY	MIXING DIFFICULTY
LOW ——O—— HIGH	LOW ——O—— HIGH

2 ounces bourbon
½ ounce dry vermouth
¼ ounce crème de cassis

Stir with cracked ice;
strain into chilled cocktail glass.
Garnish with a lemon twist.

BROOKLYN

TASTE COMPLEXITY	MIXING DIFFICULTY
LOW ——O—— HIGH	LOW ——O—— HIGH

1½ ounces bourbon
¾ ounce dry vermouth
1 dash maraschino liqueur
1 dash Amer Picon

Shake with cracked ice;
strain into chilled cocktail glass.
Garnish with a lemon squeeze.

CHARTREUSE

TASTE COMPLEXITY	MIXING DIFFICULTY
LOW ——O—— HIGH	LOW ——O—— HIGH

1½ ounces bourbon
¾ ounce green Chartreuse
½ ounce dry vermouth

Stir with cracked ice;
strain into chilled cocktail glass.
Garnish with an orange squeeze.

BUSTER BROWN

TASTE COMPLEXITY	MIXING DIFFICULTY
LOW ——O—— HIGH	LOW ——O—— HIGH

2 ounces bourbon
¾ ounce lemon juice
½ teaspoon sugar
2 dashes orange bitters

Shake with cracked ice;
strain into chilled cocktail glass.
Garnish with a maraschino cherry.

CHEERIO

TASTE COMPLEXITY	MIXING DIFFICULTY
LOW ——O—— HIGH	LOW ——O—— HIGH

2 ounces bourbon
¾ ounce curaçao
¼ ounce maraschino liqueur

Shake with cracked ice;
strain into chilled cocktail glass.
Garnish with a maraschino cherry.

194

CREOLE, NUMBER ONE

TASTE COMPLEXITY		MIXING DIFFICULTY
LOW ⟜⟜⟜⊙ HIGH	🍸	LOW ⟜⊙⟜ HIGH

1½ ounces bourbon
1½ ounces sweet vermouth
2 dashes Bénédictine
2 dashes Amer Picon

Stir with cracked ice;
strain into chilled cocktail glass.
Garnish with a lemon twist.

CREOLE, NUMBER TWO

TASTE COMPLEXITY		MIXING DIFFICULTY
LOW ⟜⟜⟜⊙ HIGH	🍸	LOW ⟜⟜⊙ HIGH

2 ounces bourbon
½ ounce curaçao
1 dash Angostura bitters
1 dash Peychaud's bitters

Swirl a few drops of Pernod in chilled
cocktail glass; toss or flick out the liqueur.
Stir ingredients with cracked ice;
strain into the prepared glass.
Garnish with an orange twist.

DERBY

TASTE COMPLEXITY		MIXING DIFFICULTY
LOW ⟜⟜⊙ HIGH	🍸	LOW ⟜⟜⟜⊙ HIGH

2 ounces Maker's Mark bourbon
¼ ounce Bénédictine
1 dash Angostura bitters

Stir with cracked ice;
strain into chilled cocktail glass.
Twist a lemon peel over drink, and
garnish with the zest.

A Paul Harrington original

DERBY FIZZ

TASTE COMPLEXITY		MIXING DIFFICULTY
LOW ⊙⟜⟜ HIGH	🍸	LOW ⟜⟜⟜⊙ HIGH

2 ounces bourbon
½ ounce lemon juice
¼ ounce simple syrup
2 teaspoons egg white
¼ ounce curaçao
Soda water

Shake ingredients except soda water
with cracked ice; strain into chilled wine
glass. Top with soda water, and
garnish with a lemon twist.

ELEGANT, NUMBER TWO

TASTE COMPLEXITY		MIXING DIFFICULTY
LOW ⟜⊙⟜ HIGH	🍸	LOW ⟜⊙⟜ HIGH

2 ounces bourbon
¾ ounce maraschino liqueur
¾ ounce lemon juice

Stir with cracked ice;
strain into chilled cocktail glass.
Garnish with a lemon twist
and a maraschino cherry.

FANCY-FREE

TASTE COMPLEXITY		MIXING DIFFICULTY
LOW ⟜⟜⊙ HIGH	🍸	LOW ⟜⊙⟜ HIGH

2 ounces bourbon
½ ounce maraschino liqueur
1 dash Angostura bitters
1 dash orange bitters

Shake with cracked ice;
strain into chilled cocktail glass.
Garnish with a maraschino cherry.

* FRISCO *

2 ounces rye
¼ ounce Bénédictine
¾ ounce lemon juice

Shake with cracked ice;
strain into chilled cocktail glass.
Garnish with a lemon wheel.

GREEN-EYED MONSTER

2 ounces Irish whiskey
½ ounce sweet vermouth
¼ ounce Pernod
1 dash Angostura bitters

Shake with cracked ice;
strain into chilled cocktail glass.
Garnish with a lemon twist.

195

FRISCO SOUR

1½ ounces bourbon
¼ ounce Bénédictine
¾ ounce lemon juice
½ ounce simple syrup
1 dash orange juice

Shake with cracked ice;
strain into chilled tumbler filled with ice.
Squeeze and then drop
an orange wheel into the drink.
Garnish with a maraschino cherry.

GROG

1½ ounces whiskey
4 ounces hot water

Pour whiskey into a warmed mug;
top with hot water.
Garnish with a cinnamon stick and/or
a lemon twist. Dust with nutmeg.

GODFATHER

1½ ounces scotch
¾ ounce amaretto

Stir with cracked ice;
strain into chilled tumbler filled with ice.
Garnish with a lemon twist.

H. G. WELLS

1½ ounces bourbon
¾ ounce dry vermouth
1 dash Pernod

Stir with cracked ice;
strain into chilled cocktail glass.
Garnish with a lemon twist.

HEARNS

TASTE COMPLEXITY		MIXING DIFFICULTY
LOW ═══○═══ HIGH		LOW ═══○═══ HIGH

1 ounce Irish whiskey
¾ ounce sweet vermouth
¼ ounce Pernod
1 dash Angostura bitters

Shake with cracked ice;
strain into chilled cocktail glass.
Garnish with a lemon twist.

IRISH ROSE

TASTE COMPLEXITY		MIXING DIFFICULTY
LOW ═○═══ HIGH		LOW ○═══ HIGH

2 ounces Irish whiskey
½ ounce lemon juice
¼ ounce grenadine

Shake with cracked ice;
strain into chilled cocktail glass.
Garnish with a lemon squeeze.

HIGHLAND

TASTE COMPLEXITY		MIXING DIFFICULTY
LOW ═══○═══ HIGH		LOW ═○═══ HIGH

1 ounce scotch
1 ounce sweet vermouth
1 dash orange bitters

Stir with cracked ice;
strain into chilled cocktail glass.
Garnish with a maraschino cherry.

JOHN COLLINS

TASTE COMPLEXITY		MIXING DIFFICULTY
LOW ═○═══ HIGH		LOW ═══○═══ HIGH

2 ounces bourbon
1 ounce lemon juice
1 teaspoon simple syrup
2 ounces soda water

Shake ingredients except soda water with
cracked ice; strain into chilled Collins glass
filled with ice. Top with soda water, and
garnish with a maraschino cherry
and an orange wheel.

HIGHLANDER

TASTE COMPLEXITY		MIXING DIFFICULTY
LOW ═══○═══ HIGH		LOW ═══○═══ HIGH

2 ounces Johnnie Walker Red Label scotch
¼ to ½ ounce Bénédictine
2 dashes Angostura bitters

Stir with ice;
strain into chilled cocktail glass.
Garnish with a lemon twist.

A Paul Harrington original

* MANHATTAN *

TASTE COMPLEXITY		MIXING DIFFICULTY
LOW ═══○═══ HIGH		LOW ═══○═══ HIGH

2 ounces rye
½ ounce sweet vermouth
1 to 2 dashes Angostura bitters (optional)

Stir with cracked ice;
strain into chilled cocktail glass.
Garnish with a maraschino cherry.

MANHATTAN (PERFECT)

TASTE COMPLEXITY		MIXING DIFFICULTY	
LOW ———O— HIGH		LOW ———O—— HIGH	

2 ounces rye
¼ ounce sweet vermouth
¼ ounce dry vermouth
1 dash Angostura bitters (optional)

Stir with cracked ice;
strain into chilled cocktail glass.
Garnish with a lemon twist.
Variation: Use bourbon instead of rye.

MILWAUKEE (WISCONSIN)

TASTE COMPLEXITY		MIXING DIFFICULTY	
LOW ——O— HIGH		LOW —O—— HIGH	

2 ounces rye
½ ounce apricot brandy

Stir with cracked ice;
strain into chilled cocktail glass.
Serve with a green maraschino cherry.

197

MIKE COLLINS

TASTE COMPLEXITY		MIXING DIFFICULTY	
LOW ——O—— HIGH		LOW —O—— HIGH	

2 ounces Irish whiskey
1 ounce lemon juice
1 teaspoon superfine sugar
2 ounces soda water

Shake ingredients without soda water with
cracked ice; strain into chilled Collins glass filled
with ice. Top with soda water, and garnish with
a maraschino cherry and an orange wheel for
East Coast drinkers, a maraschino cherry and a
lime wheel for West Coast imbibers.

• MINT JULEP •

TASTE COMPLEXITY		MIXING DIFFICULTY	
LOW —O—— HIGH		LOW ———O— HIGH	

3 ounces bourbon
6 sprigs mint
2 to 4 tablespoons simple syrup

Mix bourbon, mint, and simple syrup in a pint
glass. Add three pieces of ice; muddle for about
a minute. Let stand for several minutes. Strain
into glass filled with shaved ice. Top with soda
water and a mint sprig. For a mintier version,
remove pieces of ice, leave mint, and pour
ingredients into the glass followed by fresh ice.

• MILK PUNCH •

TASTE COMPLEXITY		MIXING DIFFICULTY	
LOW ——O—— HIGH		LOW —O—— HIGH	

3 ounces bourbon
3 ounces milk
½ teaspoon dark rum
1 tablespoon simple syrup
Nutmeg

Shake with cracked ice;
strain into chilled tumbler or highball glass.
Dust with nutmeg.

1920

TASTE COMPLEXITY		MIXING DIFFICULTY	
LOW ———O— HIGH		LOW ———O— HIGH	

1 ounce rye
½ ounce sweet vermouth
½ ounce dry vermouth
1 dash orange bitters

Stir with cracked ice;
strain into chilled cocktail glass.
Garnish with an orange twist.

OH HENRY

TASTE COMPLEXITY	MIXING DIFFICULTY
LOW ⟞⟝ HIGH	LOW ⟞⟝ HIGH

1 ounce bourbon
1 ounce Bénédictine
½ ounce ginger ale

Shake with cracked ice;
strain into chilled cocktail glass.
Garnish with a lemon squeeze.

PADDY

TASTE COMPLEXITY	MIXING DIFFICULTY
LOW ⟞⟝ HIGH	LOW ⟞⟝ HIGH

2 ounces rye
1 dash Angostura bitters
1 dash lemon juice

Stir with cracked ice;
strain into chilled cocktail glass.
Garnish with a lemon twist.

* OLD FASHIONED *

TASTE COMPLEXITY	MIXING DIFFICULTY
LOW ⟞⟝ HIGH	LOW ⟞⟝ HIGH

2 ounces whiskey
2 dashes Angostura bitters
1 teaspoon sugar
Splash soda water

In chilled Old Fashioned glass, muddle sugar,
bitters, orange wheel, and maraschino cherry
until sugar is dissolved.
Add whiskey and ice, and stir.
Optional: Garnish with a lemon twist.

PICK-UP

TASTE COMPLEXITY	MIXING DIFFICULTY
LOW ⟞⟝ HIGH	LOW ⟞⟝ HIGH

2 ounces rye
½ ounce Fernet Branca
3 dashes Pernod
1 lemon slice

Shake with cracked ice;
strain into chilled tumbler filled with ice.
Float a lemon slice.

OLD PAL

TASTE COMPLEXITY	MIXING DIFFICULTY
LOW ⟞⟝ HIGH	LOW ⟞⟝ HIGH

1 ounce bourbon
1 ounce dry vermouth
1 ounce Campari

Shake with cracked ice;
strain into chilled cocktail glass.
Garnish with an orange wheel.

ROBERT BURNS

TASTE COMPLEXITY	MIXING DIFFICULTY
LOW ⟞⟝ HIGH	LOW ⟞⟝ HIGH

2 ounces scotch
½ ounce sweet vermouth
1 dash orange bitters
1 dash Pernod

Stir with cracked ice;
strain into chilled cocktail glass.
Garnish with a lemon twist.

WHISKEY
BASE

* ROB ROY *

2 ounces scotch
½ ounce sweet vermouth
1 dash Angostura bitters (optional)

Stir with cracked ice;
strain into chilled cocktail glass.
Garnish with a lemon twist or
a maraschino cherry.

RUSTY NAIL

2 ounces scotch
½ ounce Drambuie

Stir with cracked ice;
strain into chilled tumbler
filled with ice.
Optional: Garnish with
a lemon twist.

ROB ROY (DRY)

2 ounces scotch
½ ounce dry vermouth
1 dash Angostura bitters (optional)

Stir with cracked ice;
strain into chilled cocktail glass.
Garnish with a lemon twist.

SANDY COLLINS

2 ounces scotch
1 ounce lemon juice
1 teaspoon superfine sugar
2 ounces soda water

Shake ingredients without soda water with
cracked ice; strain into a Collins glass filled
with ice. Top with soda, and
garnish with a maraschino cherry
and an orange wheel.

ROB ROY (PERFECT)

2 ounces scotch
¼ ounce sweet vermouth
¼ ounce dry vermouth
1 dash Angostura bitters (optional)

Stir with cracked ice;
strain into chilled cocktail glass.
Garnish with a lemon twist.

SANTIAGO SCOTCH PLAID

2 ounces scotch
½ ounce dry vermouth
2 dashes Angostura bitters

Stir with cracked ice;
strain into chilled cocktail glass.
Garnish with a lemon twist.

• SAZERAC •

TASTE COMPLEXITY	MIXING DIFFICULTY
LOW ⊶ HIGH	LOW ⊶ HIGH

2 ounces rye
3 dashes Peychaud's bitters
1 splash Herbsaint

Coat the inside of chilled
Old Fashioned glass with
Herbsaint, turning the glass
to coat it evenly and thoroughly.
Shake rye and bitters with
cracked ice; strain into prepared glass.
Optional: Garnish with a lemon twist.

• SCOFFLAW •

TASTE COMPLEXITY	MIXING DIFFICULTY
LOW ⊶ HIGH	LOW ⊶ HIGH

1½ ounces Canadian
1½ ounces dry vermouth
½ ounce lemon juice
1 dash grenadine
1 dash orange bitters

Shake with cracked ice;
strain into chilled cocktail glass.
Garnish with a lemon wheel.

UP-TO-DATE

TASTE COMPLEXITY	MIXING DIFFICULTY
LOW ⊶ HIGH	LOW ⊶ HIGH

1½ ounces rye
1½ ounces amontillado sherry
2 dashes Angostura bitters
2 dashes Grand Marnier

Shake with cracked ice;
strain into chilled cocktail glass.
Garnish with an orange twist.

• WARD EIGHT (SCOTTISH GUARD'S) •

TASTE COMPLEXITY	MIXING DIFFICULTY
LOW ⊶ HIGH	LOW ⊶ HIGH

2 ounces bourbon
½ ounce lemon juice
½ ounce orange juice
1 teaspoon grenadine

Shake with cracked ice;
strain into chilled cocktail glass.
Garnish with a lemon wheel.

WHISKEY SOUR

TASTE COMPLEXITY	MIXING DIFFICULTY
LOW ⊶ HIGH	LOW ⊶ HIGH

2 ounces blended whiskey
2 ounces lemon juice
½ ounce simple syrup

Shake with cracked ice;
strain into chilled tumbler filled with ice.
Garnish with a maraschino cherry and an
orange wheel. Serve with a swizzle stick.
Variation: Add a splash of orange juice
for a Stone Sour.

WILD-EYED ROSE

TASTE COMPLEXITY	MIXING DIFFICULTY
LOW ⊶ HIGH	LOW ⊶ HIGH

2 ounces Irish whiskey
1 ounce lime juice
½ ounce grenadine

Shake with cracked ice;
strain into chilled cocktail glass.
Garnish with a lime squeeze
and a maraschino cherry.

BRANDY

BASE

APPLE BLOSSOM

TASTE COMPLEXITY		MIXING DIFFICULTY	
LOW ⊢O━━┤ HIGH		LOW ⊢━━O━┤ HIGH	

1½ ounces apple brandy
¾ ounce sweet vermouth

Shake with cracked ice;
strain into chilled cocktail glass.
Garnish with a lemon twist
and a maraschino cherry.

BATIDA

TASTE COMPLEXITY		MIXING DIFFICULTY	
LOW ⊢O━━┤ HIGH		LOW ⊢━━O━┤ HIGH	

1½ ounces cachaça
1 teaspoon simple syrup
1 lime

Cut lime into quarters,
and place pieces in
the bottom of chilled
tumbler pulp side up.
Pour simple syrup over the lime,
and muddle. Add the cachaça,
and stir. Fill glass with ice.

APRICOT

TASTE COMPLEXITY		MIXING DIFFICULTY	
LOW ⊢━━O━┤ HIGH		LOW ⊢━━O━┤ HIGH	

1½ ounces apricot brandy
1 ounce gin
½ ounce lemon juice
2 dashes orange juice

Shake with cracked ice;
strain into chilled cocktail glass.
Garnish with an orange twist.

BÉNÉDICTINE

TASTE COMPLEXITY		MIXING DIFFICULTY	
LOW ⊢━━O━┤ HIGH		LOW ⊢O━━┤ HIGH	

1½ ounces cognac
½ ounce Bénédictine
½ ounce lemon juice

Shake with cracked ice;
strain into chilled cocktail glass.
Garnish with a lemon twist.

ATLAS

TASTE COMPLEXITY		MIXING DIFFICULTY	
LOW ⊢━━O━┤ HIGH		LOW ⊢━━O━┤ HIGH	

1½ ounces apple brandy
½ ounce brown rum
½ ounce Cointreau
1 dash Angostura bitters

Shake with cracked ice;
strain into chilled cocktail glass.
Garnish with a lemon squeeze.

BRANDY ALEXANDER

TASTE COMPLEXITY		MIXING DIFFICULTY	
LOW ⊢━━O━┤ HIGH		LOW ⊢O━━┤ HIGH	

¾ ounce brandy
¾ ounce crème de cacao
½ ounce cream

Shake with cracked ice;
strain into chilled snifter.
Dust with nutmeg.

BRANDY

BASE

BRANDY COLLINS

2 ounces brandy
1 ounce lemon juice
1 teaspoon superfine sugar
2 ounces soda water

Shake ingredients with
cracked ice; strain into
chilled Collins glass filled
with ice. Top with soda water,
and garnish with an orange wheel
and a maraschino cherry.

CHAMPS ELYSÉES

1½ ounces cognac
¼ ounce green Chartreuse
1 ounce lemon juice
2 dashes Angostura bitters

Shake with cracked ice;
strain into chilled cocktail glass.
Garnish with a lemon twist.

BRANDY MANHATTAN

2 ounces brandy
½ ounce sweet vermouth
1 dash Angostura bitters

Shake with cracked ice;
strain into chilled cocktail glass.
Garnish with an orange wheel.

CLASSIC COCKTAIL

1½ ounces brandy
½ ounce curaçao
¼ ounce maraschino liqueur
½ ounce lemon juice

Shake with cracked ice;
strain into chilled cocktail glass.
Garnish with a lemon squeeze.

• CAIPIRINHA •

2 ounces cachaça
¼ ounce simple syrup
1 lime

Cut lime into quarters, and place pieces in
the bottom of chilled tumbler, pulp side up.
Pour simple syrup over the lime, and muddle.
Add the cachaça, and stir.
Fill glass with ice.

COGNAC

1½ ounces cognac
¼ ounce Cointreau
¾ ounce lemon juice
1 dash bitters

Shake with cracked ice;
strain into chilled cocktail glass.
Garnish with a lemon twist.

Each recipe has TASTE COMPLEXITY and MIXING DIFFICULTY scales (LOW—HIGH).

BRANDY
BASE

• COMBUSTIBLE EDISON •

TASTE COMPLEXITY		MIXING DIFFICULTY
LOW ═══O═══ HIGH	Y	LOW ═════O HIGH

2 ounces brandy
1 ounce Campari
1 ounce lemon juice

Shake Campari and lemon juice with
cracked ice; strain into chilled cocktail glass.
Heat brandy in chafing dish. When warm,
ignite the brandy and pour in a flaming
stream into the cocktail glass. Variation: If the
brandy is chilled and shaken rather than
ignited, the drink is known as the Edisonian.

EAST INDIA

TASTE COMPLEXITY		MIXING DIFFICULTY
LOW ══O═══ HIGH	Y	LOW ══O═══ HIGH

1½ ounces brandy
½ ounce red curaçao
3 dashes maraschino liqueur
3 dashes Angostura bitters
1 teaspoon raspberry syrup

Shake with cracked ice;
strain into chilled cocktail glass.
Garnish with an orange twist.

203

CORPSE REVIVER

TASTE COMPLEXITY		MIXING DIFFICULTY
LOW ═══O═══ HIGH	Y	LOW ═══O═══ HIGH

1½ ounces cognac
½ ounce calvados or apple brandy
½ ounce sweet vermouth

Stir with cracked ice;
strain into chilled cocktail glass.
Garnish with a lemon twist.

HOURGLASS HIGHBALL

TASTE COMPLEXITY		MIXING DIFFICULTY
LOW ═════O HIGH	▌	LOW ══O═══ HIGH

1 ounce cognac
1 ounce Cointreau
½ ounce Pernod

Shake ingredients with cracked ice;
strain into chilled highball glass.
Add a lump of ice, and top with soda water.
Garnish with a lemon twist.

COUNTRY GENTLEMAN

TASTE COMPLEXITY		MIXING DIFFICULTY
LOW ══O═══ HIGH	Y	LOW ══O═══ HIGH

1½ ounces apple brandy
¾ ounce curaçao
¼ ounce lemon juice
1 teaspoon simple syrup

Shake with cracked ice;
strain into chilled cocktail glass.
Garnish with a lemon twist.

JACK COLLINS

TASTE COMPLEXITY		MIXING DIFFICULTY
LOW O═════ HIGH	▌	LOW ══O═══ HIGH

2 ounces applejack
1 ounce lemon juice
1 teaspoon superfine sugar
2 ounces soda water

Shake ingredients with cracked ice;
strain into chilled Collins glass filled
with ice. Top with soda, and
garnish with a maraschino cherry
and an orange wheel.

BRANDY

BASE

• JACK ROSE •

TASTE COMPLEXITY		MIXING DIFFICULTY
LOW ⊢═══O═══⊣ HIGH		LOW ⊢═══O═══⊣ HIGH

2 ounces applejack
1 ounce lime juice
½ ounce grenadine

Shake with cracked ice;
strain into chilled cocktail glass.
Garnish with a lime wheel.

OLYMPIC

TASTE COMPLEXITY		MIXING DIFFICULTY
LOW ⊢═══O═══⊣ HIGH		LOW ⊢═O═══⊣ HIGH

1 ounce brandy
½ ounce curaçao
½ ounce orange juice
½ ounce lemon juice

Shake with cracked ice;
strain into chilled cocktail glass.
Garnish with a maraschino cherry.

NEWTON'S SPECIAL

TASTE COMPLEXITY		MIXING DIFFICULTY
LOW ⊢══O═══⊣ HIGH		LOW ⊢═O═══⊣ HIGH

2 ounces brandy
½ ounce Cointreau
1 dash Angostura bitters

Shake with cracked ice;
strain into chilled cocktail glass.
Garnish with an orange twist.

PARK AVENUE

TASTE COMPLEXITY		MIXING DIFFICULTY
LOW ⊢═══O══⊣ HIGH		LOW ⊢═O═══⊣ HIGH

1 ounce brandy
½ ounce Grand Marnier
4 ounces champagne or sparkling wine

Stir brandy and Grand Marnier with cracked
ice; strain into chilled champagne flute.
Top with chilled champagne.
Garnish with a lemon twist.

• NICKY FINN •

TASTE COMPLEXITY		MIXING DIFFICULTY
LOW ⊢════O═⊣ HIGH		LOW ⊢═══O══⊣ HIGH

1 ounce brandy
1 ounce Cointreau
1 ounce lemon juice
1 dash Pernod

Shake with cracked ice;
strain into chilled cocktail glass.
Garnish with a maraschino cherry
or a lemon twist.

PEACOCK

TASTE COMPLEXITY		MIXING DIFFICULTY
LOW ⊢════O═⊣ HIGH		LOW ⊢═══O═══⊣ HIGH

2 ounces brandy
¼ ounce Amer Picon
1 dash Pernod

Shake with cracked ice;
strain into chilled cocktail glass.
Garnish with an orange squeeze.

PISCO PUNCH

TASTE COMPLEXITY		MIXING DIFFICULTY	
LOW ——O—— HIGH		LOW —O——— HIGH	

2 ounces pisco
½ ounce lemon juice
½ ounce pineapple juice
Soda water

Stir pisco and juices with ice,
strain into chilled wine glass filled with ice.
Top with soda water, and
garnish with a pineapple wheel
or a maraschino cherry.

• PISCO SOUR •

TASTE COMPLEXITY		MIXING DIFFICULTY	
LOW ——O—— HIGH		LOW —O——— HIGH	

2 ounces pisco
1 ounce lemon juice
½ ounce simple syrup
1 dash bitters
1 dollop egg white

Shake with cracked ice;
strain into chilled champagne flute.
Optional: Garnish with a lemon twist
or a mint sprig.

• SIDECAR •

TASTE COMPLEXITY		MIXING DIFFICULTY	
LOW —O——— HIGH		LOW ———O— HIGH	

1½ ounces cognac
¾ ounce Cointreau
¾ ounce lemon juice

Shake with cracked ice;
strain into chilled cocktail glass.
Garnish with a lemon wheel.

SIR KNIGHT

TASTE COMPLEXITY		MIXING DIFFICULTY	
LOW ——O—— HIGH		LOW ——O—— HIGH	

2 ounces cognac
½ ounce Cointreau
¼ ounce Chartreuse
1 dash Angostura bitters

Shake with cracked ice;
strain into chilled cocktail glass.
Garnish with a lemon twist.

• STINGER •

TASTE COMPLEXITY		MIXING DIFFICULTY	
LOW ——O—— HIGH		LOW —O——— HIGH	

2 ounces brandy
½ ounce white crème de menthe

Stir with cracked ice;
strain into chilled cocktail glass.
Garnish with mint sprigs and
serve with a glass of ice water.

SUN

TASTE COMPLEXITY		MIXING DIFFICULTY	
LOW ——O—— HIGH		LOW ———O— HIGH	

1½ ounces brandy
½ teaspoon curaçao
2 dashes maraschino liqueur
2 drops Angostura bitters
½ ounce lemon juice
1 dash pineapple syrup

Shake with cracked ice;
strain into chilled cocktail glass.
Garnish with a lemon squeeze.

206

ANN SHERIDAN

TASTE COMPLEXITY		MIXING DIFFICULTY	
LOW ══O═══ HIGH		LOW ═══O═══ HIGH	

1½ ounces dark rum
¾ ounce orange curaçao
¾ ounce lime juice

Shake with cracked ice;
strain into chilled cocktail glass.
Garnish with a lime squeeze.

• BACARDI COCKTAIL •

TASTE COMPLEXITY		MIXING DIFFICULTY	
LOW ══O═══ HIGH		LOW ══O═══ HIGH	

1¾ ounces Bacardi light rum
1 ounce lime juice
½ teaspoon simple syrup
1 dash grenadine

Shake with cracked ice;
strain into chilled cocktail glass.
Garnish with a lime squeeze.

APPLE PIE

TASTE COMPLEXITY		MIXING DIFFICULTY	
LOW ═════O═ HIGH		LOW ═══O═══ HIGH	

1½ ounces dark rum
1 ounce sweet vermouth
½ ounce lemon juice
⅛ ounce grenadine

Shake with cracked ice;
strain into chilled cocktail glass.
Garnish with a lemon wheel.

BACARDI HIGHBALL

TASTE COMPLEXITY		MIXING DIFFICULTY	
LOW ══O═══ HIGH		LOW O═════ HIGH	

2 ounces Bacardi light rum
Soda water

Stir with ice; strain into pint glass.
Add ice cubes, and top with soda water.
Garnish with a lemon twist.

ARAK

TASTE COMPLEXITY		MIXING DIFFICULTY	
LOW ═════O═ HIGH		LOW ═════O═ HIGH	

1½ ounces dark rum
1½ ounces sherry
1 dash Angostura bitters

Stir with cracked ice;
strain into chilled cocktail glass.
Garnish with a lemon twist.

BACARDI PEACH

TASTE COMPLEXITY		MIXING DIFFICULTY	
LOW ══O═══ HIGH		LOW ═════O═ HIGH	

1½ ounces Bacardi light rum
1 ounce peach brandy
½ ounce lemon juice
½ ounce simple syrup
1 mint sprig

Shake with cracked ice;
strain into chilled cocktail glass.
Garnish with frosted mint.

RUM

BASE

BACARDI SPECIAL

TASTE COMPLEXITY		MIXING DIFFICULTY
LOW ⊢━○━━┤ HIGH	Y	LOW ⊢━━○━┤ HIGH

1½ ounces Bacardi light rum
¾ ounce gin
¾ ounce lime juice
1 dash grenadine

Shake with cracked ice;
strain into chilled cocktail glass.
Garnish with a lime squeeze.

BEE'S KISS

TASTE COMPLEXITY		MIXING DIFFICULTY
LOW ⊢━○━━┤ HIGH	Y	LOW ⊢━━━○━┤ HIGH

1½ ounces light rum
½ ounce dark rum
¾ ounce cream
1 barspoon honey

Shake with cracked ice;
strain into chilled cocktail glass.
Dust with nutmeg.

207

BARBARESQUE

TASTE COMPLEXITY		MIXING DIFFICULTY
LOW ⊢○━━━┤ HIGH	Y	LOW ⊢━○━━┤ HIGH

1½ ounces light rum
¾ ounce lemon juice
½ ounce Cointreau

Shake with cracked ice;
strain into chilled cocktail glass.
Garnish with a lemon squeeze.

BIRDIE

TASTE COMPLEXITY		MIXING DIFFICULTY
LOW ⊢━○━━┤ HIGH	Y	LOW ⊢━━○━┤ HIGH

1½ ounces brown rum
¼ ounce curaçao
¼ ounce pineapple juice
¼ ounce orange juice
1 dash grenadine

Shake with cracked ice;
strain into chilled cocktail glass.
Garnish with an orange wheel.

BEACHCOMBER

TASTE COMPLEXITY		MIXING DIFFICULTY
LOW ⊢━○━━┤ HIGH	♦	LOW ⊢━━○━┤ HIGH

1½ ounces light rum
½ ounce Cointreau
¾ ounce lime juice
2 dashes maraschino liqueur

Flash blend ingredients with shaved ice;
pour unstrained into wine glass.
Garnish with a lime squeeze.

BLUE BOY

TASTE COMPLEXITY		MIXING DIFFICULTY
LOW ⊢━━○━┤ HIGH	Y	LOW ⊢━━━○━┤ HIGH

2 ounces dark rum
¾ ounce sweet vermouth
½ ounce orange juice
1 dash Angostura bitters

Shake with cracked ice;
strain into chilled cocktail glass.
Garnish with an orange wheel.

COCKTAIL

BROOKLYNITE

TASTE COMPLEXITY		MIXING DIFFICULTY
LOW ⊢──O──┤ HIGH		LOW ⊢─O───┤ HIGH

2 ounces dark rum
1 ounce lime juice
1 barspoon honey
1 dash Angostura bitters

Shake with cracked ice;
strain into chilled cocktail glass.
Garnish with a lime squeeze.

CORAL

TASTE COMPLEXITY		MIXING DIFFICULTY
LOW ⊢──O──┤ HIGH		LOW ⊢─O───┤ HIGH

1½ ounces light rum
¼ ounce apricot brandy
½ ounce lemon juice
¼ ounce grapefruit juice

Shake with cracked ice;
strain into chilled cocktail glass.
Garnish with a lemon twist.

CAPTAIN'S BLOOD

TASTE COMPLEXITY		MIXING DIFFICULTY
LOW ⊢───O──┤ HIGH		LOW ⊢──O───┤ HIGH

1½ ounces dark rum
½ ounce lime juice
2 dashes Angostura bitters

Shake with cracked ice;
strain into chilled cocktail glass.
Garnish with a lime squeeze.

* CUBA LIBRE (IMPROVED) *

TASTE COMPLEXITY		MIXING DIFFICULTY
LOW ⊢O─────┤ HIGH		LOW ⊢O─────┤ HIGH

1 ounce light rum
½ ounce gin
¼ ounce lime juice
2 to 3 ounces Coca-Cola
2 dashes bitters

Pour ingredients except Coca-Cola
over ice into chilled Collins glass.
Top with cola and stir.
Garnish with a lime squeeze.

COLUMBIA

TASTE COMPLEXITY		MIXING DIFFICULTY
LOW ⊢─O────┤ HIGH		LOW ⊢──O───┤ HIGH

1½ ounces light rum
¾ ounce lemon juice
¼ ounce raspberry syrup

Shake with cracked ice;
strain into large wine glass filled with ice.
Garnish with a lime squeeze.

CUBA LIBRE (ORIGINAL)

TASTE COMPLEXITY		MIXING DIFFICULTY
LOW ⊢O─────┤ HIGH		LOW ⊢O─────┤ HIGH

1½ ounces light rum
4 ounces Coca-Cola

Pour ingredients over ice into
chilled Collins glass.
Garnish with a lime squeeze.

CUBAN, NUMBER ONE

TASTE COMPLEXITY		MIXING DIFFICULTY	
LOW ⊢O⊣ HIGH		LOW ⊢O⊣ HIGH	

1½ ounces light rum
¼ ounce maraschino liqueur
½ ounce lemon juice
1 dash grenadine
1 dash orange bitters

Shake with cracked ice;
strain into chilled cocktail glass.
Garnish with a lemon twist.

CUBANO

2 ounces dark rum
¾ ounce lime juice
¼ ounce pineapple juice

Shake with cracked ice;
strain into chilled cocktail glass.
Garnish with a lime twist
or pineapple wheel.

CUBAN, NUMBER TWO

TASTE COMPLEXITY		MIXING DIFFICULTY	
LOW O⊣ HIGH		LOW O⊣ HIGH	

1½ ounces light rum
¾ ounce lemon juice
1 teaspoon sugar

Shake with cracked ice;
strain into chilled cocktail glass.
Garnish with a lemon squeeze.

CUBAN PRESIDENTE

TASTE COMPLEXITY		MIXING DIFFICULTY	
LOW ⊢O⊣ HIGH		LOW ⊢O⊣ HIGH	

2 ounces light rum
½ ounce dry vermouth
¼ ounce Cointreau
1 dash grenadine

Shake with cracked ice;
strain into chilled cocktail glass.
Garnish with a maraschino cherry
and a lemon twist.

CUBAN, NUMBER THREE

TASTE COMPLEXITY		MIXING DIFFICULTY	
LOW ⊢O⊣ HIGH		LOW ⊢O⊣ HIGH	

2 ounces light rum
½ ounce apricot brandy
½ ounce lime juice

Shake with cracked ice;
strain into chilled cocktail glass.
Garnish with a lime squeeze.

• DAIQUIRI •

TASTE COMPLEXITY		MIXING DIFFICULTY	
LOW O⊣ HIGH		LOW ⊢O⊣ HIGH	

1½ ounces light rum
½ ounce lime juice
¼ ounce simple syrup

Shake with cracked ice;
strain into chilled cocktail glass.
Garnish with a lime wheel.

RUM
BASE

DEL MONTE

TASTE COMPLEXITY		MIXING DIFFICULTY	
LOW ⊢O————⊣ HIGH	Y	LOW ⊢——O———⊣ HIGH	

1½ ounces light rum
¾ ounce lemon juice
¼ ounce grenadine

Shake with cracked ice;
strain into chilled cocktail glass.
Garnish with a maraschino cherry.

FLORIDA PUNCH

TASTE COMPLEXITY		MIXING DIFFICULTY	
LOW ⊢——O———⊣ HIGH	♟	LOW ⊢——O———⊣ HIGH	

1 ounce brown rum
1 ounce brandy
½ ounce Cointreau
½ ounce lime juice
½ ounce grapefruit juice

Shake with cracked ice;
strain into a wine glass filled with ice.
Garnish with a lime wheel.

FIG LEAF

TASTE COMPLEXITY		MIXING DIFFICULTY	
LOW ⊢——O———⊣ HIGH	Y	LOW ⊢——O———⊣ HIGH	

1½ ounces light rum
1 ounce dry vermouth
½ ounce lime juice
1 dash Angostura bitters

Shake with cracked ice;
strain into chilled cocktail glass.
Garnish with a lime twist.

* FLORIDITA *

TASTE COMPLEXITY		MIXING DIFFICULTY	
LOW ⊢——O———⊣ HIGH	Y	LOW ⊢————O⊣ HIGH	

1½ ounces light rum
½ ounce lime juice
½ ounce sweet vermouth
1 dash white crème de cacao
1 dash grenadine

Shake with cracked ice;
strain into chilled cocktail glass.
Garnish with a lime wheel.

FLORIDA DAIQUIRI

TASTE COMPLEXITY		MIXING DIFFICULTY	
LOW ⊢O————⊣ HIGH	Y	LOW ⊢——O———⊣ HIGH	

2 ounces light rum
¾ ounce curaçao
½ ounce orange juice
½ ounce lime juice

Shake with cracked ice;
strain into chilled cocktail glass.
Garnish with an orange squeeze.

FLORIDITA SPECIAL

TASTE COMPLEXITY		MIXING DIFFICULTY	
LOW ⊢——O———⊣ HIGH	Y	LOW ⊢——O———⊣ HIGH	

1½ ounces light rum
½ ounce maraschino liqueur
¾ ounce lime juice

Shake with cracked ice;
strain into chilled cocktail glass.
Garnish with a lime squeeze.

FOX TROT

TASTE COMPLEXITY		MIXING DIFFICULTY	
LOW ⊢○──────┤ HIGH		LOW ⊢─○──┤ HIGH	

2 ounces light rum
¼ ounce Cointreau
½ ounce lime juice

Shake well with cracked ice;
strain into chilled cocktail glass.
Garnish with a lime wheel.

HAVANA CLUB RICKEY

TASTE COMPLEXITY		MIXING DIFFICULTY	
LOW ⊢─○──┤ HIGH		LOW ⊢────○─┤ HIGH	

1½ ounces light rum
½ ounce lime juice
1 dash simple syrup
Soda water

Squeeze lime into chilled Old Fashioned glass;
drop in hull of lime.
Add rum and cracked ice;
top with soda water. Simple syrup may be
added with the lime juice for a sweeter drink.
Garnish with a mint sprig or a lime wheel.

HAVANA

TASTE COMPLEXITY		MIXING DIFFICULTY	
LOW ⊢──────○──┤ HIGH		LOW ⊢──○──┤ HIGH	

1½ ounces light rum
1½ ounces sweet sherry
½ ounce lemon juice

Shake with cracked ice;
strain into chilled cocktail glass.
Garnish with a lemon twist.

HAVANA SIDECAR

TASTE COMPLEXITY		MIXING DIFFICULTY	
LOW ⊢─○──┤ HIGH		LOW ⊢────○─┤ HIGH	

1½ ounces brown rum
¾ ounce Cointreau
¾ ounce lemon juice

Shake with cracked ice;
strain into chilled cocktail glass.
Garnish with a lemon twist.

HAVANA BEACH

TASTE COMPLEXITY		MIXING DIFFICULTY	
LOW ⊢─○──┤ HIGH		LOW ⊢────○─┤ HIGH	

1½ ounces light rum
1 ounce pineapple juice
½ ounce lime juice
¼ ounce simple syrup

Shake with cracked ice;
strain into chilled cocktail glass.
Garnish with a pineapple wheel.

• HEMINGWAY DAIQUIRI •

TASTE COMPLEXITY		MIXING DIFFICULTY	
LOW ⊢─○──┤ HIGH		LOW ⊢○──────┤ HIGH	

1½ ounces light rum
¼ ounce maraschino liqueur
¾ ounce lime juice
¼ ounce grapefruit juice

Shake with cracked ice;
strain into chilled cocktail glass.
Garnish with a lime wheel.

• HENESSEY DAIQUIRI •

TASTE COMPLEXITY		MIXING DIFFICULTY	
LOW ⊨O━━⊨ HIGH	Y	LOW ⊨━━O━⊨ HIGH	

2 ounces light rum
¾ ounce lime juice
½ ounce Rene Niel Tangerine liqueur

Shake with cracked ice;
strain into chilled cocktail glass.
Garnish with a tangerine wheel.

A Paul Harrington original

JAMAICA RUM

2 ounces dark rum
¾ ounce lime juice
1 teaspoon simple syrup

Shake with cracked ice;
strain into chilled cocktail glass.
Garnish with a lime squeeze.

HOOVER

TASTE COMPLEXITY		MIXING DIFFICULTY	
LOW ⊨━O━⊨ HIGH	Y	LOW ⊨━O━━⊨ HIGH	

1½ ounces brown rum
1½ ounces sweet vermouth
1 dash curaçao

Shake with cracked ice;
strain into chilled cocktail glass.
Garnish with an orange twist.

JOURNALIST (PERIODISTA)

TASTE COMPLEXITY		MIXING DIFFICULTY	
LOW ⊨━O━⊨ HIGH	Y	LOW ⊨━━━O⊨ HIGH	

1½ ounces light rum
¼ ounce Cointreau
¼ ounce apricot brandy
¾ ounce lime juice
¼ ounce simple syrup

Shake with cracked ice;
strain into chilled cocktail glass.
Garnish with a lime squeeze.

HURRICANE

1 ounce light rum
1 ounce dark rum
1 ounce lime juice
½ ounce passion-fruit syrup

Shake with cracked ice;
strain into hurricane glass filled with ice.
Garnish with a lime wheel and an umbrella.

LAND'S END

1½ ounces dark rum
¾ ounce curaçao
½ ounce lemon juice
1 dash raspberry wine

Shake with cracked ice;
strain into chilled cocktail glass.
Garnish with a lemon twist.

RUM

BASE

LEAVE-IT-TO-ME

TASTE COMPLEXITY		MIXING DIFFICULTY
LOW ⊢O—⊣ HIGH		LOW ⊢—O—⊣ HIGH

1½ ounces light rum
½ ounce maraschino liqueur
¾ ounce lime juice
¼ ounce raspberry syrup

Shake with cracked ice;
strain into chilled cocktail glass.
Garnish with a lime wheel.

MILLIONAIRE

TASTE COMPLEXITY		MIXING DIFFICULTY
LOW ⊢—O—⊣ HIGH		LOW ⊢—O—⊣ HIGH

1½ ounces light rum
1 dash sloe gin
½ ounce apricot brandy
½ ounce lemon juice

Shake with cracked ice;
strain into chilled cocktail glass.
Garnish with a lemon squeeze.

213

* MAI TAI *

TASTE COMPLEXITY		MIXING DIFFICULTY
LOW ⊢O—⊣ HIGH		LOW ⊢——O—⊣ HIGH

2½ ounces dark rum
¾ ounce lime juice
½ ounce curaçao
1 splash grenadine or simple syrup
1 splash orgeat

Shake with cracked ice;
strain into wine goblet or Collins glass filled
with ice. Top with ½ ounce dark rum.
Garnish with a paper umbrella or
a cherry and a flower blossom.

* MOJITO *

TASTE COMPLEXITY		MIXING DIFFICULTY
LOW ⊢—O—⊣ HIGH		LOW ⊢————O⊣ HIGH

2 to 3 ounces light rum
1 lime
½ ounce simple syrup
8 to 10 mint sprigs
Soda water

Place sugar, mint, and splash of soda water in
chilled 16-ounce glass. Muddle mint until the
sugar dissolves. Squeeze both halves of lime
into the glass, leaving a hull in the mixture.
Add rum, stir, and fill with ice. Top with soda
water, and garnish with a mint sprig.

MIAMI

TASTE COMPLEXITY		MIXING DIFFICULTY
LOW ⊢O—⊣ HIGH		LOW ⊢—O—⊣ HIGH

2 ounces light rum
¾ ounce Cointreau
½ ounce lemon juice

Shake with cracked ice;
strain into chilled cocktail glass.
Garnish with a lemon squeeze.

NATIONALE

TASTE COMPLEXITY		MIXING DIFFICULTY
LOW ⊢—O—⊣ HIGH		LOW ⊢—O—⊣ HIGH

2 ounces light rum
½ ounce apricot brandy
1 ounce lime juice

Shake with cracked ice,
strain into chilled cocktail glass.
Garnish with a lime squeeze.

PALMETTO

TASTE COMPLEXITY		MIXING DIFFICULTY
LOW ⊙ HIGH		LOW ⊙ HIGH

1 ounce brown rum
½ ounce Cointreau
½ ounce apricot brandy
1 ounce lemon juice

Shake with cracked ice;
strain into chilled cocktail glass.
Garnish with a lemon twist
and a maraschino cherry.

PARDO BAR

TASTE COMPLEXITY		MIXING DIFFICULTY
LOW ⊙ HIGH		LOW ⊙ HIGH

2 ounces brown rum
½ ounce Amer Picon
1 dash Pernod

Shake with cracked ice;
strain into chilled cocktail glass.
Garnish with a lemon twist.

PAULINE

TASTE COMPLEXITY		MIXING DIFFICULTY
LOW ⊙ HIGH		LOW ⊙ HIGH

1½ ounces light rum
½ ounce Cointreau
1 ounce lemon juice
1 dash Pernod

Shake with cracked ice;
strain into chilled cocktail glass.
Garnish with a lemon twist.

PEDRO COLLINS

TASTE COMPLEXITY		MIXING DIFFICULTY
LOW ⊙ HIGH		LOW ⊙ HIGH

2 ounces light rum
1 ounce lemon juice
1 teaspoon superfine sugar
2 ounces soda water

Shake rum, juice, and sugar with cracked ice;
strain into chilled Collins glass filled with ice.
Top with soda. For East Coast imbibers,
garnish with a maraschino cherry and
an orange wheel. West Coast drinkers
get a cherry and a lime wheel.

PEG O' MY HEART

TASTE COMPLEXITY		MIXING DIFFICULTY
LOW ⊙ HIGH		LOW ⊙ HIGH

2 ounces light rum
1 ounce lime juice
¼ ounce grenadine

Shake with cracked ice;
strain into chilled cocktail glass.
Garnish with a maraschino cherry.

PET

TASTE COMPLEXITY		MIXING DIFFICULTY
LOW ⊙ HIGH		LOW ⊙ HIGH

1½ ounces dark rum
½ ounce Cointreau
½ ounce lemon juice
1 dash grenadine

Shake with cracked ice;
strain into chilled cocktail glass.
Garnish with a lemon twist.

PIKAKI

2 ounces dark rum
½ ounce orange juice
½ ounce lemon juice
½ ounce raspberry syrup

Shake with cracked ice;
strain into chilled cocktail glass.
Garnish with a lemon twist
and a maraschino cherry.

PLANTER'S

2 ounces dark rum
1 ounce orange juice
½ ounce lemon juice
1 dash grenadine

Shake with cracked ice;
strain into chilled cocktail glass.
Garnish with a lemon twist.

215

PINK GOODY

1 ounce light rum
1 ounce gin
¾ ounce lime juice
¼ ounce maraschino liqueur

Shake with cracked ice;
strain into chilled cocktail glass.
Garnish with a lime twist.

• PLANTER'S PUNCH •

2 ounces dark rum
1 ounce lemon juice
1 dash orange juice
1 dash simple syrup

Shake with cracked ice;
strain into large wine goblet filled with ice.
Garnish with a lemon twist.

PLANTATION

2 ounces dark rum
1 ounce lemon juice
1 dash orange juice

Shake with cracked ice;
strain into chilled cocktail glass.
Garnish with a lemon squeeze.

PRESIDENTE

1½ ounces light rum
½ ounce dry vermouth
½ ounce Cointreau
½ ounce lemon juice
1 dash grenadine

Shake with cracked ice;
strain into chilled cocktail glass.
Garnish with a lemon twist.

RANGER

TASTE COMPLEXITY		MIXING DIFFICULTY
LOW ⊢─O─⊣ HIGH	Y	LOW ⊢─O─⊣ HIGH

1 ounce light rum
1 ounce gin
½ ounce lemon juice
1 dash simple syrup

Shake with cracked ice;
strain into chilled cocktail glass.
Garnish with a lemon twist.

SANTIAGO

TASTE COMPLEXITY		MIXING DIFFICULTY
LOW ⊢─O─⊣ HIGH	Y	LOW ⊢──O─⊣ HIGH

2 ounces light rum
¾ ounce lime juice
¼ ounce grenadine

Shake with cracked ice;
strain into chilled cocktail glass.
Garnish with a lime squeeze.

RILEY

TASTE COMPLEXITY		MIXING DIFFICULTY
LOW ⊢O─⊣ HIGH	Y	LOW ⊢──O─⊣ HIGH

1 ounce Mount Gay Barbados Eclipse Rum
½ ounce Cointreau
½ ounce lemon juice
½ ounce orange juice
½ ounce lime juice
1 dash crème de cassis
1 dash raspberry syrup

Shake first six ingredients with cracked ice;
strain into chilled cocktail glass. Add raspberry
syrup. Garnish with a lime squeeze.

SANTIAGO JULEP

TASTE COMPLEXITY		MIXING DIFFICULTY
LOW ⊢O─⊣ HIGH		LOW ⊢──────O⊣ HIGH

2 ounces light rum
1 ounce lime juice
1 ounce pineapple juice
½ ounce grenadine
6 mint sprigs

Muddle mint with grenadine in pint glass;
add lime and pineapple juices with rum.
Pack with shaved ice.
Garnish with mint sprigs.

RUM JULEP

TASTE COMPLEXITY		MIXING DIFFICULTY
LOW ⊢O─⊣ HIGH		LOW ⊢──────O⊣ HIGH

3 ounces light rum
½ ounce simple syrup
5 mint sprigs

Put cubed ice, simple syrup, mint,
and rum in pint glass; muddle thoroughly.
Fill chilled serving glass with shaved ice,
and strain ingredients into glass.
Garnish with a mint sprig and a lemon slice.

SOUTHERN CROSS

TASTE COMPLEXITY		MIXING DIFFICULTY
LOW ⊢O─⊣ HIGH	Y	LOW ⊢──O─⊣ HIGH

1 ounce light rum
1 ounce brandy
½ ounce lime juice
¼ ounce simple syrup
1 dash curaçao

Shake with cracked ice;
strain into chilled cocktail glass.
Garnish with a lime squeeze.

RUM
BASE

SOUTH SEA

TASTE COMPLEXITY		MIXING DIFFICULTY
LOW ⊙ HIGH		LOW ⊙ HIGH

2 ounces brown rum
¾ ounce curaçao
¾ ounce lime juice

Shake with cracked ice;
strain into chilled cocktail glass.
Garnish with a lime squeeze.

TROPICAL

TASTE COMPLEXITY		MIXING DIFFICULTY
LOW ⊙ HIGH		LOW ⊙ HIGH

1½ ounces light rum
¾ ounce curaçao
¾ ounce lime juice

Shake with cracked ice;
strain into chilled cocktail glass.
Garnish with a lime squeeze.

SUNSHINE

TASTE COMPLEXITY		MIXING DIFFICULTY
LOW ⊙ HIGH		LOW ⊙ HIGH

1 ounce light rum
1 ounce dry vermouth
½ ounce crème de cassis
½ ounce lemon juice

Shake with cracked ice;
strain into chilled cocktail glass.
Garnish with a lemon twist.

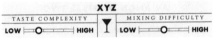

XYZ

TASTE COMPLEXITY		MIXING DIFFICULTY
LOW ⊙ HIGH		LOW ⊙ HIGH

1½ ounces light rum
¾ ounce Cointreau
¾ ounce lemon juice

Shake with cracked ice;
strain into chilled cocktail glass.
Garnish with a lemon twist.

TAMPA

TASTE COMPLEXITY		MIXING DIFFICULTY
LOW ⊙ HIGH		LOW ⊙ HIGH

1½ ounces light rum
¾ ounce gin
¾ ounce lemon juice

Shake with cracked ice;
strain into chilled cocktail glass.
Garnish with a lemon twist.

• ZOMBIE •

TASTE COMPLEXITY		MIXING DIFFICULTY
LOW ⊙ HIGH		LOW ⊙ HIGH

1½ ounces brown rum
¾ ounce Jamaican dark rum
¾ ounce light rum
¾ ounce pineapple juice
¾ ounce papaya juice
1 ounce lime juice • ¼ ounce simple syrup

Shake with cracked ice; strain into
chilled tumbler or hurricane glass. Garnish
with a pineapple wheel and a cherry.
Float Demerara rum.

218

Some of you may find this selection of vodka cocktails slight, particularly when you consider the popularity of this spirit. We chose to keep it short, because nearly all the cocktails included in this book could be made with vodka instead of the prescribed base spirit. So if vodka is your spirit of choice, experiment with any recipe you wish.

AVIATION, NUMBER TWO

TASTE COMPLEXITY		MIXING DIFFICULTY	
LOW ⊢O⊣ HIGH		LOW ⊢O⊣ HIGH	

1½ ounces citrus-flavored vodka
½ ounce maraschino liqueur
½ ounce lemon juice

Shake with cracked ice;
strain into chilled cocktail glass.
Garnish with a lemon twist.

BLOODY MARY

TASTE COMPLEXITY		MIXING DIFFICULTY	
LOW ⊢O⊣ HIGH		LOW ⊢O⊣ HIGH	

1½ ounces vodka
3 ounces tomato juice
½ ounce lemon juice
7 drops Worcestershire sauce
3 drops Tabasco sauce
Several shakes of freshly ground pepper
1 dash celery salt
Freshly grated horseradish

Shake with cracked ice; pour into chilled Old Fashioned glass filled with ice. Garnish with a pickled asparagus sprig or a celery stalk.

* CAESAR *

TASTE COMPLEXITY		MIXING DIFFICULTY	
LOW ⊢O⊣ HIGH		LOW ⊢O⊣ HIGH	

1½ ounces vodka
4 ounces Clamato juice
1 dash Worcestershire sauce
2 to 3 dashes horseradish
1 pinch of salt and pepper
Celery salt
Celery stalk

Shake first five ingredients with cracked ice;
strain into chilled pint glass.
Coat the rim of the glass with celery salt.
Garnish with a celery stalk and a lemon wheel.

CAJUN KAMIKAZE

TASTE COMPLEXITY		MIXING DIFFICULTY	
LOW ⊢O⊣ HIGH		LOW ⊢O⊣ HIGH	

1½ ounces pepper-flavored vodka
½ ounce Cointreau
¼ ounce Rose's lime juice
½ ounce fresh-squeezed lime juice

Shake with cracked ice;
strain into chilled cocktail glass.
Garnish with a lime squeeze.

* COSMOPOLITAN *

TASTE COMPLEXITY		MIXING DIFFICULTY	
LOW O⊣ HIGH		LOW ⊢O⊣ HIGH	

1½ ounces vodka
¾ ounce Cointreau
½ ounce lime juice
1 splash cranberry juice

Shake with cracked ice;
strain into chilled cocktail glass.
Garnish with a lime wheel.

VODKA

BASE

• THE DRINK WITHOUT A NAME •

TASTE COMPLEXITY		MIXING DIFFICULTY
LOW ⟜⟜⊙ HIGH		LOW ⟜⟜⊙⟜ HIGH

2 ounces vodka
¼ ounce Cointreau
⅛ ounce Chartreuse

Stir with cracked ice;
strain into chilled cocktail glass.
Garnish with an orange twist.

A Paul Harrington original

• LEMON DROP •

TASTE COMPLEXITY		MIXING DIFFICULTY
LOW ⊙⟜⟜ HIGH		LOW ⟜⟜⊙⟜ HIGH

1½ ounces citrus-flavored vodka
¾ ounce lemon juice
1 teaspoon simple syrup

Shake with cracked ice;
strain into chilled cocktail glass
rimmed with sugar.
Garnish with a lemon wheel.

EVAN

TASTE COMPLEXITY		MIXING DIFFICULTY
LOW ⊙⟜⟜ HIGH		LOW ⟜⟜⊙⟜ HIGH

2 ounces citrus-flavored vodka
½ ounce Cointreau
½ ounce lemon juice
1 splash of cranberry juice

Shake with cracked ice;
strain into chilled cocktail glass.
Garnish with a lemon twist.

A Paul Harrington original

• MOSCOW MULE •

TASTE COMPLEXITY		MIXING DIFFICULTY
LOW ⟜⊙⟜ HIGH		LOW ⟜⊙⟜ HIGH

2 ounces vodka
1 ounce lime juice
4 ounces ginger beer

Stir vodka and juice in chilled Collins glass.
Add cracked ice and a swizzle stick;
top with chilled ginger beer.
Garnish with a lime squeeze.

KAMIKAZE

TASTE COMPLEXITY		MIXING DIFFICULTY
LOW ⟜⊙⟜ HIGH		LOW ⟜⊙⟜ HIGH

1½ ounces vodka
½ ounce Cointreau
½ ounce lime juice
½ ounce Rose's lime juice

Shake with cracked ice;
strain into chilled cocktail glass.
Garnish with a lime squeeze.

• PETIT ZINC •

TASTE COMPLEXITY		MIXING DIFFICULTY
LOW ⟜⊙⟜ HIGH		LOW ⟜⟜⊙ HIGH

1 ounce vodka
½ ounce Cointreau
½ ounce sweet vermouth
½ ounce orange juice

Shake with cracked ice;
strain into chilled cocktail glass.
Garnish with an orange wheel
or a maraschino cherry.

BLOODY MARIA

TASTE COMPLEXITY		MIXING DIFFICULTY	
LOW — HIGH		LOW — HIGH	

1½ ounce tequila or light rum
3 ounces tomato juice
½ ounce lime juice
Pinch of salt and pepper
1 dash Worcestershire sauce
2 to 3 dashes horseradish
Celery stalk

Shake with cracked ice; strain into chilled pint
glass filled with ice and rimmed with salt.
Garnish with a celery stalk and a lime wheel.

MAURI

TASTE COMPLEXITY		MIXING DIFFICULTY	
LOW — HIGH		LOW — HIGH	

1 ounce pepper-flavored vodka
1 ounce Silver Patrón tequila
¼ ounce brine from cocktail onions
1 dash lime juice

Shake with cracked ice;
strain into chilled cocktail glass.
Garnish with a cocktail onion
and a lime squeeze.

A Paul Harrington original

• DIABLO •

TASTE COMPLEXITY		MIXING DIFFICULTY	
LOW — HIGH		LOW — HIGH	

1½ ounces tequila
¾ ounce crème de cassis
½ ounce lime juice
Ginger ale

Stir tequila and cassis with cracked ice;
strain into chilled Collins glass filled with ice.
Top with ginger ale, and
garnish with a lime wheel.

TEQUILA GIMLET

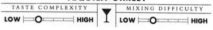

TASTE COMPLEXITY		MIXING DIFFICULTY	
LOW — HIGH		LOW — HIGH	

2 ounces white tequila
½ ounce Rose's lime juice
½ ounce lime juice

Shake with cracked ice;
strain into chilled cocktail glass.
Garnish with a lime squeeze.

• MARGARITA •

TASTE COMPLEXITY		MIXING DIFFICULTY	
LOW — HIGH		LOW — HIGH	

1½ ounces tequila
¾ ounce Cointreau
½ ounce lemon juice
½ ounce lime juice

Shake with cracked ice;
strain into chilled wine goblet
or cocktail glass with kosher salt on its rim.
Garnish with a lime wheel.

TEQUILA SUNRISE

TASTE COMPLEXITY		MIXING DIFFICULTY	
LOW — HIGH		LOW — HIGH	

1½ ounces tequila
2 ounces orange juice
¼ ounce lime juice
1 dash grenadine

Shake with cracked ice;
strain into chilled Collins glass filled with ice.
Garnish with a lime wheel.

ABSINTHE FRAPPÉ

TASTE COMPLEXITY		MIXING DIFFICULTY
LOW ⊢──O── HIGH		LOW ⊢─O── HIGH

1 ounce Pernod
1 teaspoon simple syrup

Shake with cracked ice;
strain into a highball glass.
Pack with cracked ice.

BLACK AND TAN

TASTE COMPLEXITY		MIXING DIFFICULTY
LOW ⊢──O── HIGH	⏶	LOW ⊢O─── HIGH

1½ ounces sweet vermouth
¼ ounce Pernod
¾ ounce crème de cassis

Shake with cracked ice;
strain into chilled cocktail glass.
Garnish with a thin lemon slice.

* AMERICANO *

TASTE COMPLEXITY		MIXING DIFFICULTY
LOW ⊢───O─ HIGH		LOW ⊢─O── HIGH

1 ounce Campari
½ ounce sweet vermouth
Soda water

Add Campari and sweet vermouth
over ice in chilled Collins glass.
Top with chilled soda water, and stir.
Garnish with an orange wheel.

DUBONNET FIZZ

TASTE COMPLEXITY		MIXING DIFFICULTY
LOW ⊢──O── HIGH		LOW ⊢──O── HIGH

2 ounces Dubonnet
½ ounce cherry brandy
1 ounce orange juice
½ ounce lemon juice
Soda water

Shake first four ingredients with cracked ice;
strain into chilled highball glass.
Top with chilled soda water.
Garnish with a lemon twist.

AMER PICON FIZZ

TASTE COMPLEXITY		MIXING DIFFICULTY
LOW ⊢───O─ HIGH	▮	LOW ⊢───O─ HIGH

2 ounces Amer Picon
½ ounce lemon juice
¾ ounce grenadine
1 teaspoon egg white
Soda water

Flash blend first three ingredients
with cracked ice; strain into chilled tumbler.
Top with chilled soda water, and
garnish with a lime squeeze.

KISS-ME-QUICK

TASTE COMPLEXITY		MIXING DIFFICULTY
LOW ⊢────O HIGH	⏶	LOW ⊢─O── HIGH

2 ounces Pernod
2 dashes Angostura bitters
3 dashes curaçao

Shake with cracked ice;
strain into chilled cocktail glass.
Garnish with a lemon twist.

BITTER
BASE

• NEGRONI (CAMPARINETE) •

TASTE COMPLEXITY		MIXING DIFFICULTY	
LOW ⊢━━O━⊣ HIGH		LOW ⊢━━O━━⊣ HIGH	

1 ounce gin
1 ounce sweet vermouth
1 ounce Campari

Shake with cracked ice;
strain into chilled cocktail glass.
Garnish with an orange slice.

• PICON PUNCH •

1½ ounces Amer Picon
1 dash grenadine
Soda water
Float of brandy

Coat inside of chilled 16-ounce glass with
grenadine. Add Amer Picon and ice;
top with soda water, and stir.
Float brandy, and garnish
with a lemon twist.

PICON-CURAÇAO HIGHBALL

1½ ounces Amer Picon
¾ ounce curaçao
Soda water

Shake Amer Picon and curaçao
with cracked ice;
strain into Collins glass filled with ice.
Top with soda water, and
garnish with a lemon squeeze.

PICON WHISKEY

1 ounce bourbon
1 ounce Amer Picon
1 dash simple syrup

Shake with cracked ice;
strain into chilled cocktail glass.
Garnish with a lemon twist
or an orange twist.

• PICON-LIMÓN •

TASTE COMPLEXITY		MIXING DIFFICULTY	
LOW ⊢━━O━⊣ HIGH		LOW ⊢━O━━⊣ HIGH	

1½ ounces Amer Picon
½ ounce crème de cassis or grenadine
½ ounce Rose's lime juice
Soda water

Stir first three ingredients with cracked ice;
strain into chilled 16-ounce glass.
Top with soda water, and
garnish with a lemon twist.

• PIMM'S CUP •

2 ounces Pimm's No. 1
3 ounces ginger ale
Cucumber

Pour Pimm's into chilled pint glass;
fill with ice. Top with chilled ginger ale.
Garnish with a lemon wheel
and a cucumber slice.

ADONIS

TASTE COMPLEXITY		MIXING DIFFICULTY
LOW ⊙ HIGH		LOW ⊙ HIGH

2 ounces dry sherry
1 ounce sweet vermouth
2 dashes orange bitters

Stir with cracked ice;
pour into chilled cocktail glass.
Garnish with a lemon twist.

• BLACK VELVET •

TASTE COMPLEXITY		MIXING DIFFICULTY
LOW ⊙ HIGH		LOW ⊙ HIGH

4 ounces champagne or sparkling wine
1 ounce chilled Guinness stout

Pour chilled Guinness into frosted flute.
Add chilled champagne, and
garnish with a lemon twist.

• BELLINI •

TASTE COMPLEXITY		MIXING DIFFICULTY
LOW ⊙ HIGH		LOW ⊙ HIGH

4 ounces *prosecco* (Italian sparkling wine)
1 ounce white peach purée

Peel and purée 3 to 4 very ripe white
peaches; mix nectar with 1 ounce simple
syrup. Strain through coarse cheesecloth;
refrigerate until chilled. Pour 1 ounce of
nectar into a frosted champagne flute;
top with *prosecco*.

BRUT

TASTE COMPLEXITY		MIXING DIFFICULTY
LOW ⊙ HIGH		LOW ⊙ HIGH

1½ ounces dry vermouth
¾ ounce Amer Picon
1 dash Peychaud's bitters

Shake with cracked ice;
strain into chilled cocktail glass.
Garnish with a thin lemon slice.

BISHOP

TASTE COMPLEXITY		MIXING DIFFICULTY
LOW ⊙ HIGH		LOW ⊙ HIGH

3 ounces red wine
2 ounces lemon juice
2 teaspoons simple syrup

Shake with cracked ice;
strain into chilled wine glass.
Garnish with an orange twist.

CHAMPAGNE COCKTAIL

TASTE COMPLEXITY		MIXING DIFFICULTY
LOW ⊙ HIGH		LOW ⊙ HIGH

5 ounces champagne
1 sugar cube
Angostura bitters

Soak sugar cube with Angostura bitters.
Place cube in bottom of chilled champagne
flute. Fill with chilled champagne.
Garnish with a lemon twist.

DEATH IN THE AFTERNOON

TASTE COMPLEXITY		MIXING DIFFICULTY	
LOW ═══○═══ HIGH		LOW ═══○═══ HIGH	

5 ounces champagne
½ ounce Pernod

Pour Pernod into chilled flute.
Top with chilled champagne,
and garnish with a lemon twist.

Credited to Ernest Hemingway

SHERRY TWIST

TASTE COMPLEXITY		MIXING DIFFICULTY	
LOW ═══○═══ HIGH		LOW ═══○═══ HIGH	

1 ounce amontillado sherry
½ ounce dry vermouth
½ ounce Cointreau
½ ounce brandy
½ ounce lemon juice

Shake with cracked ice;
strain into chilled cocktail glass.
Garnish with a lemon twist.

* FRENCH 75 *

TASTE COMPLEXITY		MIXING DIFFICULTY	
LOW ═══○═══ HIGH		LOW ═══○═══ HIGH	

4 ounces champagne
¼ ounce gin
¼ ounce Cointreau
¼ ounce lemon juice

Shake gin, Cointreau, and
lemon juice with cracked ice;
strain into chilled flute.
Top with chilled champagne, and
garnish with a lemon twist.

VERMOUTH CASSIS

TASTE COMPLEXITY		MIXING DIFFICULTY	
LOW ═══○═══ HIGH		LOW ═══○═══ HIGH	

1½ ounces dry vermouth
½ ounce crème de cassis
Soda water

Stir with ice cubes;
strain into chilled wine glass filled with ice.
Top with soda water.
Garnish with a lemon twist.

PRINCE OF WALES

TASTE COMPLEXITY		MIXING DIFFICULTY	
LOW ═══○═══ HIGH		LOW ═══○═══ HIGH	

1 ounce Madeira
1 ounce brandy
1 dash Angostura bitters
1 teaspoon curaçao
Champagne

Shake with cracked ice;
strain into chilled wine glass filled with ice.
Top with champagne, and
garnish with a lemon twist.

VERMOUTH AND CURAÇAO

TASTE COMPLEXITY		MIXING DIFFICULTY	
LOW ═══○═══ HIGH		LOW ○═══ HIGH	

1½ ounces dry vermouth
¾ ounce curaçao
Soda water

Stir with ice cubes;
strain into chilled wine glass filled with ice.
Top with soda water and
garnish with a lemon twist.

• COMBUSTIBLE EDISON •

TASTE COMPLEXITY		MIXING DIFFICULTY	
LOW ⊶—O—⊶ HIGH		LOW ⊶——O ⊶ HIGH	

2 ounces brandy
1 ounce Campari
1 ounce lemon juice

Shake Campari and lemon juice with
cracked ice; strain into chilled cocktail glass.
Heat brandy in chafing dish. When warm,
ignite the brandy and pour in a flaming
stream into the cocktail glass.

• FISH HOUSE PUNCH •

TASTE COMPLEXITY		MIXING DIFFICULTY	
LOW ⊶—O—⊶ HIGH		LOW ⊶——O—⊶ HIGH	

36 ounces dark rum
24 ounces lemon juice
25 ounces brandy
4 ounces peach brandy
¾ pound superfine sugar
40 ounces water

Dissolve sugar in a little water. Add lemon
juice and remaining water; stir. Two hours
before serving, add spirits and refrigerate.
Serve in chilled glasses. Makes 30 servings.

HOT BONNIE

TASTE COMPLEXITY		MIXING DIFFICULTY	
LOW ⊶—O—⊶ HIGH		LOW ⊶—O——⊶ HIGH	

1½ ounces bourbon
1 teaspoon honey
¼ ounce lemon juice
4 ounces hot water

Stir ingredients in warmed snifter or mug.
Garnish with a lemon squeeze.

SANGRIA

TASTE COMPLEXITY		MIXING DIFFICULTY	
LOW ⊶—O—⊶ HIGH		LOW ⊶—O——⊶ HIGH	

64 ounces dry red wine
12 ounces brandy or light rum
8 ounces orange juice
4 ounces lemon juice
8 ounces soda water
4 slices each of lemon, lime, and orange

In a pitcher or bowl, stir ingredients with ice
molds. For effervescence, splash with champagne. Serve in chilled wine glass. Garnish
with a lemon twist. Makes 30 servings.

225

SINGAPORE SLING

TASTE COMPLEXITY		MIXING DIFFICULTY	
LOW O—⊶ HIGH		LOW ⊶——O—⊶ HIGH	

1½ ounces gin
½ ounce cherry brandy
½ ounce crème de cassis
½ ounce lemon juice
½ ounce lime
1 dash grenadine

Shake with cracked ice; strain into chilled
Collins glass fill with cracked ice.
Top with soda water.

• TOM AND JERRY •

TASTE COMPLEXITY		MIXING DIFFICULTY	
LOW ⊶—O—⊶ HIGH		LOW ⊶————O ⊶ HIGH	

1½ ounces bourbon, rye, or brandy
¾ ounce rum
1 egg, chilled
1 teaspoon superfine sugar
1 dash allspice
Milk or water

Stir egg yolk, spirits, sugar, and spice in warmed
mug or wine goblet. Whip egg white until it
stiffens; stir into mixture. Add hot milk or water
to taste, and serve. Garnish with grated nutmeg.

BULLSHOT

TASTE COMPLEXITY		MIXING DIFFICULTY
LOW ⊶○⊶ HIGH	Y	LOW ⊢○⊶ HIGH

1½ ounces vodka
3 ounces beef bouillon
1 to 3 dashes Worcestershire sauce
1 dash A-1 sauce
1 dash Tabasco
1 dash Angostura bitters
Celery salt

Shake with cracked ice; strain into chilled
cocktail glass rimmed with celery salt.
Garnish with a lemon squeeze.

EYE-OPENER

TASTE COMPLEXITY		MIXING DIFFICULTY
LOW ⊢○ HIGH	Y	LOW ⊢○ HIGH

1½ ounces light rum
¼ ounce Pernod
¼ ounce curaçao
½ teaspoon sugar
1 teaspoon egg yolk

Shake well with cracked ice;
strain into chilled cocktail glass.

HAIR OF THE DOG

TASTE COMPLEXITY		MIXING DIFFICULTY
LOW ⊶○⊶ HIGH	Y	LOW ⊶○⊶ HIGH

2 ounces scotch
½ ounce cream
1 teaspoon honey

Shake with shaved ice or
blend with an electric mixer;
strain into chilled cocktail glass.

PICK-ME-UP

TASTE COMPLEXITY		MIXING DIFFICULTY
LOW ⊶○⊶ HIGH	❘	LOW ⊶○⊶ HIGH

1 ounce brandy
¼ ounce Cointreau
1 dash Pernod
1 dash orange juice
3 ounces sparkling wine

Chill champagne flute with cracked ice and
dash of Pernod. Shake brandy, Cointreau, and
juice with ice. Empty flute of ice, and strain
into chilled flute. Top with chilled sparkling
wine, and garnish with a lemon twist.

• RAMOS GIN FIZZ •

TASTE COMPLEXITY		MIXING DIFFICULTY
LOW ⊢○⊶ HIGH	❘	LOW ⊢○ HIGH

1½ ounces gin
½ ounce lemon juice
3 to 4 drops orange-flower water
1 teaspoon simple syrup
2 ounces cream
1 egg white
Soda water

Place first six ingredients in blender with one
scoop of cracked ice; flash blend for 15 to 30
seconds. Pour into chilled wine goblet; top with
soda water. Garnish with a flower blossom.

STOMACH REVIVER

TASTE COMPLEXITY		MIXING DIFFICULTY
LOW ⊢○ HIGH	Y	LOW ⊶○⊶ HIGH

1½ ounces brandy
½ ounce Kümmel
¼ ounce Fernet Branca
¼ ounce Angostura bitters

Stir with cracked ice;
strain into chilled cocktail glass.
Garnish with a lemon twist.

⟝ GLOSSARY ⟞

A

ABSINTHE
(AB-sinth) • A bitter, anis-flavored distillate, also known as "the notorious green muse" and blamed for making men sterile, virgins randy, and the nicest folk murderous. This LIQUEUR, made from herbs steeped in high-proof spirits, is said to derive its reported narcotic and addictive qualities from *Artemisia absinthium*, or WORMWOOD. Absinthe is no longer legal in some countries – including the United States, France, and Switzerland – but absinthe substitutes (such as New Orleans' Herbsaint, Spain's Ojen, and France's Pernod) are commonly available, as are numerous recipes for making this CORDIAL at home.

This elixir was invented in Switzerland as a stomachic and general cure-all by Pierre Ordinaire, a French physician, in 1792. Several years later, Henri-Louis Pernod began promoting the liqueur, and his family name remains closely linked with absinthe.

AGAVE
(ah-GAH-vay) • See TEQUILA.

AGUARDIENTE
(ah-gwar-dee-YEN-tay) • The term used in Spanish-speaking countries for distilled SPIRITS that have not been aged. Raw-tasting, colorless liquids, *Aguardientes* can be produced from either grapes or molasses. The name means "burning water."

AKVAVIT, AQUAVIT
(ahk-vah-VEET) • The favored drink of the Scandinavian countries, and one best sipped cold and fast. Flavored mainly with caraway seeds, some brands of akvavit also smack of citrus and herbs. This clear, high-proof spirit, distilled from potatoes or grain, has a history going back centuries. Legend has it (as reported in Peter Hallgarten's *Spirits & Liqueurs*) that "if a man be bereft of speech in death, give him akvavit on his lips, and he shall at once regain his tongue." Similar in taste to flavored VODKAS.

AMER PICON
(a-mer PEE-con) • A bitter orange spirit that does wonders for the appetite and works well as a stomachic. Frenchman Gaëtan Picon concocted Amer Picon in 1837 while living in Philippeville, Belgium. Made with orange peel, gentian, and cinchona, Amer Picon is one of the few orange BITTERS readily available today.

AÑEJO
(an-YAY-ho) • A Spanish word for *old*, *añejo* is a term applied to RUMS aged more than six years and TEQUILAS aged more than three.

ANGOSTURA
(ang-oh-STOOR-ah) • See BITTERS.

ANIS, ANISE
(AN-ihss) • A French or Spanish licorice-flavored LIQUEUR made with aniseed. These cordials are sweet, are usually colorless or yellow, and range in PROOF from 60 to 100.

APÉRITIF
(ah-pehr-uh-TEEF) • The general term (from the French) for beverages enjoyed before a meal to stimulate the appetite. These potables can be wine-based, alcohol-based, BITTERS-based, or a mixture of the three. A good apéritif is to its drinker what a ringing bell was to Pavlov's dog.

APPLEJACK
Jersey lightning – what Americans call their traditional apple BRANDY and everyone else considers the uncouth counterpart to French CALVADOS. Applejack contains less than 50 percent apple brandy; the remaining spirits may be any NEUTRAL SPIRIT. There's only one licensed applejack distiller left in the world: Laird & Company in Scobeyville, New Jersey.

AQUAVIT
(AHK-wuh-veet) • See AKVAVIT.

ARMAGNAC
(ar-mahn-YAK) • BRANDY from the Armagnac region of Gascony, France. Distilled at lower PROOFS than most cognacs, this robust brandy is often considered second only to cognac itself.

B

BACARDI
See RUM.

BARSPOON
A long-handled stainless steel spoon, about 14 inches in length. Most hold between one-half and one teaspoonful and have a "twirled" handle that aids in stirring.

BÉNÉDICTINE
(ben-eh-DIHK-teen) • A COGNAC-based herbal LIQUEUR with a tradition as distinctive as its taste. A closely guarded secret, the recipe for this cordial is known only to a few. First devised in the 16th century by Bénédictine monks in Fécamp, Normandy, it is said to contain angelica root, arnica blooms, lemon peels, thyme, cardamom, peppermint, cassia, hyssop, and cloves blended in water, sweeteners, and cologne spirits before aging. The D.O.M. on the label stands for *Deo Optimo Maximo*, meaning "to God, most good, most great."

BITTERS
The general term for highly aromatic, bitter-tasting SPIRITS containing herbs, spices, roots, and plant extracts. Bitters are used as medicinal tonics, as APÉRITIFS, and as accents in mixed drinks. Bars used to produce their own brands of bitters, but now only a handful of manufacturers make these high-PROOF tonics. AMER PICON, FERNET BRANCA, and CAMPARI, though not packaged like other bitters, can be used in the same fashion. The most notable brands and types of traditional bitters include:

—ANGOSTURA
(ang-oh-STOOR-ah) • A well-known brand of bitters dating back to 1830, Angostura was created in Venezuela as a malaria tonic by Dr. Johann Gottlieb Benjamin Siegert, a Prussian military surgeon. Now made in Trinidad and bottled at 90 proof, Angostura reportedly contains more than 40 herbs and extracts, including QUININE and orange rind.

—ORANGE BITTERS
The most difficult to find of all bitters, orange bitters, flavored principally with the skins of bitter oranges, are called for in many of the great classic cocktails. The Fee Brothers of

Rochester, New York, may very well be the last makers of orange bitters in the United States.

—PEYCHAUD'S
Essential to the Sazerac, Peychaud's – a child of New Orleans – was first made by the famous alchemist Antoine Amédée Peychaud in the early 1800s.

BLENDED WHISKEY, WHISKY
See WHISKEY, WHISKY.

BOURBON
See WHISKEY, WHISKY.

BRANDY
This term is Esperanto for distillates made from fermented fruit. The finest brandies are still made in Cognac, a region in the south of France near Bordeaux. In California, a few small distilleries produce superior brandies for the price of an average cognac. Carneros Alambic Distillery and Germain Robin make wonderful brandies using the same processes as their French counterparts.

BUCK
A tall mixed drink with a name derived from its supposed kick. Unlike such tall drinks as the COLLINS, the FIZZ, and the RICKEY, the Buck doesn't include sugar, and is mixed with ginger ale and a citrus wedge.

BYRRH
(bir) • A French wine-based APÉRITIF produced on the Mediterranean coast. Fortified with BRANDY, byrrh gets its color from red wine and its bitter taste from QUININE.

C

CACAO, CRÈME DE
(krehm deuh kah-KAH-oh) • A LIQUEUR flavored with cacao and sometimes with vanilla beans. Cacao, as the sweet-toothed are aware, is also used to make cocoa and chocolate. Always remember that a little of this goes a long way in a cocktail. Most drink recipes call for the colorless version for mixing.

CACHAÇA
(kah-SHAH-sah) • A fiery Brazilian BRANDY that tastes like a cross between TEQUILA and RUM. Distilled from sugarcane grown in the country's northeast region, cachaça was originally considered firewater for the poor, but is now sipped neat or mixed in a Caipirinha along Rio de Janeiro's Copacabana by moneyed Brazilians and tourists alike.

CALVADOS
(KAL-vah-dohs) • A fruit BRANDY distilled from fermented apple cider, made in Normandy, France.

CAMPARI
(kahm-PAH-ree) • An aromatic Italian LIQUEUR made from herbs and most noticeably flavored with QUININE. The recipe for Campari has remained a closely guarded secret ever since Gaspare Campari invented this BITTER in 1860, after 18 years of mixing liqueurs.

CANADIAN WHISKY
See WHISKEY, WHISKY.

CASSIS, CRÈME DE
(krehm deuh kah-SEES) • A LIQUEUR steeped from black currants, crème de cassis dates from the 16th century, when

monks near Dijon, France, produced this cordial as a cure for snakebite, jaundice, and general wretchedness. The modern-day formula was developed by L. Lagoute in Dijon.

CHAMPAGNE
(sham-PAYN) • Sparkling wine produced in the Champagne region of France. As COGNAC is the best of brandies, champagne is the paragon of sparkling wines.

CHARTREUSE
(shar-TROOZ) • A rich herbal DIGESTIF available in pale green and in yellow. The green version is 110 proof and is said to contain 130 herbs and essences, including sweet flag, orange peel, peppermint oil, dried tops of hyssop, balm, angelica seeds and root, tonka bean, and cardamom. Classic cocktails usually call for the yellow version, but nowadays the green is more popular.

Chartreuse was first made in 1605 by the Carthusian monks of La Grande Chartreuse, a monastery in the French Alps founded by St. Bruno in 1084. As members of a strict contemplative order of the Catholic Church, the monks can neither beg nor work, and subsist solely on the royalties they receive for each bottle of Chartreuse sold. Compagnie Française de la Grande Chartreuse bottles and distributes the cordial, though its executives occasionally grumble about the difficulties of turning a profit for overscrupulous monks.

CHASER
A mild drink taken after a PONY of WHISKEY, TEQUILA, or some other spirit. Chasers can be soda, water, juice from squeezes of citrus, "bites" of salt, or beer.

CHERRY HEERING
A well-known brand of cherry liqueur that's been produced commercially in Denmark for about two centuries.

CHIMNEY GLASS
A tall, thin glass holding about 10 to 14 ounces. Similar to a COLLINS glass.

COCKTAIL
Traditional APÉRITIF cocktails – sleek, refined, and limitless in variation – are typically composed of a base, a modifier, and an accent. The ideal cocktail is 3 to 4 ½ ounces in volume, and is served well chilled in a stemmed glass holding no more than 6 ounces. It is never sweet and always elegant.

As for the word's origin, H. L. Mencken mentions several possibilities in his fine tome *The American Language*. Among the most notable are the hypotheses that the word derives from the French *coquetier*, or egg cup, and was first used in New Orleans, perhaps by Antoine Amédée Peychaud of BITTERS fame, or that the word comes from *coquetel*, "the name of a mixed drink known in the vicinity of Bordeaux and introduced to America by French officers during the Revolution." More amusing are conjectures that the term *cocktail* comes from *cock ale*, bitters and spirits given to cocks training for a fight, or from *cock tailings*, a mixture of leftover spirits sold for cheap. Of course, as Mencken was careful to note, all these rationales are "somewhat fishy."

COGNAC
(KON-yak) • A wine-producing region of France, best known for its superior BRANDY.

COINTREAU

(KWAHN-troh) • An especially fine TRIPLE SEC produced by the French company of the same name. Less cloying than other versions of this clear, orange-flavored liqueur, Cointreau is a perfect mixer in a cocktail, provided it's not poured with a heavy hand.

The brand was created in the mid-1800s by the Cointreau family, and remains an 80-PROOF BRANDY-based LIQUEUR made with the peels of both bitter and sweet oranges.

COLLINS

A family of mixed drinks made with a primary spirit, lemon juice, soda water, and sugar. A Collins should be served with ice in its namesake glass, which holds 10 to 14 ounces.

CORDIAL

The American term for LIQUEUR.

CRÈME DE

(krehm deuh) • The telltale stem of a LIQUEUR'S name, typically modified by its dominant flavor, as in CRÈME DE MENTHE and CRÈME DE VIOLETTE.

CURAÇAO

(KYOOR-uh-soh) • A LIQUEUR made from bitter oranges, BRANDY, and sugar, this is really just another type of TRIPLE SEC. Although curaçao plays second fiddle to COINTREAU, it's preferable to any other triple sec because it's not overly sweet. Curaçao comes in red, white, and blue, and shares its name with an island in the South Caribbean.

D

DARK AGE OF AMERICAN DRINKING

The era of drink – from 1969 to 1989 – that we'd most like to forget. Epitomized by the FERN BARS of the '70s, this dark age gave little to the world of drink but sugary concoctions owing more to the Slurpee than to the classic cocktail. The Lemon Drop and the Caesar constitute this era's only saving graces.

DASH

One-eighth of a teaspoon, or roughly 1/2 centiliter.

DEMERARA

(dehm-uh-REHR-ah) • See RUM.

DIGESTIF

(dee-zheh-STEEF) • An after-dinner drink that aids digestion and acts as a nightcap, warming the stomach while soothing the senses.

The royalty of the digestifs are the BRANDIES, with cognac the highest majesty of all. Other traditional digestifs include PORTS, SHERRIES, GRAPPAS, and CRÈME LIQUEURS.

DISTILLATION

Distillation is the art of purifying spirits. If you understand how a liquid turns into a vapor and back into a liquid again, you understand the basics of distillation: First, a mixture is heated to separate its volatile parts from its less active parts. Next, the vapor is cooled and condensed to be used later to produce a refined spirit. Distillation is why certain alcohols have different tastes and aromas.

DRAMBUIE

(dram-BOO-ee) • A venerable scotch named after the Gaelic phrase *An Dram Buidheach* – meaning "the drink that satisfies." Made from 30 to 60 malt whiskeys and three or four grain whiskeys, Drambuie is flavored with honey and herbs, following a recipe originally held by Bonnie Prince Charlie.

DRY

An adjective that describes a cocktail based on the type of VERMOUTH used or the degree of sweetness desired. Dry is the opposite of sweet. In a cocktail that calls for vermouth, the less vermouth you use, the drier the drink will be. See WET.

DUBONNET

(doo-boh-NAY) • Originally a French wine-based APÉRITIF made with herbs and QUININE and possessing a rich, slightly sweet taste, Dubonnet is now produced in California and is available in a fruity red and a dry white version.

E

ERA OF THE RAT PACK

During this era of drink, from 1955 to 1968, the first so-called swingers inspired the creation of only a few drinks but did sip plenty of classics. According to Joseph Lanza's *The Cocktail: The Influence of Spirits on the American Psyche*: "The Rat Pack was indeed a Hollywood product, spawned by the supreme film noir couple Humphrey Bogart and Lauren Bacall. Bacall, who became Mrs. Bogart, supposedly coined the term *Rat Pack* during the late '50s when it was still a small cabal of swingers hanging out in Los Angeles' Holmby Hills.... [It] included Sinatra, Irving 'Swifty' Lazar, Sid Luft, Judy Garland, Joey Bishop, Sammy Davis Jr., Shirley MacLaine, and others...."

EAU DE VIE

(oh deuh VEE) • A trade term applied to all clear distillates, but typically dropped after the product has been aged or processed. Most often associated with fruit BRANDIES, the term *eau de vie* can be further modified by adding the suffixes *de cidre, de poire, de marc,* and so on. Each *eau de vie* has unique qualities, though they all share a not-so-subtle burn when tossed quickly down the gullet.

F

FERN BAR

The quintessential singles bar. The fern bar dates back to 1969, when Norman Hobday moved to San Francisco, reinvented himself as Henry Africa, and opened the first fern-filled bar on record. Fern bars capitalized on the Age of Aquarius and thrived into the early '80s, when Hard Rock Cafes lured their trend-happy clientele away. Decorated with electric trains, mounted wildebeests, and Tiffany-style lamps, fern bars picked up where Trader Vic – creator of the Mai Tai – left off. These bars must bear the blame for the "disco cocktails" of the DARK AGE OF AMERICAN DRINKING.

FERNET BRANCA

An Italian bitter DIGESTIF made with QUININE, popular in the States as well as in Italy. This bitter LIQUEUR, enjoyed over ice or with GIN, is often prescribed as a hangover cure.

FIFTH
A fifth of a gallon or ⅕ of a quart. The metric equivalent of a fifth is the 750-milliliter bottle.

FIZZ
A family of mixed drinks made with a primary spirit, lemon or lime juice, soda water, and sugar. A fizz should be served without ice and in a tall glass that holds less than 9 ounces. Although GIN is most commonly used in a fizz, any spirit higher than 80 PROOF will work.

FLASH BLENDING
A mechanical method of chilling large batches of drinks made with egg, cream, or fruit juice. Flash blending is also the method used in making soda fountain milkshakes.

FLOAT
An additional layer resting atop the drink. To "float" a liquid ingredient is to break its fall, notably in layered drinks such as POUSSE-CAFÉS. The easiest way to float a liquid is to use the back side of a BARSPOON: Turn the spoon upside down and lower it into the glass until it touches the liquid; pour the liquid slowly over the convex side of the spoon and let it flow gently into the glass. A cherry with a long stem can be used instead of a spoon, in which case the cherry is lowered in the same manner as the spoon and the liquid is poured slowly over the fruit.

FRAPPÉ
A type of potion made by pouring a drink over finely cracked ice in a cocktail glass. A warning: If you're in a New England dive bar, frappe (without the accent) means "milkshake."

FROSTED
The term for a glass whose rim has been coated with some granulated foodstuff, such as superfine sugar or celery salt. To frost a glass, moisten its rim with the appropriate citrus juice, taking care not to wet the rim too much. Then invert the glass and place it on a saucer covered evenly with either sugar or salt, pressing gently. Carefully shake the excess granules from the glass and fill it with the drink. Always frost less than half the circumference of the rim to give the imbiber the option of avoiding the sugar or salt.

G

GILL
An English liquid measurement, equal to ¼ pint, 4 ounces, or .1183 liter.

GIN
The classiest of the clear spirits, gin is distilled as a NEUTRAL SPIRIT and flavored primarily with JUNIPER berries, though countless herbs contribute to its pungent flavor. Gin's bite can be jarring and its extended use taxing, but like all things sublime, gin can truly transport.
—GENEVER GIN
See HOLLANDS.
—HOLLANDS
Gin produced by the Dutch, often called *Genever gin*. More robust than London Dry gin, Hollands is distilled in a manner that largely preserves the character of the malt and grains

used for distillation. Typically sipped cold and fast, Genever is overpowering in a Martini but well suited to a Pink Gin.
—LONDON DRY
What we generally think of when ordering gin. Unsweetened and tasting predominantly of JUNIPER berries, this is the SPIRIT that makes great Martinis.
—OLD TOM
An English gin similar to London Dry, but sweeter. A good choice for a Tom Collins, this gin – unlike most – rarely requires additional sweeteners.
—PLYMOUTH
Produced in England, Plymouth gin is heavier in body than London Dry gin. Rarely used in cocktails.

GIRL DRINKS
Don't blame us for this term – we've never liked its implications either. Historically, poor-quality bathtub liquors from the PROHIBITION era led to the creation of these drinks – sickly-sweet concoctions that completely mask the taste of the liquor. Today, men and women alike order girl drinks in the false hope of catching a cheap buzz. Girl drinks are the gourmet jellybeans of the cocktail world.

GOLDEN AGE OF AMERICAN DRINKING
The era of drink from 1865 to 1900, a time that was just as good as it sounds. This phrase was almost certainly coined by H. L. Mencken in *The American Language*: "…the new drinks of the 1865–1900 era, the Golden Age of American drinking, were largely eponymous and hence relatively decorous, e.g., rickey and Tom Collins." Other classics of this period include the Astoria, the Bronx, the Manhattan, and the Gimlet.

GOTHIC AGE OF AMERICAN DRINKING
The era of drink from 1775 to 1865, a period that boldly highlighted a drink's spirituous strength and little else. Compared to the men and women of that time, we are of weak gullets and flimsy stomachs. This term, too, was probably first used by H. L. Mencken in *The American Language*: "In the Gothic Age of American drinking and word making, between the Revolution and the Civil War, many fantastic drinks were invented, and given equally fantastic names: *stone fence, blue blazer,* and *stinkibus*…. The touring Englishmen of those days always spread news of such grotesque drink names, some of these Columbuses embellished the list with outlandish inventions of their own…." Classics from this heroic time include the Black Velvet, the Fish House Punch, and the Tom and Jerry.

GRAND MARNIER
(GRAN mahr-NYAY) • A French LIQUEUR with a rich COGNAC base and an orange flavor, this cordial has been popular for more than a century despite its high cost. Grand Marnier is used much like COINTREAU, a rival French TRIPLE SEC.

GRAPPA
(GRAHP-ah) • An Italian pomace BRANDY distilled from the refuse (skins, pips, and stalks) of grapes after they have been pressed to make wine. Rarely used in cocktails or mixed drinks, this crude spirit was once considered moonshine, but is now sipped at even the most respectable tables.

Many grappas today – marketed in hand-blown, 750-milliliter bottles – go for more than $100.

GRENADINE
A modern-day scientific miracle about as natural as a maraschino cherry, grenadine is a syrup that sets out to mimic the taste of pomegranates, usually without containing any. This mixer, which rarely contains alcohol, is most often called for in sweet cocktails.

H

HERBSAINT
An absinthe substitute from New Orleans – and, according to City of Sin locals, the recommended edge to the Sazerac.

HIGHBALL
The most popular tall drink. A highball is any mixed drink composed of one spirit and one mixer (traditionally soda water or ginger ale) that is served in a highball glass – short and stubby by nature and typically holding 10 to 12 ounces.
In *The Official Mixer's Manual*, Patrick Gavin Duffy claims to have created this drink: "It is one of my fondest hopes that the highball will again take its place as the leading American drink. I admit to being prejudiced about this – it was I who first brought the highball to America, in 1895. Although the distinction is claimed by the Parker House in Boston, I was finally given due credit for this innovation in the *New York Times* of not many years ago."

I

IRISH WHISKEY
See WHISKEY, WHISKY.

J

JIGGER
The bar term for 1½ ounces; also the name of a measuring device holding up to 1½ ounces of liquid. The best jiggers are really two cups end to end, one of which holds half the volume of the other.

JULEP
A family of drinks mixing water, sugar, and SPIRITS. English pharmacists of the 1400s prescribed juleps as a tonic to disguise bad-tasting medicine. In 1634, the julep was ennobled in literature by English poet John Milton's musings on the "cordial Julep."

JUNIPER
An evergreen that produces fruit essential to GIN'S flavor. The acrid oil of juniper berries is added to gin during distillation.

K

KÜMMEL
(KIHM-uhl) • A caraway-flavored LIQUEUR available in a variety of brands. Some claim the first kümmel was distilled in Holland during the late 16th century by one Erven Lucas Bols. Still known as Bolskümmel, this fine liqueur is reported (at least by *The Esquire Drink Book* of 1956) to have been so tasty that a Russian czar took the recipe back to his native

land, eventually making Russia a principal producer and consumer of kümmel.

L

LILLET
(lee-LAY) • A French wine-based APÉRITIF made from fruits and herbs, with a subdued bitter-orange taste. Dating from the late 19th century, this mixer was first made in the French village of Podensac. Lillet Blanc (or blonde) is made from dry white wine and Lillet Rouge (or red) from red wine.

LIQUEUR
The French term for the syrupy-sweet spirits known in the U.S. as CORDIALS. Liqueurs originated centuries ago as medicinal treatments to stimulate the heart. The base ingredient is high-proof *eau de vie* or neutral grain spirits.

M

MADEIRA
An unfortified wine originally exported from the tiny island of the same name. Shippers of the late 1700s noticed that wine stored in overheated ship hulls often became unpalatable by a voyage's end. To increase the wine's stability, BRANDY was added to this dessert wine.

MARASCHINO LIQUEUR
A clear, semi-dry LIQUEUR made from Marasca cherries grown along the Adriatic coasts of Italy and the former Yugoslavia. Because of its distillation process, maraschino imparts a slight flowery nose to many libations. Of all the cherry brandies and liqueurs, this is COINTREAU'S one rival as a sweetening agent.

MARC
French pomace BRANDY distilled from the refuse – skins, pips, and stalks – of grapes and other fruits.

MENTHE, CRÈME DE
(krehm deuh MENTH) • A peppermint-tasting LIQUEUR made from several varieties of mint. Originally much drier than the cloying stuff available today, crème de menthe comes in green and clear (called white) varieties. Use only white crème de menthe in cocktails.

MESCAL
(mehs-KAL) • A North American distillation derived from the various species of the agave plant. Mescal is a more general term for the spirit TEQUILA.

MOCKTAIL
A silly-sounding word for a cocktail made without alcohol. The term came about in recent times and – considering its predecessors – could have been far worse.
Historically, we blame the term on the politician Mr. Pussyfoot – no better remembered by his real name, William Eugene Smith. Had his behavior been more appealing to the public and the press during the early 1900s, such drinks might have garnered a more respectable name than "pussyfoots," and there would never have been any need for a replacement. *Pussyfoot's* original meaning ("indecisive" or "weak") was soon applied to any drink made with little or no liquor. The oldest "dry" cocktail is, in fact, called the

231

Pussyfoot. During the early '30s, the similarly undesirable moniker "Shirley Temple" was adopted as a more wholesome name for a drink even a child could enjoy.

MUDDLER
A bar tool made of wood, similar in shape and function to a pestle.

N

NEUTRAL SPIRITS
Ethyl alcohol distilled to 190 PROOF or higher. Neutral spirits can be distilled from any source – sugar, beets, cane, potatoes, corn, other grains – but because they're distilled to such a high purity, it's nearly impossible to tell what they're made from by their taste.

O

OLD SCHOOL OF AMERICAN BARTENDING
The era of drink from 1897 to 1919, which produced the best-known and most enduring classics, the Aviation and the Mojito among them. Not surprisingly, that time frame mirrors the heyday of the Old Waldorf Bar. According to Albert S. Crockett's *The Old Waldorf-Astoria Bar Book*: "A school of drinking, and a distinctive one, the old Waldorf Bar undoubtedly was. And – which may surprise many – it was a real school of art – a school in which more than one connoisseur who has since spent hundreds of thousands in collecting paintings and sculpture, got his first tuition from the pictures on the Bar walls, whose appeal was often emphasized by the cumulative indulgence of cocktails or highballs."

ON THE ROCKS
A drink served with ice. A cocktail on the rocks stays colder longer but will change color and strength as the ice melts. To make a drink on the rocks, follow the same steps as you would in serving it up, and then strain the mixture into a tumbler or goblet filled with ice. When serving a spirit on the rocks, simply pour the liquid over the ice and serve.

ORANGE BITTERS
See BITTERS.

ORANGE-FLOWER WATER
A French *parfumeur distillateur* occasionally used as an accent in cocktails. Few have seen the illustrious orange flower that, when steeped, metamorphoses into the Ramos Gin Fizz's most exotic ingredient, but that flower's derivative – typically packaged in 6-ounce bottles and sold for less than two bucks – can be found at most fine liquor stores.

ORGEAT
(OHR-zhat) • A sweet, nonalcoholic almond syrup traditionally made in France with barley and orange flowers; used for flavoring cocktails, coffee, and foods.

P

PARFAIT AMOUR
(pahr-FAY a-MOUR) • A purple CORDIAL similar to CRÈME DE VIOLETTE, Parfait Amour – French for "perfect love" – works best in a POUSSE-CAFÉ or as a not-so-subtle hint offered to a cocktail companion.

PASTIS
(pas-TEES) • A French APÉRITIF made with 1 part ABSINTHE substitute (HERBSAINT, PERNOD, or Ricard) and 5 parts water. Perfect for hot afternoons.

PERFECT
An adjective applied to drinks containing VERMOUTH. "Perfect" defines a drink made with equal parts dry and sweet vermouth.

PERNOD
(pehr-NOH) • A high-PROOF APÉRITIF LIQUEUR whose name was once synonymous with ABSINTHE. Pernod, made by one of the early distillers of the now illegal green muse, contains many of absinthe's original ingredients – minus the WORMWOOD, of course. Pernod is commonly sipped in PASTIS.

PEYCHAUD'S
See BITTERS.

PICK-ME-UP
A type of mixed drink rumored to remedy a hangover or low spirits. These drinks are traditionally spirituous.

PIMM'S
A GIN SLING made with herbs (such as QUININE) and LIQUEURS. First mixed in the 1880s as a digestive tonic by James Pimm, who started Pimm's No. 1 as the house specialty of his London oyster bar. About twenty years later, Mr. Pimm began distributing his drink more broadly, and by the 1920s it was being sold throughout England.

PISCO
(PIHS-koh) • A nearly clear, unaged high-PROOF BRANDY distilled from wine grapes of the muscatel variety in Chile and Peru. This youthful spirit was first produced in the 16th century in Peru's Pisco Valley, though many Chileans will be happy to dispute that fact.

POIRE WILLIAM
(pwahr WEEL-yahm) • An *eau de vie* BRANDY distilled from pears and said to stave off hangovers. This spirit's key ingredient, a pear, is often grown inside its bottle, which is secured to the fruit's tree – making for a drink that looks nearly as good as it tastes.

PONY
A short glass most often used to serve LIQUEURS. "Pony" also refers to the amount the glass holds – 1 ounce.

POT STILL
The most basic type of still, also known as the alembic still, and consisting of a heat source, a large pot to hold the fermentation, and a gooseneck-shaped arm and coil that collect and condense the vapor into distilled spirits. Though crude, this still produces the richest spirits, most notably fine brandies and whiskeys.

POUSSE-CAFÉ
(poos ka-FAY) • A drink family that boasts layers of differently colored cordials and syrups, usually in three, five, or seven layers. The layering effect of a pousse-café results from the different densities of the various liqueurs or syrups in the drink. There's one rule to know when making these drinks: The higher the sugar content, the higher the density of the liquid, and the lower in the glass its layer will go.

PROHIBITION

The era in the United States from 1920 to 1933, when Federal law prohibited the manufacture, transportation, and sale of spirituous beverages. Charles H. Baker Jr., in his *Gentleman's Companion* of 1939, calls Prohibition "the ridiculous drought," President Herbert Hoover dubbed it the "Noble Experiment" in a letter to Senator William E. Borah, and just about everyone else agrees that the government's attempt to stamp out strong drink did little good. Most imbibers just switched to bathtub gin and then went on to GIRL DRINKS. Bootlegging became big business, and legal enforcement and teetotalers were thwarted by SPEAKEASIES, moonshiners, rum-runners, and so-called medicinal alcohols.

Although more than 300,000 lawbreakers were convicted under the Volstead Act, which enforced Prohibition at the federal level, Americans spent nearly $40 billion on bootleg liquor, and the lineage of many classic cocktails – such as the Floridita, the Maiden's Prayer, and the Monkey Gland – can be traced to this time. On December 5, 1933, the United States decided to cash in on this lost revenue, and the 21st Amendment was ratified, repealing the 18th Amendment and ending Prohibition.

PROOF

The measure of alcohol in any distilled liquid. In the U.S., a liquid's proof is twice its percentage of alcohol (100 proof equals 50 percent alcohol). In France, proof is measured in degrees known as "Guy-Lussac" (named after the French chemist credited with establishing the classic method of fermentation). In this standard of measure, proof is equal to the concentration of alcohol expressed as a percentage (50 G.L. equals 50 percent alcohol, or 100 proof). To confuse matters further, England has yet another form of measurement, stemming from a curious practice. The English found that liquids of 57 percent alcohol would ignite when mixed with black powder. This concentration was designated as 100 proof, and measurement of alcohol content was then based on that benchmark. If you do the math, you'll find that 50 G.L. equals 100 proof in the U.S., which equals 70 proof in the U.K. Of course, you don't need to know any of this when buying spirits in the States, because U.S. trade regulations require importers to list the U.S. proof on every label.

PUNCH

A family of drinks – typically comprised of five ingredients, not all of them spirits – that's especially forgiving to novice mixers. There are two types of punch, the party punch and the single-serving punch; the latter, despite its similarity to a COLLINS or a JULEP, is often overlooked. Many modern drinks making the rounds of the singles bars would be considered punches by classic standards.

PUNT E MES

(punt eh mes) • A proprietary LIQUEUR distilled by Carpono with a bitter taste derived from QUININE. This BITTER'S name comes from the old Milanese stockbrockers' term *punt e mes*, meaning "point and a half." According to *Playboy's Host & Bar Book*, Punt e Mes is a "deep, dark Italian

APÉRITIF wine known for its provocative bitterness…. [It will] cause you first to shudder, then instantly to ask for more."

QUININE

(KWAI-nine) • A bitter extract made from cinchona bark, often used for such medicinal purposes as the treatment of malaria. During the 1930s, tonic water was referred to as quinine water, which is why commercial soda guns (or squirt guns) have a trigger labeled Q. Though very little quinine is used in flavoring modern tonic water, this abbreviation has stuck.

REVIVAL OF AMERICAN DRINKING

The current era of drink, which began in 1990. This designation admittedly verges on presumptuous, but given such modern-day classics as the Combustible Edison and the Jasmine, it's not without merit. For further evidence, note *The American Forecaster Almanac* of 1997: "Generation Xers, who rediscovered the Martini in recent years, are leading the revival of the cocktail party…." Scripps Howard News Service has chimed in from the mainstream with this observation: "Suddenly, the quintessential American cocktail is back in style."

RICKEY

A drink family with similarities to the SOUR and the FIZZ, though here the citrus juice is always lime. This drink is usually served in a glass holding less than 9 ounces.

ROSE'S LIME JUICE

An English creation containing more than its name implies. Aside from fruit-juice concentrate, this venerable syrup includes high-fructose corn syrup, sodium metabisulfite, and Blue No. 1. Stocked by most bars and by the world's few remaining soda fountains, Rose's is used in the States as an accent to cocktails.

RUM

A spirit distilled from the byproducts of sugar refinement, notably molasses. Because of differences in climate, soil, and method of distillation, rum is classed by country of origin and labeled by color.

—BARBADOS

The easternmost island of the West Indies, well known for its production of rum. Mount Gay is one of the better-known distillers of Barbados rum.

—CUBA

Just off the Florida panhandle, the island of Cuba is known for its superior production of rum and cigars. Very light in style, Cuban rums are recognized as the best in the world, but because of the American government's decades-old embargo, they are not available in the U.S.

—DEMERARA

(dehm-uh-REHR-ah) • The name of a river in Guyana, and of the rums produced in this region. Demerara rums are heavier and darker than the similarly styled Jamaican rums.

—HAITI

Part of a Caribbean island, sandwiched between Cuba and Puerto Rico, known for producing light-bodied rums. Haitian rum is slightly more aromatic than either of its neighbors' products, owing to the French influence on the island.

—JAMAICA

A small island south of Cuba that produces rums valued for their strong molasses aroma and flavor. Naturally brown in color, some of the more popular brands of Jamaican rum contain caramel, which gives them a rich, dark color. Notable for their long fermentations and low-proof distillations, Jamaican rums are aged about seven years before being bottled and shipped.

—MARTINIQUE

A Caribbean island, heavily influenced by the French, that produces rums enjoyed by drinkers who appreciate more peculiar flavors. Varying in color from very light to quite dark, Martinique rum should be sampled straight before being considered as an addition to a cocktail.

—PUERTO RICO

An island most noted among imbibers for the production of Bacardi rum. Puerto Rico is known for its neutral, light-bodied rums, similar in style to Cuban rums.

S

SCHNAPPS

(SHNAHPS) • From the German word for *mouthful*, this term originally signified GENEVER GIN. Nowadays, in the U.S., the term *schnapps* includes just about any spirituous LIQUEUR that's overly sweet and artificially flavored. Fortunately, the fine people of northern and eastern Europe have maintained their drier, more biting version – it's just harder to find.

SEC, SECO, SECCO

(SEHK, SEHK-oh) • French, Spanish, and Italian words meaning *dry*; often found on bottles of spirits and wine.

SHERRY

A fortified wine produced in Jerez, Spain, sold in varying styles. Sherry is not bottled at a specific vintage; instead, it's a blend of different wines from different vintages. This drink is aged and blended in an intricate system known as the *solera*. As the wine matures, each barrel in the system takes on qualities from the wine. These barrels are then placed into a tiered blending system that lets the older wines "educate" the younger ones through fractional blending. Sherries are of two types, either *fino* or *oloroso*.

—AMONTILLADO

(ah-mon-teh-LAH-doh) • Dark-colored *finos*, *amontillados* are identified early in the aging process and developed to highlight their superior color and nuttiness. To preserve a promising *amontillado*, the master blender marks the wine so it will not be refreshed or blended with others. This sherry is a good accent in cocktails.

—AMOROSO

A type of *oloroso* that is richer, sweeter, and darker than *amontillado*. Created for the English palate, this sherry is best served in cold weather or as a DIGESTIF. Its rich flavor suits cocktails calling for BRANDY or WHISKEY.

—FINO

(FEE-noh) • The paler and lighter of the two main types of sherry. Owing to its delicate nature, *fino* should be sipped within a few years of bottling. Once opened, a *fino* will fade rapidly, so it's best to purchase this sherry in small quantities. A lovely APÉRITIF in its own right, this wine is also a good substitute for dry VERMOUTH in many cocktails.

—MANZANILLA

(mahn-zuh-NEE-yuh) • The lightest of *finos*. This sherry is greatly appreciated by the Spanish, who typically serve it with tapas, but because of its light nature, it's not a good mixer in cocktails.

—OLOROSO

(oh-loh-ROH-soh) • The darker and richer of the two main sherry types. Intrinsically dry, some *olorosos* make good accents in cocktails. A bottle of this fine sherry will be a valued asset to your cocktail cabinet.

SIMPLE SYRUP

Dissolved sugar used in drinkmaking. The recipe for simple syrup is 2 cups of sugar dissolved in 1 cup of boiling water. Let it cool before using it.

SLING

Any tall, icy drink made with a liquor such as GIN, RUM, BRANDY, or WHISKEY, water (still or bubbly), sugar, and lemon or lime juice. Some sling recipes are bottled and sold, like PIMM'S, though not particularly popular. Others, such as the Singapore Sling and the Tom Collins, are easily mixed at home or obtained at a bar.

SLOE GIN

Not a GIN, but a mawkish LIQUEUR flavored with sloe berries. Use it as an accent to a particularly tart, colorless cocktail.

SOUR

A tall drink closely related to the FIZZ. Some, in fact, would argue that a fizz is merely a sour with soda water. Made with a distilled spirit, sugar, and lemon juice (and occasionally a DASH of orange juice), a sour is shaken with cracked ice and is usually served in a sour glass – a short, squat vessel holding about 6 ounces.

SPACER

That glass of water or other alcohol-free drink ordered between cocktails in hopes of keeping (or regaining) one's composure.

SPEAKEASY

A place where drinks containing liquor are sold illegally. Although most commonly associated with PROHIBITION, the term goes back to the 1800s – when, to gain entrance to such an establishment, you had to "speak easy" and credit whomever sent you. Speakeasies were often fronted by such chaste establishments as barbershops and ice cream parlors. John F. Mariani, in *The Dictionary of American Food and Drink*, claims the English, with their "speak-softly shops" selling the wares of smugglers, should be credited with the word.

Speakeasies defeated the Volstead Act, opened bars to women, and romanticized the mob. Interestingly enough, it's been argued that the speakeasy destroyed the profession of bartending. The speakeasy crowd typically brought its own bottles of liquor, safely stashed in coat pockets and purses; bar backs merely distributed glasses, ice, and sodas – called "setups." The only requirements of the job were to remain calm during police raids and to keep a straight face while serving crappy drinks.

SPIRITS
Alcoholic liquids produced by distillation and fit for human consumption.

SPLASH
One-fourth ounce, or roughly 1 centiliter.

STRAIGHT UP
Shaken or stirred in a mixer and strained into a cocktail glass. The only debris permissible in a drink served up is tiny slivers and flecks of ice. A drink served straight up will not surprise you; it will never change color or strength. It is reliable.

SUZE
(SOOZ) • This French herbal LIQUEUR is made from the bitter root of the yellow gentian, a root that's been used as a gastrointestinal tonic for centuries. A caramel-colored BITTER, suze is similar to GRAND MARNIER.

SWEET
An adjective used to describe the type of VERMOUTH to be used in a cocktail: a request for "sweet" means the imbiber prefers Italian vermouth over its French, or dry, counterpart.

T

TABLESPOON
One-half ounce, or roughly 2 centiliters.

TALL DRINK
The drink classification that includes all libations made with carbonated water or soda, a distilled spirit, and citrus juice. The best-known members of this drink family include the COLLINS, the FIZZ, the RICKEY, the BUCK, the JULEP, the SOUR, and the HIGHBALL. These refreshing coolers are usually served in tall, thin glasses holding more than 8 ounces.

TEETOTALER
Credit the temperance society for this term. According to *The Morris Dictionary of Word and Phrase Origins*, teetotaler dates back to 1807, when newbies to the Carry Nation signed a *T* by their names, signifying total abstinence from liquor.

TEQUILA
(tuh-KEE-luh) • A North American distillate steeped from the blue-gray maguey plant. Tequila – or, more accurately, *agave tequilana* – may be produced only in the central region of Jalisco, Mexico. As with COGNAC and BOURBON, whose production are also tied to a particular locale, "tequila" made anywhere else is given another name: *mescal* (me SKAL´). There are four types of tequila or mescal: white or silver, gold, *reposado*, and *añejo*.

TODDY
The family of drinks made with spirituous liquors diluted with hot water, sweeteners, spices, and juices. Similar to the grog.

TRAPPISTINE
(trap-eh-STEEN) • A pale yellow-green LIQUEUR made at the Abbaye de Grace de Dieu in the French department of Doubs. Originally made by Trappist monks in Normandy around 1670, this bitter, BRANDY-based herbal cordial will add kick to any drink.

TRIPLE SEC
(TRIH-pl sehk) • A semisweet, orange-flavored, colorless LIQUEUR, used as an accent to cocktails. COINTREAU is the most notable brand, though generic triple sec is acceptable for drinkmaking.

U

UP
A drink served in a cocktail glass without ice. See STRAIGHT UP and ON THE ROCKS.

V

VERMOUTH
A white-wine-based APÉRITIF infused with herbs and fortified with BRANDY, vermouth is classified as either sweet (Italian) or dry (French). There is no difference between "dry" and "extra dry" vermouth.

Years ago, French and Italian vermouths were quite different. "French vermouth" implied the dry version, made with white wines and a slew of herbs – most notably QUININE. The traditional Italian – or "sweet" – type is more bittersweet, made with brandy and herbs. Nowadays, though, each type is made in both countries, as well as elsewhere, so the distinction by country has been muddied. The confusion is best addressed by referring to the two types as "dry" and "sweet." The large vermouth houses, such as Cinzano, Boissiere, and Martini & Rossi, bottle both varieties.

For most Americans, vermouth is merely a component in their cocktails. For Europeans, though, it's the drink the Americans, with their extra dry Martinis, have never truly appreciated. An order for a Martini in Italy or France will often get you a glass of Martini & Rossi vermouth.

VIOLETTE, CRÈME DE
(krehm deuh vee-oh-LET) • A sweet liquor made almost exclusively in France, though the brand Crème d'Yvette – named after the turn-of-the-century French actress Yvette Gilbert – is still made in all its purple-hued splendor by Jacquin in Philadelphia. Both cordials are said to taste of violet petals dipped in vanilla.

VODKA
A colorless, flavorless distillate that makes a perfectly acceptable DIGESTIF and an excellent accompaniment to meals of caviar, smoked salmon, and black bread. Regrettably, vodka is one spirit that offers little to the art of drinkmaking.

W

WELL DRINKS
The default brands an establishment uses for drink orders that don't mention a specific brand. These default brands are stored in the "well," which is kept right behind the bar,

always within easy reach of the drinkmaker. Gin and tonic would be the "well" equivalent of a Tanqueray and tonic.

WET

An adjective that describes a cocktail based on the type of VERMOUTH used or the degree of sweetness desired. In making a cocktail that calls for vermouth, the more vermouth used, the "wetter" the drink will be. See DRY.

WHISKEY, WHISKY

A distillate from a mash of grains (barley, rye, or corn) often wasted on home brews and pigs. There are a number of whiskey types – bourbon, rye, scotch, Irish, and Canadian – as well as further variations, such as blended and sour mash.

We won't argue about the "correct" spelling of the word *whiskey*, which dates back to the 16th century and is derived from the Gaelic word *uisgebeatha,* for "water of life." But in general, the Irish and the Americans spell whiskey with an *e*; the Scots, the English, and the Canadians go without.

—BLENDED

Whiskey consisting of a blend of two or more straight whiskeys or a mix of whiskey with neutral spirits. Blended whiskeys are lighter in body than straight whiskeys and are therefore more palatable to the masses, both in price and in taste. Scotland, Ireland, Canada, and the U.S. all produce blended whiskeys.

—BOURBON

An American whiskey distilled at less than 160 PROOF from fermented mash of no less than 51 percent corn and then aged in new charred oak containers. After aging, typically for at least two years, this whiskey may be bottled or blended with other bourbons before bottling. The charred casks are what give bourbon its distinctive color and taste. Although bourbon is most closely associated with Bourbon County, Kentucky, its distinctive taste may well have originated in Virginia. Most accounts agree that during the late 1700s, a Baptist minister named Reverend Elijah Craig was the first to distill whiskey in Kentucky, and coined the name "bourbon whiskey."

—CANADIAN

As the name implies, whiskeys made in Canada – specifically, blended whiskeys with a flavor reminiscent of rye. The popularity of Canadian whiskey can be attributed largely to PROHIBITION. During this infamous dry period, Canadian whiskey practically poured down from the north into America's illicit SPEAKEASIES.

—IRISH

A POT-STILL distillate produced in Ireland that's much lighter in body than scotch. Irish whiskey is made with grains blended with fermented malt before distillation. After distillation, it may be blended with other whiskeys, neutral spirits, and/or water. Before the advent of blended scotches, the lighter taste of Irish whiskey was popular with the masses.

—RYE

A type of whiskey that by U.S. law must be distilled from a fermented mash of at least 51 percent rye grain. Though rye has slipped in popularity, it should not be considered an also-ran. Many classic whiskey cocktails first called for straight rye.

—SCOTCH

A smoky, complex whiskey distilled only in Scotland. Each single malt has its own distinctive taste, but all scotches are made from 100 percent barley. As with all whiskeys, uniqueness is achieved by adding something extra in the distillation process. Scotland's abundance of fresh water, barley, and peaty soil have contributed to the great variety of distinct flavors produced. Of course, other factors can also affect the flavor, from the charring of oak casks to sheep peeing into the local spring.

—SOUR MASH

Grain mash made with mash from a previous batch, used in the distillation of some whiskeys.

—TENNESSEE

A sour mash whiskey similar to bourbon. Tennessee whiskeys such as Jack Daniel's and George Dickel set themselves apart from their Kentucky neighbors by using charcoal produced from maple trees, which adds a sweet finish to their distillates.

WHITE LIGHTNING

Homemade whiskey, rarely aged and seldom palatable. Since it hasn't been aged in charred oak barrels, this distillation – unlike most whiskeys – is clear. Also known as moonshine.

WHITE WHISKEY

This phrase was spawned by yet another marketing ploy on VODKA'S behalf. John G. Martin, the man who first promoted this distillation in the States, stumbled across it while calling on one of his distributors of spirits in South Carolina. The salesman had hung signs in the warehouse boasting: "Smirnoff White Whiskey. No Smell. No Taste." After World War II, vodka was shipped with whiskey stoppers due to cork shortages; the bottles had reportedly reminded the salesman of his own down-home white lightning.

WORMWOOD

Any of 250 strong-smelling plants with white or yellow flowers, generally classed as weeds, which were once used in making ABSINTHE and other BITTERS. It's specifically the Eurasian perennial *Artemisia absinthium* that's so notorious in the cocktail world. When steeped, *Artemisia absinthium* makes for an oil that's forest green in color and bitter in taste.

Hippocrates sipped wormwood steeped in wine for jaundice and rheumatism, and others throughout history have used it as an aphrodisiac. In the early 18th century, however, the Swiss and the French led an anti-absinthe crusade that eventually managed to ban the use of wormwood in food and drink.

Y

YEARS OF REFORM

The era of drink, lasting from 1934 to 1949, that followed the havoc of PROHIBITION. "During what facetious American newspaper columnists sometimes referred to as the Period of the Great Drought – that is to say, during the days of the Noble Experiment," explains Albert S. Crockett in *The Old Waldorf-Astoria Bar Book* of 1934, "the art of mixing cocktails as known and practiced up to 1919 lapsed into a sort of desuetude, even if that could not be described as 'innocuous' or even innoxious."

Allen, Frederick. *Secret Formula*. New York: HarperBusiness, 1995.

Altschul, Ira D. *Drinks as They Were Made before Prohibition*. Schauer Printing Studio, 1934.

American Heritage Cookbook. New York: American Heritage Publishing Co., Inc., 1964.

Amis, Kingsley. *On Drink*. London: Jonathan Cape, 1972.

Asbury, Herbert, ed. *The Bon Vivant's Companion, or How to Mix Drinks*, by Professor Jerry Thomas. New York: Knopf, 1928.

Ayto, John. *The Diner's Dictionary*. New York: Oxford University Press, 1994.

"Drinks' Roots Steeped in History: Origins of Popular Cocktails." *Nation's Restaurant News*, September 18, 1989.

Baker, Charles H. *The Gentleman's Companion: An Exotic Drinking Book*. New York: Crown Publishers, 1946.

_____. *The South American Gentleman's Companion: Being an Exotic Drinking Book*. New York: Crown Publishers, 1951.

The Balance, May 13, 1806.

" 'Scofflaw' Wins Word Contest." *The Boston Herald*, January 16, 1924.

"Bellini, Giovanni." Britannica Online. *www.britannica.com*. Cited November 21, 1997.

Bergeron, Victor J. *Trader Vic's Bartender's Guide*. Garden City, N.Y.: Doubleday, 1972.

_____. *Trader Vic's Book of Foods & Drink*. Garden City, N.Y.: Doubleday, 1946.

Beveridge, N. E. *Cups of Valor*. Harrisburg: Stackpole Books, 1968.

Bierce, Ambrose. *The Devil's Dictionary*. 1911. Reprint, New York: Dover Publications, Inc., 1993.

Birmingham, Frederic A., ed. *The Esquire Drink Book*. New York: Harper & Brothers, 1956.

Brady, James. "Korean Vets Carry Memories in Their Hearts." *Washingtonian*, March 1995.

Brooks, Johnny. *My 35 Years behind Bars*. New York: Exposition Press, 1954.

Brown, Erica. "Pimm's Cup, Once Just Posh, Has Become Popular." *The New York Times*, August 15, 1984.

Brown, John Hull. *Early American Beverages*. New York: Bonanza Books, 1966.

Brown, Jr., R.G. "Sazerac Whiskey Cocktail." *The Glass Packer: Little Biographies of Famous Products*, February 1939.

Browne, Charles. *The Gun Club Drink Book*. New York: Charles Scribner's Sons, 1939.

Byron, O. H. *The Modern Bartender's Guide*. New York: Excelsior Publishing House, 1884.

Caen, Herb. *Don't Call It Frisco*. New York: Doubleday, 1953.

Calip, Howard. "Smirnoff Vodka – From Czarist Moscow to Hartford." *Business Times*, February 1987.

Cenzato, Giovanni. *Campari 1860–1960*. Milan: Campari, 1960.

Chandler, Raymond. *The Long Goodbye*. 1953. Reprint, New York: Vintage Books, 1992.

Cipriani, Arrigo. *Harry's Bar: The Life and Times of the Legendary Venice Landmark*. New York: Arcade Publishing, 1996.

Coates, James. "Gonzo Tale of Drugs Is No Hallucination." *Chicago Tribune*, March 18, 1990.

Conrad III, Barnaby. *The Martini*. San Francisco: Chronicle Books, 1995.

Craddock, Harry. *The Savoy Cocktail Book*. 1930. Reprint: London: Constable & Co., Ltd., 1933.

Cress, Doug. "True South Mint Juleps: Kentucky Stables May Change Hands, But Drink Is Forever Steeped in South." *Atlanta Journal and Constitution*, May 1, 1994.

Crockett, Albert S. *The Old Waldorf-Astoria Bar Book*. New York: Dodd, Mead and Company, 1934.

Curry, Dale. "Signature Dishes Made New Orleans Famous." *Chicago Sun-Times*, November 20, 1994.

Dardis, Tom. *The Thirsty Muse: Alcohol and the American Writer*. New York: Ticknor & Fields, 1989.

Deacon, Mary R. *The Clover Club of Philadelphia*. Philadelphia: Avil Printing Company, 1897.

Dempsey, Mary A. "Henry Ford's Amazonian Suburbia: Belterra and Fordlandia, Brazil." *Americas*, March 1996.

DeRasor, Roberto. *Alcohol Distiller's Manual for Gasohol and Spirit*. San Antonio, Tex.: Doña Carolina Distiller, 1980.

DeVoto, Bernard. *The Hour*. Riverside Press, 1948.

Dobbs, Kildare. "The Genie in the Bottle." *The Financial Post* (Toronto), July 1, 1996.

Dooley, Susan. "A Happening on Oscar Night." *The Washington Post*, April 10, 1980.

_____. "Summer Fizzes," *The Washington Post*, June 22, 1987.

Downard, William L. *Dictionary of the History of the American Brewing and Distilling Industries*. Westport, Conn.: Greenwood Press, 1980.

Duffy, Patrick Gavin. *The Official Mixer's Manual*. New York: Blue Ribbon Books, 1934.

Edmunds, Lowell. *The Silver Bullet: The Martini in American Civilization*. Westport, Conn.: Greenwood Press, 1981.

Egan, Pierce. *Life in London*. London: John Camden Hotten, Picadilly, 1821.

Eksteins, Mordis. *Rites of Spring*. New York: Doubleday, 1989.

Embury, David A. *The Fine Art of Mixing Drinks*. 1948. Reprint, New York: Doubleday, 1961.

Emerson, Edward R. *Beverages, Past and Present*. G. P. Putnam's Sons, 1908.

Esquire's Handbook for Hosts. New York: Grosset & Dunlap, 1949.

Evans, Christopher. "Hi from Margaritaville! A Special Clip-and-Save Investigative Report," *The Plain Dealer* (Cleveland), August 17, 1997.

Fisher, John. *The Rough Guide to Mexico*. New York: Rough Guides, 1997.

Fitzgerald, F. Scott. *This Side of Paradise*. New York: Cambridge University Press, 1920. Reprint, New York: Bantam Classics, 1996.

Fleming, Ian. *Casino Royale*. London: Jonathan Cape, 1953.

_____. *A View to a Kill*. CD edition. Baker & Taylor Video: 1994.

Gaige, Crosby. *Crosby Gaige's Cocktail Guide and Lady's Companion*. New York: M. Barrows, 1941.

Grimes, William. *Straight Up or On the Rocks*. New York: Simon & Schuster, 1993.

Grossman, Harold J. *Grossman's Guide to Wines, Spirits and Beer*. New York: Charles Scribner's Sons, 1943.

Haimo, Oscar. *Cocktail and Wine Digest: The Barman's Bible*. 1945. Reprint, New York: Oscar Haimo, 1963.

Hallgarten, Peter. *Spirits and Liqueurs*. London: Faber and Faber, 1983.

Hannum, Hurst and Robert S. Blumberg. *Brandies and Liqueurs of the World*. New York: Doubleday, 1976.

Harland, Marion. *Breakfast, Luncheon, & Tea*. New York: Scribner, Armstrong & Co., 1875.

Harwell, Richard B. *The Mint Julep*. Charlottesville: University Press of Virginia, 1975.

Haslip, Joan. *The Crown of Mexico: Maximilian and His Empress Carlota*. New York: Henry Holt & Co., 1972.

Heath, Ambrose. *Good Drinks*. London: Faber & Faber Ltd., 1939.

Hemingway, Ernest. *A Farewell to Arms*. 1929. Reprint, New York: Charles Scribner's Sons, 1993.

_____. *Islands in the Stream*. New York: Charles Scribner's Sons, 1970.

_____. *The Sun Also Rises*. New York: Charles Scribner's Sons, 1954.

Hendrickson, Robert. *Dictionary of Eponyms: Names That Became Words*. New York: Dorset Press, 1972.

Hines, Mary Anne, Gordon Marshall, and William Woys Weaver. *The Larder Invaded*. Philadelphia: The Historical Society of Pennsylvania, 1987.

Hunter, William "The Offbeat Life of George Orwell: An Original Who Fits No Pattern." *Houston Chronicle*, December 1, 1991.

Indiana, Gary. *Gone Tomorrow*. New York: Pantheon Books, 1993.

Jackson, Michael. *Michael Jackson's Bar & Cocktail Companion*. Philadelphia: Running Press Books, 1995.

Jefford, Andrew. "Downing the Pink: They May Not Bother in the Navy Any More, but in Yacht-Club Bars All Over Britain Glasses Are Still Raised in Salute to the Pinking Hour." *Evening Standard* (London), August 24, 1993.

Kaplan, Karen. "Boston Tradition." *Bon Appétit*, November 1991.

Knefel, Don. "Animal Farm Tells Tale of Corrupt Politics." *Telegraph Herald* (Dubuque), June 30, 1996.

Kump, Peter. "Making the Holidays Special: Invite in a Crowd to a New Orleans Brunch." *Chicago Tribune*, December 20, 1992.

Lanza, Joseph. *The Cocktail: The Influence of Spirits on the American Psyche*. New York: St. Martin's Press, 1995.

Leibling, A. J. *The Honest Rainmaker*. 1952. Reprint, San Francisco: North Point Press, 1989.

Lichine, Alexis. *Alexis Lichine's Encyclopedia of Wines & Spirits*. New York: Alfred A. Knopf, 1967.

Lipinsky, Robert A. and Kathleen A. Lipinsky. *Professional Guide to Alcoholic Beverages*. New York: Van Nostrand Reinhold, 1989.

Lockhart, Sir Robert Bruce. *Scotch: The Whiskey of Scotland in Fact and Story*. London: Putnam's Sons, 1970.

Lord, Tony. *The World Guide to Spirits, Apéritifs and Cocktails*. New York: Sovereign Books, 1979.

Lott, Lt.Cdr. Arnold S. and Raymond J. McHugh. *A New Century Beckons: A History of the Army and Navy Club*. Washington, D.C.: Printing, Inc. of Virginia, 1988.

MacElhone, Harry. *Harry's ABC of Mixing Cocktails*. London: Souvenir Press, 1919.

Maclean, Neil. "A Taste of Mexico, However You Pronounce It." Times Newspapers Ltd., February 21, 1993, *Sunday Times*.

Madison J. Gray. "Hidden Treasures: Statue Pays Homage to Scottish Poet." *The Detroit News*, March 20, 1996.

Mariani, John F. *The Dictionary of American Food and Drink*. New York: Hearst Books, 1983, 1994.

Mario, Thomas. *Playboy's Host & Bar Book*. Chicago: Playboy, 1971.

Masse, William E. *Wine & Spirits: A Complete Buying Guide*. New York: McGraw-Hill Book Company Inc., 1961.

Mencken, H. L. *The American Language*. 1919. Reprint, New York: Alfred A. Knopf, 1995.

Mendelsohn, Oscar A. *Drinking with Pepys*. New York: Macmillan & Co Ltd., 1963.

Moore, Caroline. "First Lady of English Literature." Times Newspapers Ltd., January 14, 1993.

Morago, Greg. "Pimm's Cup: Summer Refresher from England," *The Hartford Courant*, May 29, 1997.

Morris, Eleanor S. "Gran Plaza Is the Centerpiece of Bustling Monterrey." *Austin American-Statesman*, August 31, 1997.

Naccarato, Michael. "Bloody Caesar: Canada's Cocktail." *The Toronto Star*, May 11, 1994.

Nicklès, Sara, ed. *Drinking, Smoking & Screwing*. San Francisco: Chronicle Books, 1994.

North, Sterling and Carl Kroch. *So Red in the Nose*. New York: Farrar & Rinehart, 1935.

Orwell, George. *1984*. 1949. Reprint, New York: New American Library, 1990.

_____. *Shooting an Elephant and Other Essays*. New York: Martin Secker & Warburg Ltd., 1950.

Plotkin, Robert. "Coffee Drinks Take Chill out of Fall," *Nation's Restaurant News*, September 18, 1989.

Prial, Frank J. "Spirits: Cooling and Relaxing." *The New York Times*, July 7, 1985.

Regan, Gary and Mardee Haidin Regan. *New Classic Cocktails*. New York: Macmillan, 1997.

"Robert," of the Embassy Club, London. *Cocktails: How to Mix Them*. Ebenezer Baylis and Son, Limited (date unknown).

Rogers, Paul. "A Strange Case of Smirnoff." Independent Newspaper Publishing PLC, 1995.

Rorabaugh, W. J. *The Alcoholic Republic*. New York: Oxford University Press, Inc., 1979.

Ryan, Bill. "Smirnoff White Whiskey – No Smell, No Taste." *Connecticut Weekly Desk*.

Schumann, Charles A. *American Bar*. New York: Abbeville Press, 1995.

_____. *Tropical Bar Book*. New York: Stewart, Tabori & Chang, 1995.

Simon, André. *A Dictionary of Wines, Spirits and Liqueurs*. New York: The Citadel Press, 1963.

Tasker, Fred. "Aperitifs for Summer Are the Essence of Cool." *Orange County Register*, July 21, 1994.

Thomas, Jerry. *The Bon Vivant's Companion*. New York: Alfred A. Knopf, 1862.

Thomson, Ian. "Continental Drifters." Times Newspapers Ltd., October 23, 1994.

Villas, James. "The Social Status of the Martini." *Esquire*, April 1973.

Vivant, Don. "Rolling with the Punches." *Forbes*, November 20, 1995.

The Weasel. "Two Things Will Inevitably Ruin Any Mint Julep, the First of Which Is Too Much Sugar, the Second Too Little Whiskey." *Independent* (London), May 25, 1996.

Weingarten, Paul. "Baron of Books Lets the Discount Wars Rage." *Chicago Tribune*, December 28, 1986.

Wilkinson, Donna. "Pride of the South." *Colonial Homes*, June 1993.

239

240

241